EVERYONE
IS AWFUL

EVERYONE IS AWFUL

HOW PEOPLE FAIL—AND SO CAN YOU!

NATALYA LOBANOVA

A TarcherPerigee Book

tarcherperigee

an imprint of Penguin Random House LLC
penguinrandomhouse.com

Most TarcherPerigee books are available at special quantity discounts for bulk purchase for sales promotions, premiums, fund-raising, and educational needs. Special books or book excerpts also can be created to fit specific needs. For details, write: SpecialMarkets@penguinrandomhouse.com.

Library of Congress Cataloging-in-Publication Data

Names: Lobanova, Natalya, author.
Title: Everyone is awful: how people fail—and so can you! / Natalya Lobanova.
Description: New York: TarcherPerigee, [2022] Identifiers: LCCN 2022010675 (print) |
LCCN 2022010676 (ebook) | ISBN 9780593420720 (trade paperback) | ISBN 9780593543092 (epub)
Subjects: LCSH: Failure (Psychology) | Self-acceptance.
Classification: LCC BF575.F14 L63 2022 (print) | LCC BF575.F14 (ebook) |
DDC 158.1—dc23/eng/20220401
LC record available at https://lccn.loc.gov/2022010675
LC ebook record available at https://lccn.loc.gov/2022010676

Printed in the United States of America
1st Printing

Book design by Laura K. Corless

HELLO!

WELCOME TO MY BOOK.

I'M SO GLAD YOU COULD MAKE IT.

HERE, HAVE A SEAT.

HERE'S A BLANKET IF YOU GET COLD.

WHAT **WOULD** YOU LIKE TO DRINK?

(CIRCLE THE ONE YOU WANT. YOU CAN EVEN
HAVE MORE THAN ONE, I CAN'T STOP YOU.
I'M JUST A DISEMBODIED VOICE IN YOUR HEAD.)

WATER   TEA   COFFEE   MYSTERIOUS GOBLET   JUICE

HOW HAVE YOU BEEN? YOU LOOK WELL!

MMM...

YEAH.

WELL, **THAT'S** GREAT/AWFUL.

(DELETE **AS** APPROPRIATE.)

AND HOW'S YOUR MOTHER?

MM... YEAH, WOW.

I'M SO PLEASED/SO SORRY TO HEAR THAT.
(DELETE AS APPROPRIATE.)

RIGHT, WELL, LET'S GET A START ON THIS BOOK.

I HOPE YOU ENJOY IT!

IF YOU DON'T, THEN I DON'T KNOW WHAT TO
TELL YOU.

MAYBE YOU SHOULD HAVE SAID SOMETHING EARLIER.

IT'S FINE, I'M SURE WE CAN MOVE PAST THIS.

I THINK OUR RELATIONSHIP IS STRONG ENOUGH.

ANYWAY, ENJOY!

HOW TO USE THIS BOOK:

- YOU DON'T HAVE TO READ IT IN ANY SPECIFIC ORDER, I DON'T MIND.

- I RECOMMEND READING LEFT TO RIGHT. YOU MAY GET CONFUSED OTHERWISE.

- JUST BE YOURSELF AND HAVE FUN. ♡

WHAT DO YOU NEED TO HEAR TODAY?

CLOSE YOUR EYES AND POINT TO A PAGE NUMBER.
THAT IS WHAT YOU NEED TO HEAR TODAY.*

```
 5   6   7   8   9  10  11  12  13  14  15  16  17  18  19
20  21  22  23  24  25  26  27  28  29  30  31  32  33  34
35  36  37  38  39  40  41  42  43  44  45  46  47  48  49
50  51  52  53  54  55  56  57  58  59  60  61  62  63  64
67  68  69  70  71  72  73  74  75  76  77  78  79  80  81
82  83  84  85  86  87  88  89  90  91  92  93  94  95  96
97  98  99 100 101 102 103 104 105 106 107 108 109 110 111
112 113 114 115 116 117 118 119 120 121 122 123 124 125 126
127 128 129 130 131 135 136 137 138 139 140 141 142 143 144
145 146 147 148 150 151 152 153 154 155 156 157 158 159 160
161 162 163 164 165 166 167 168 169 170 171 172 173 174 175
176 177 178 179 180 181 182 183 184 185 186 187 188 189 190
191 192 193 194 195 196 197 198 199 200 201 202 203 204 205
206 207 208 209 210 211 212 213 214 215 216 217 218 219 222
```

* MAY NOT NECESSARILY BE WHAT YOU NEED TO HEAR
TODAY, OR EVER.
EITHER WAY, I TAKE NO RESPONSIBILITY.

INTRODUCTION

EVERYTHING AND EVERYONE IS AT LEAST A LITTLE BIT AWFUL, AND THERE'S NOTHING WE CAN DO ABOUT IT

We are told that every cloud has a silver lining. This is a lie. Clouds do not contain any precious metals, otherwise they wouldn't be floating in the sky. The other more implicit lie is that all situations have a positive side. But no, sometimes they're simply a shitty situation. Of course, they probably will have positive outcomes later on down the line that you're not aware of—but other times the only good outcome is that they're over.

My point is—some things are bad and we need to stop lying to ourselves and claiming that they're still somehow secretly good. No! Some things are just simply *bad*, with each side being negative, no matter which angle you look at it. Sit with it, and then get on with life. What other option is there? To be stripped of your basic human right to occasionally wallow in self-pity? To not treat yourself to a little tantrum?! That's an absolute travesty. If you have to go through a tough time, at the very least you should be allowed to complain for the entire duration.

And on top of that, you too, I'm sorry to say, are flawed. Awful, even. At this point, you're probably expecting me to say, "And that's OK." But I'm not going to do that, because it's an entirely useless sentiment. It won't magically make you OK with your flaws. Instead it'll make you obsess over your *new* flaw of not being perfectly content with your flawed self, which will inevitably make you feel even worse than before.

No. Your only option is to be flawed, to cause your own problems sometimes, and then to feel bad about it until you stop feeling so bad, but then you're just going to make some other mistake and repeat the cycle. And that's it. That is the human condition.

So—I'm not here to tell you how to live life, mostly because I don't think I'm particularly good at it. Nor can I tell you how to become a better person, or even a more resilient one. My comics may not resonate with each and every one of your experiences, but I hope they validate a lot of emotions that actually are universal to the human experience—predominantly embarrassment—and make you feel a bit better about being a part of the collective human failure.

AWFUL AT WORK

NO ONE EVER REALLY KNOWS WHAT THEY'RE DOING, BUT YOU GET BETTER AT HIDING IT

I have no idea what I'm doing. How the hell do you write a book? I've never done this, and yet people trust me to do it, and have even given me money for it?? And, worse still, actually expect me to do it?? Via a legally binding agreement???

Presumably I have now successfully done it somehow, seeing as you're reading this, but rest assured: I had no idea what I was doing while I was doing it. At this point in my life, I have realized that this is normal and no reason to panic.

When I was little, I always assumed everything big was organized in a very specific way. There were rules and procedures and everything behind the scenes was carefully planned and smoothly run. Everyone who was given a task knew exactly how to complete it, and they did so identically across the entire industry. Then I actually started working, and I was the one who suddenly needed to complete tasks. Granted, I'm a freelance creative, and there's never truly a "correct" way to create a work of art. There are definitely stupid, difficult, and inefficient ways to make it, but these aren't exactly *wrong*. Nevertheless, it took me several years to realize that no one was going to come along and tell me the proper way to have something commissioned, write a book, or organize an exhibition. This is horrifying, but on the positive side, it also means no one can tell you off for doing it incorrectly, as long as the final product is at least somewhat passable. And from that point on I aimed for everything I do to be "somewhat passable."

The Two Golden Rules of Having (and Keeping) a Job Are:

- Handle the basic day-to-day tasks with some level of competency.
- Sound like you are capable of handling the day-to-day tasks with some level of competency.

Over time, the tasks that scared you at first become second nature. But here's the thing: there are always going to be new tasks. Life is relentless, and so is work. And the whole time, you're aging and can't escape the feeling that there ought to be more to life, that surely your job is supposed to make you fulfilled and accomplished and give you purpose, right?

Wrong!

It's not that you'll never feel accomplished or that you'll always be terrified of messing up. It's more that you'll never permanently feel like you've "arrived." But, as I said earlier, this is normal and no reason to panic. Enjoy the brief nuggets of fulfillment, accomplishment, and success you feel in your life, and the rest of the time, just aim for "somewhat passable."

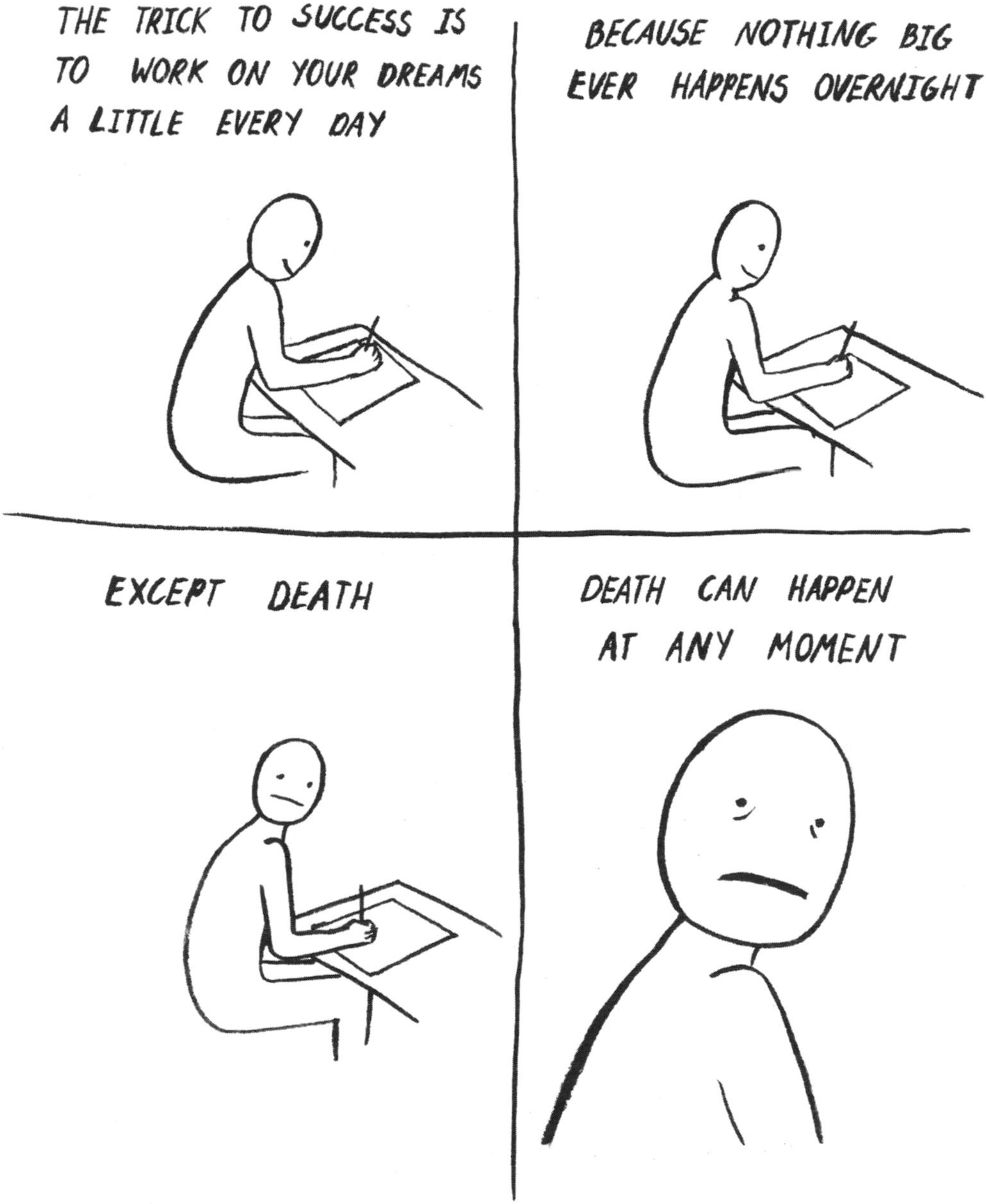
THE TRICK TO SUCCESS IS TO WORK ON YOUR DREAMS A LITTLE EVERY DAY
BECAUSE NOTHING BIG EVER HAPPENS OVERNIGHT
EXCEPT DEATH
DEATH CAN HAPPEN AT ANY MOMENT

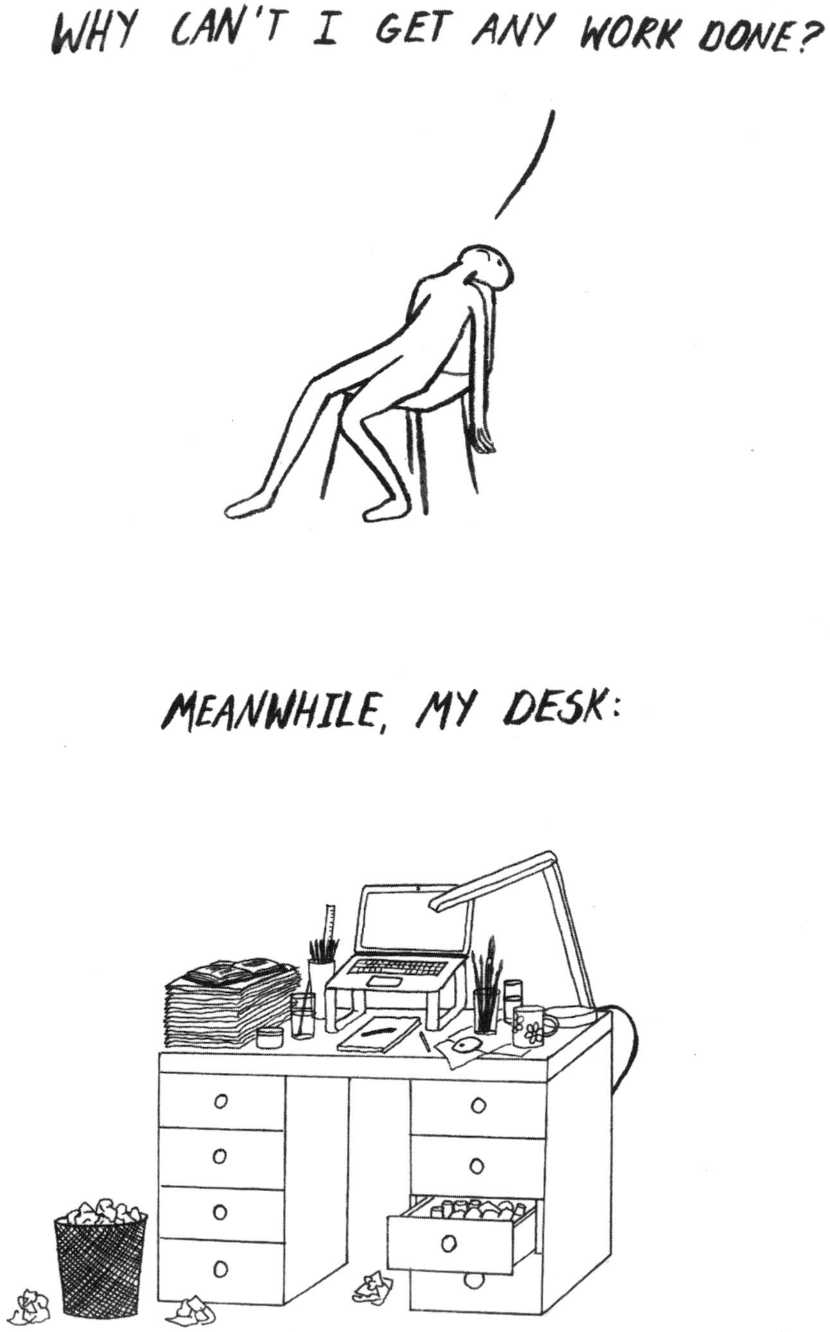
WHY CAN'T I GET ANY WORK DONE?
MEANWHILE, MY DESK:

RATING YOUR MOTIVATION

"SUCCESS IS AN INHERENT GOOD, ALWAYS WORTHY OF PURSUIT"

2/10

I DOUBT EVEN YOU BELIEVE THIS YOURSELF.

"I WANT TO MAKE MY LOVED ONES PROUD"

5/10

NOBLE, BUT DO YOU TAKE THE TIME TO MAKE THEM HAPPY AND LOVED?

"I WANT TO BE CONTENT, AND STRIVING TOWARDS MY GOALS WILL HELP ME ACHIEVE THIS"

7/10

DISCONTENTMENT IS THE HUMAN CONDITION, BUT I ADMIRE YOU NONETHELESS.

"I SIMPLY WANT TO SPITE ALL THOSE WHO HAVE EVER WRONGED ME"

10/10

HONEST, TRUE, AND VERY EFFECTIVE.

LITERALLY NO ONE, EVER, ACROSS ALL OF HUMAN HISTORY, ON THEIR DEATHBED:

"MY ONLY REGRET IS NOT WORKING UNTIL MIDNIGHT EVERY DAY AT A JOB I HATE SO I COULD GET THAT PROMOTION 3-6 MONTHS EARLIER, MAYBE."

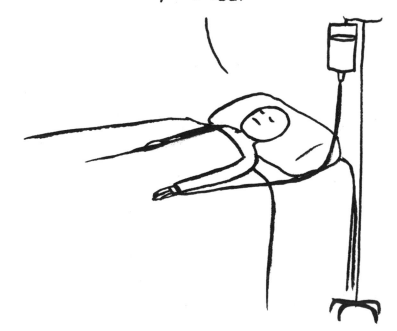

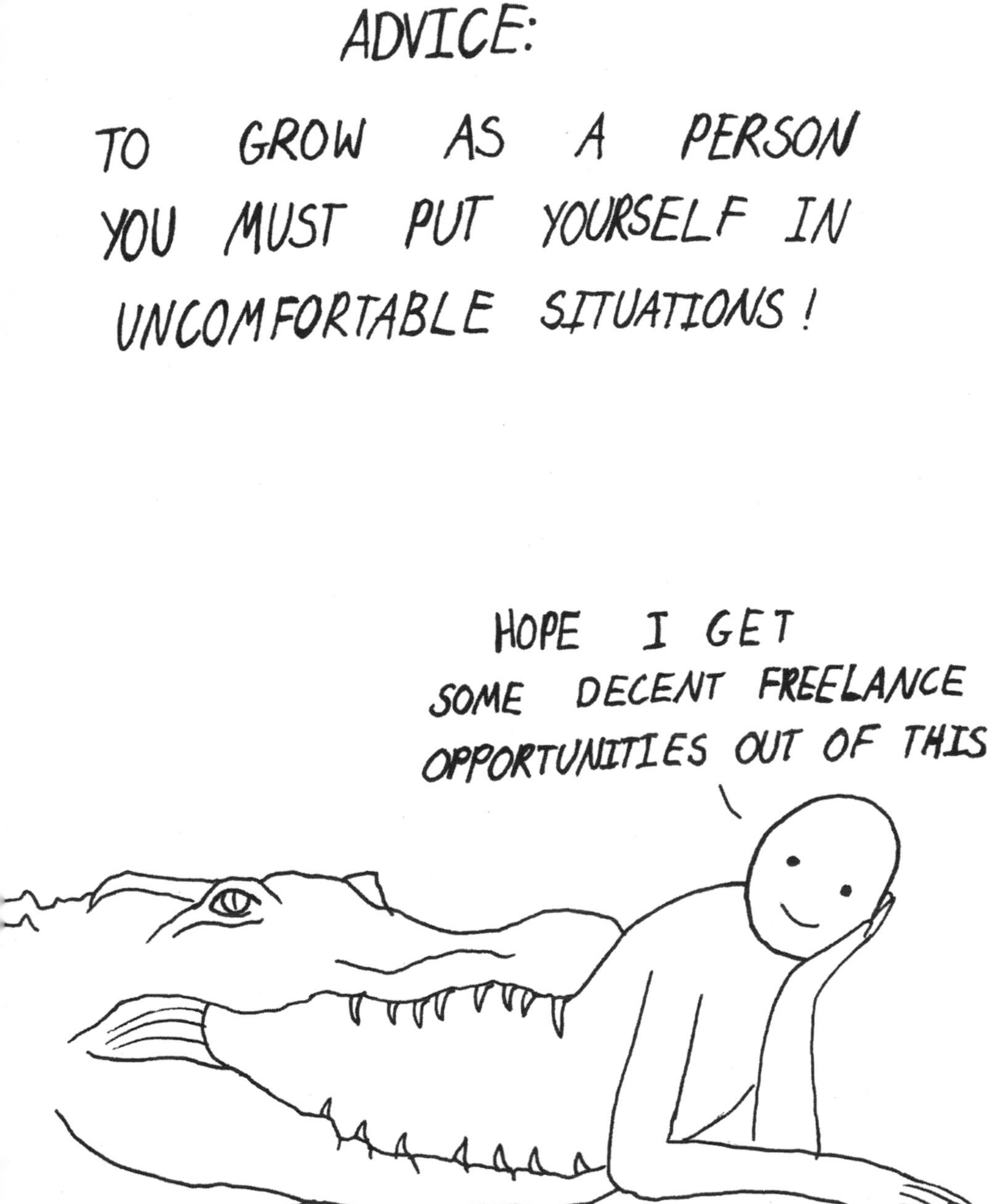
ADVICE:
TO GROW AS A PERSON
YOU MUST PUT YOURSELF IN
UNCOMFORTABLE SITUATIONS!
HOPE I GET
SOME DECENT FREELANCE
OPPORTUNITIES OUT OF THIS

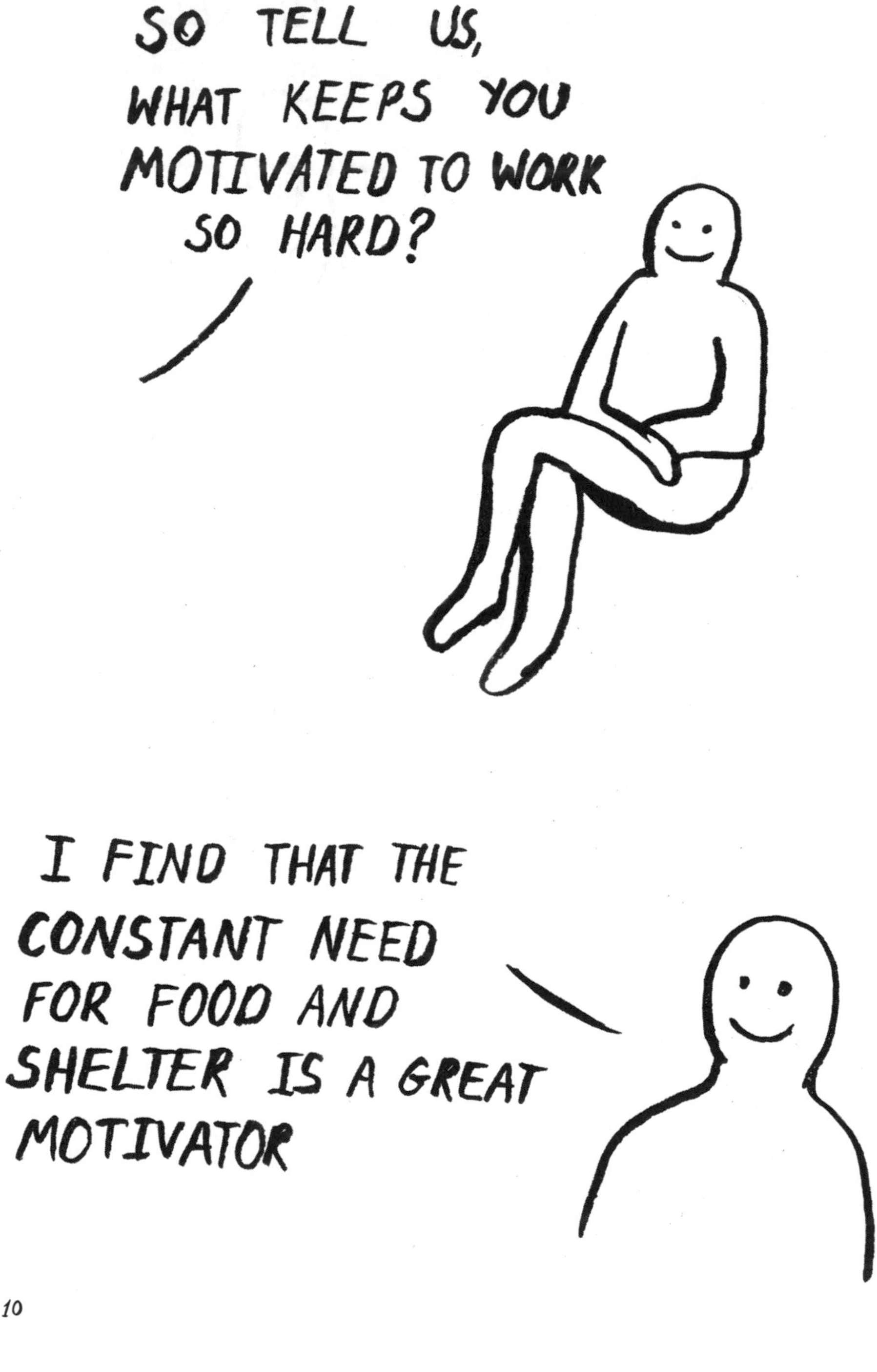
SO TELL US, WHAT KEEPS YOU MOTIVATED TO WORK SO HARD?
I FIND THAT THE CONSTANT NEED FOR FOOD AND SHELTER IS A GREAT MOTIVATOR

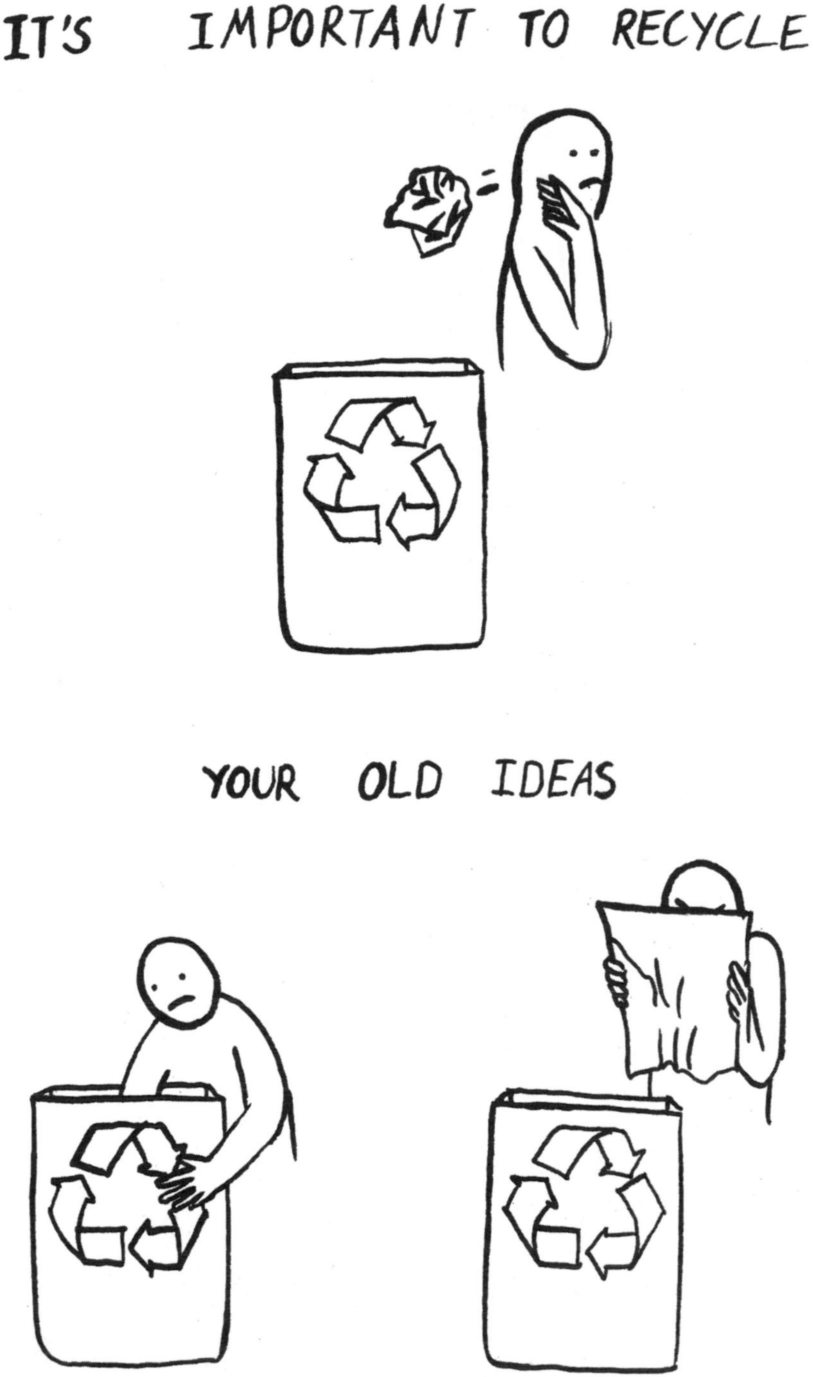
IT'S IMPORTANT TO RECYCLE
YOUR OLD IDEAS

WORKING

RELAXING

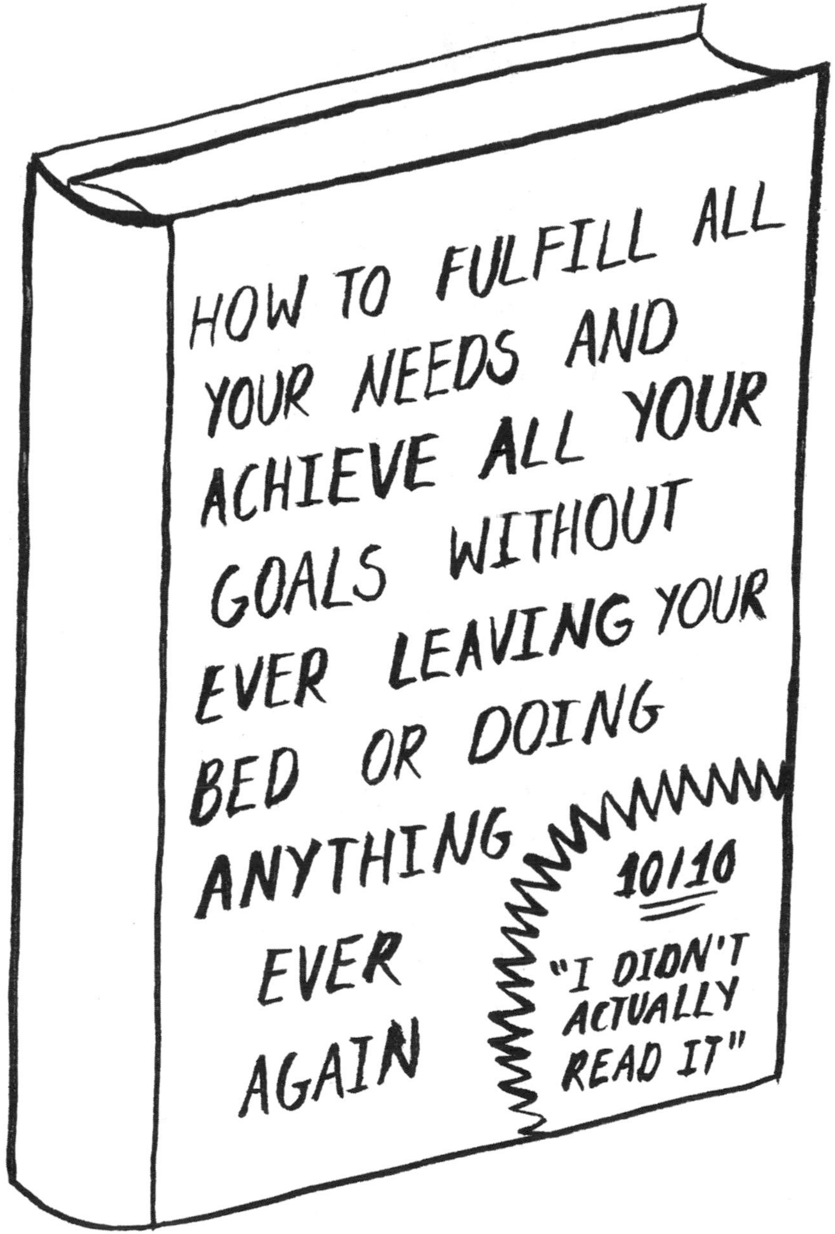
HOW TO FULFILL ALL YOUR NEEDS AND ACHIEVE ALL YOUR GOALS WITHOUT EVER LEAVING YOUR BED OR DOING ANYTHING EVER AGAIN
10/10
"I DIDN'T ACTUALLY READ IT"

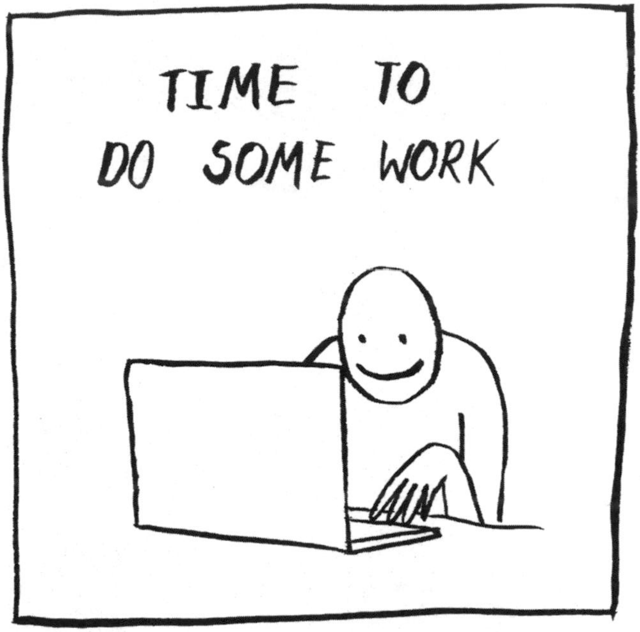
TIME TO
DO SOME WORK

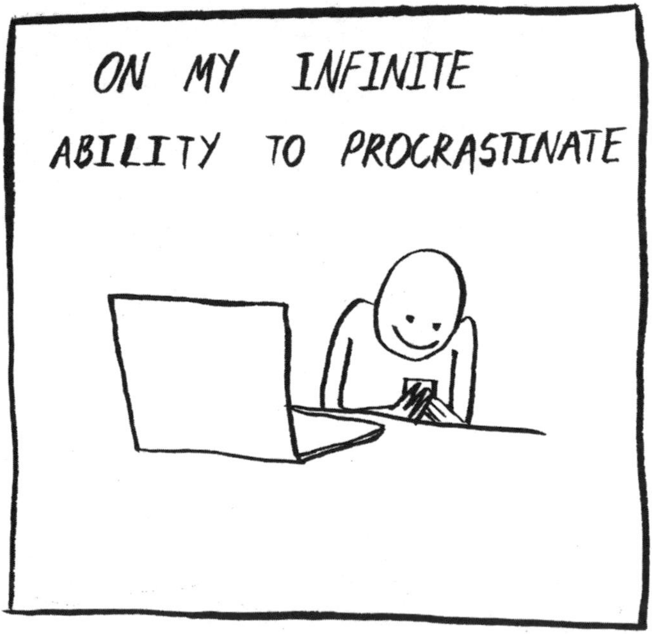
ON MY INFINITE
ABILITY TO PROCRASTINATE

WHAT TO ASK YOURSELF WHEN CHOOSING YOUR CAREER

WHICH OF THESE SCENARIOS WOULD YOU LEAST BE ABLE TO LIVE WITH?

1. FEELING CONSTANTLY UNSTABLE, WORRYING ABOUT MONEY, AND DEALING WITH AN UNCLEAR CAREER TRAJECTORY. YEARS OF HARD WORK AND TOIL NOT GUARANTEEING ANY SORT OF RETURN.

2. MONOTONY, FEELING LIKE YOU'RE PART OF A SYSTEM, A STRICT HIERARCHY. CODES OF CONDUCT AND LIMITATIONS TO YOUR PERSONAL EXPRESSION.

3. FEELING LIKE YOU HAVE GIVEN MOST OF YOUR LIFE TO WORK AND SOMETHING YOU'RE NOT PASSIONATE ABOUT. REGRETTING NOT EXPERIENCING MORE OF LIFE AND SPENDING TIME WITH YOUR FAMILY.

WHAT WE THINK SUCCESS AND HARD WORK LOOK LIKE:

I WAKE UP AT 5AM EVERY DAY, WORK OUT FOR AN HOUR, CHECK ON MY INVESTMENTS, WORK SOLIDLY FOR 10 HOURS, THEN IN THE EVENING I READ AN ENTIRE BOOK TO RELAX. I'M 95% ALLOY AND I WAS MADE IN A LAB!

WHAT SUCCESS AND HARD WORK CAN ACTUALLY LOOK LIKE:

I'VE MANAGED TO COMPLETE ALL MY TASKS IN HALF THE TIME BY WORKING SMARTER, NOT HARDER.

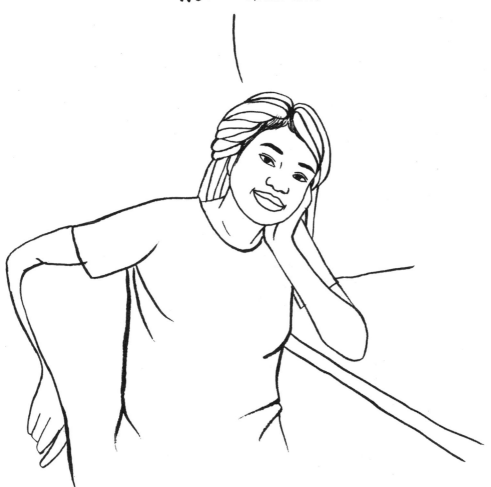

OR IT CAN LOOK LIKE:

I SPEND MOST OF THE DAY DOING NOTHING AT ALL, THEN IN THE EVENING I ENTER A MANIC CREATIVE STATE AND WORK UNTIL 4AM!

OR, OF COURSE:

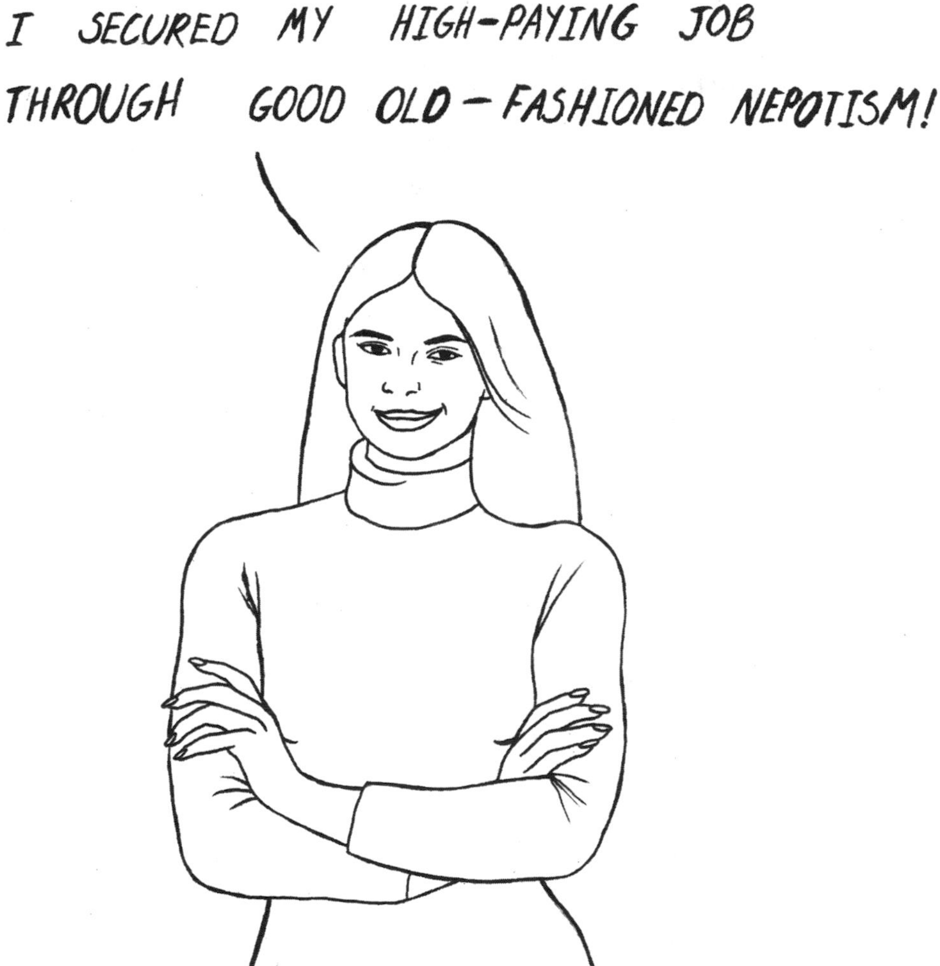
I SECURED MY HIGH-PAYING JOB THROUGH GOOD OLD-FASHIONED NEPOTISM!

IF YOU CHOSE...

1: AVOID CREATIVE CAREERS WITH LITTLE STABILITY (ANYTHING FREELANCE, BEING AN ARTIST, MUSICIAN, CONTENT CREATOR).

2: AVOID HIGHLY DEMANDING CAREERS IN CORPORATE SETTINGS SUCH AS FINANCE AND CORPORATE LAW.

3: AVOID CAREERS THAT YOU'RE ONLY CONSIDERING BECAUSE THEY SEEM SENSIBLE — YOU WILL ONLY RESENT IT.

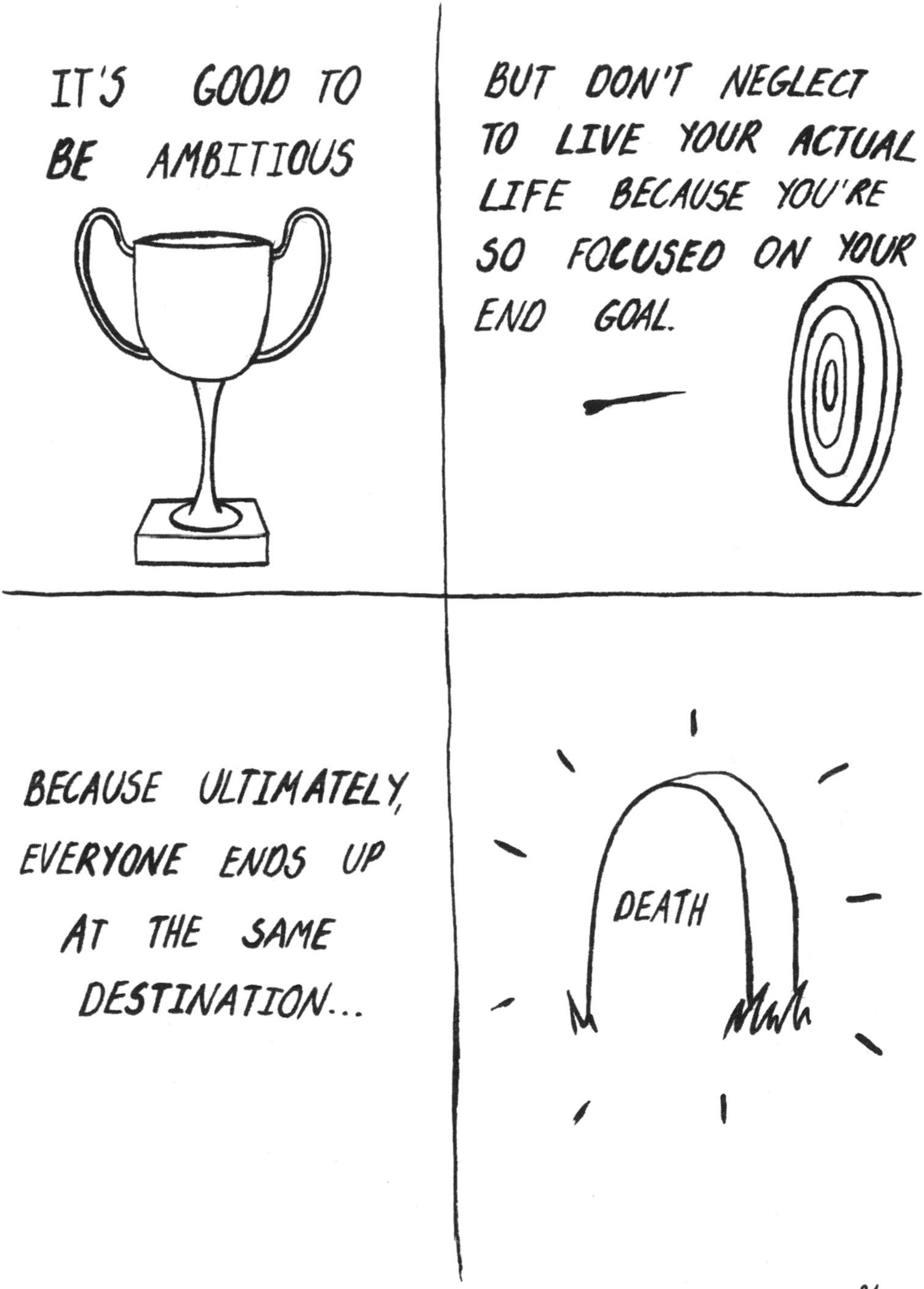
IT'S GOOD TO BE AMBITIOUS
BUT DON'T NEGLECT TO LIVE YOUR ACTUAL LIFE BECAUSE YOU'RE SO FOCUSED ON YOUR END GOAL.
BECAUSE ULTIMATELY, EVERYONE ENDS UP AT THE SAME DESTINATION...
DEATH

INSTAGRAM

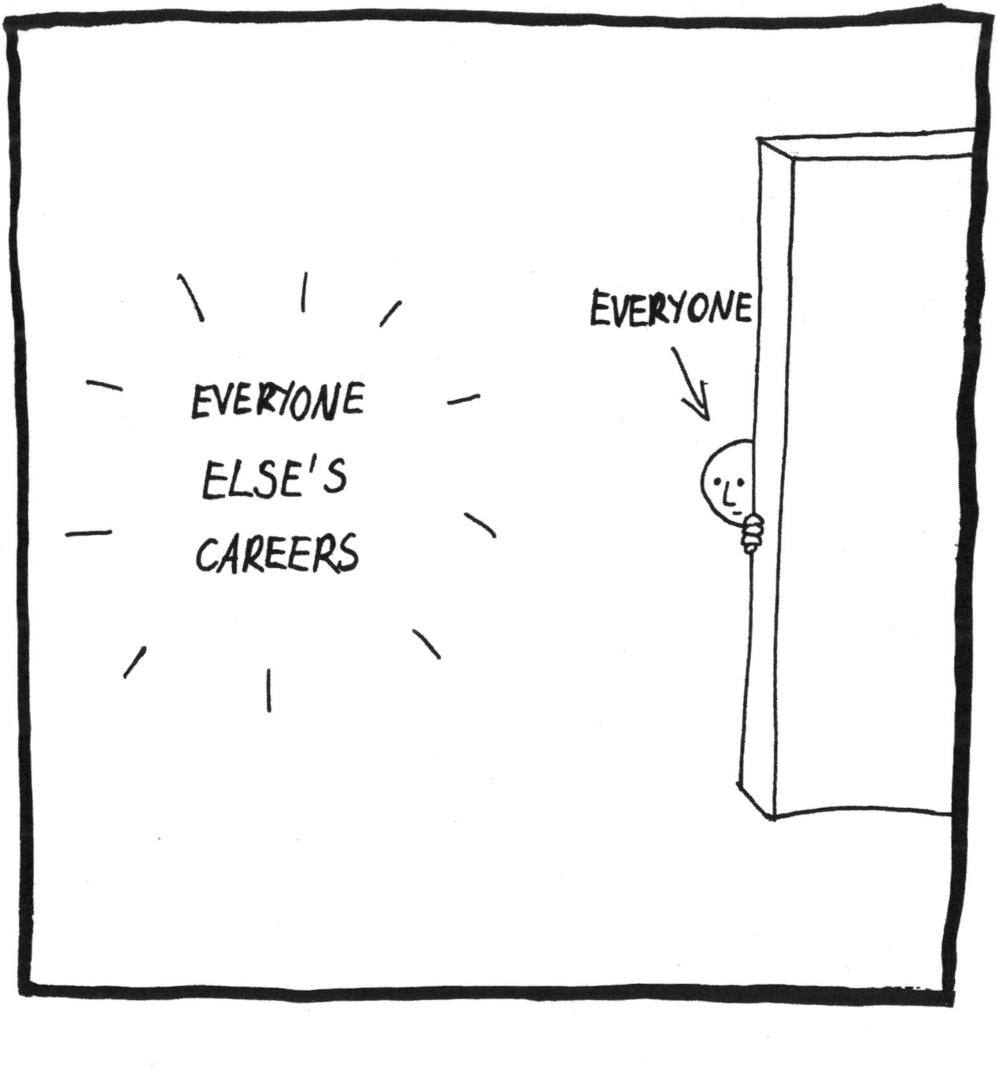

THIS IDEA
IS EXCELLENT

LATER, IN THE COLD LIGHT OF DAY

THIS IDEA
WAS
TERRIBLE

WHEN SUCCESSFUL:

THIS IS THE RESULT
ONLY OF MY TALENTS
AND STRENGTH OF
CHARACTER,
NOT LUCK

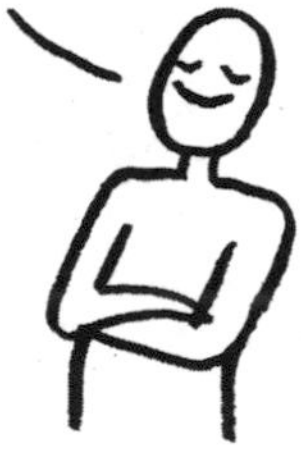

WHEN UNSUCCESSFUL:

THIS IS A REFLECTION
ONLY OF MY BAD LUCK,
AND THE WORLD'S PERSONAL
VENDETTA AGAINST ME,
NOTHING TO DO WITH ANY
OF MY FLAWS

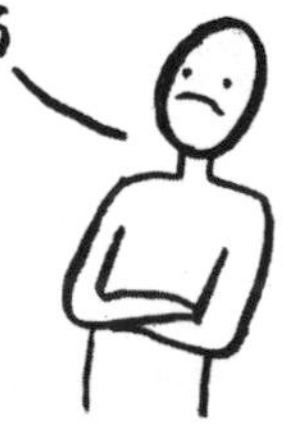

TIRED OF BEING TOO DAMN EFFICIENT?

- DO YOU WANT TO FEEL BAD ABOUT YOURSELF MOST EVENINGS?
- DO YOU PREFER TO DO ALL YOUR WORK IN A MAD RUSH THE NIGHT BEFORE?
- WOULD YOU LIKE TO HAVE AN AVERAGE SCREEN TIME OF 12 HOURS A DAY?

WHY NOT TRY...

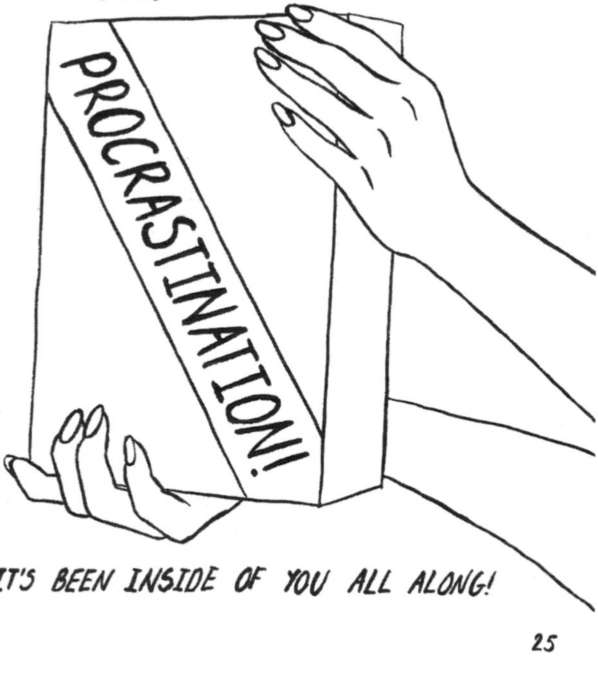
PROCRASTINATION!

* MADE WITH 100% ORGANIC BURNOUT!
* NOW WITH 20% MORE GUILT!
* GENTLY PASTEURIZED

NO PURCHASE NECESSARY, IT'S BEEN INSIDE OF YOU ALL ALONG!

MY WORK IS TERRIBLE

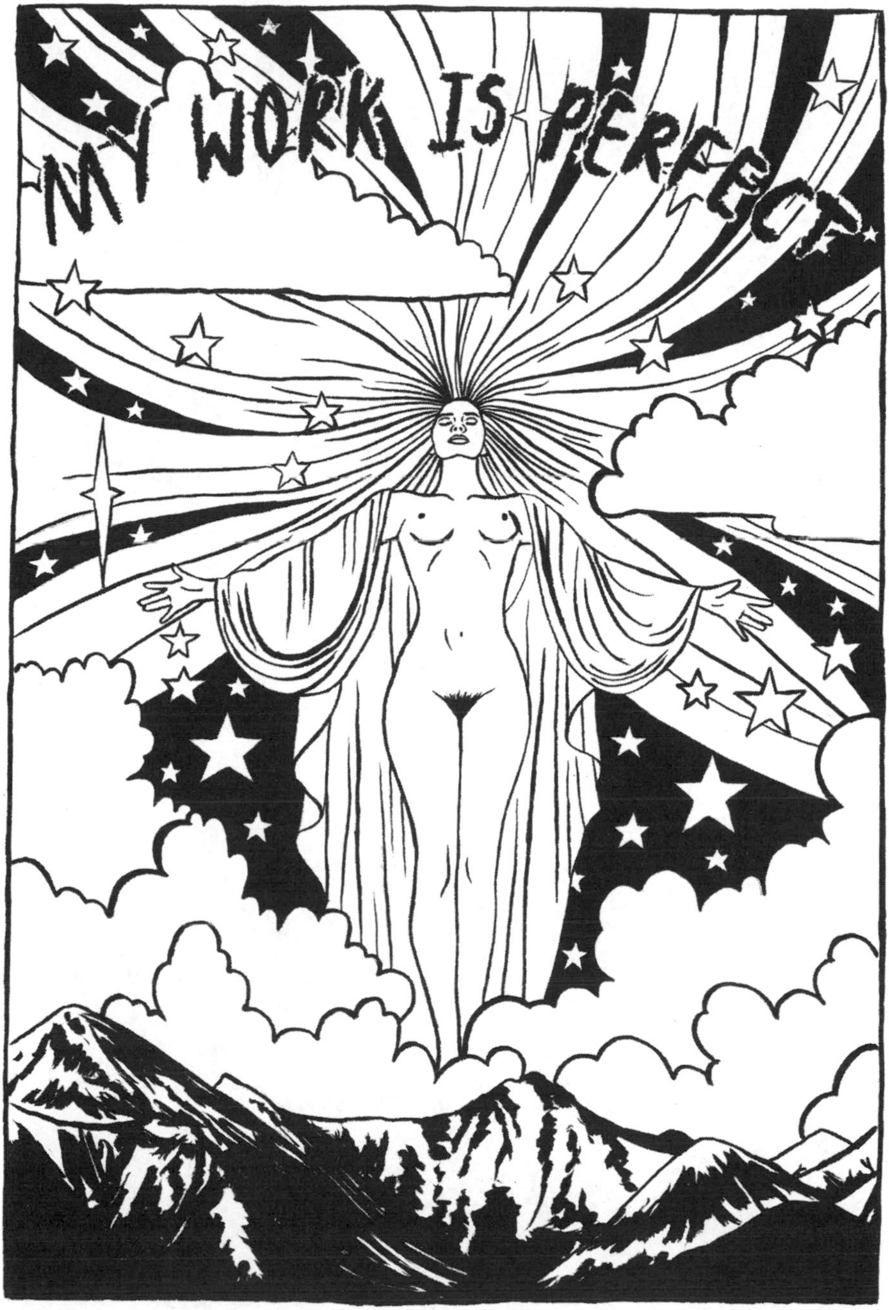
MY WORK IS PERFECT

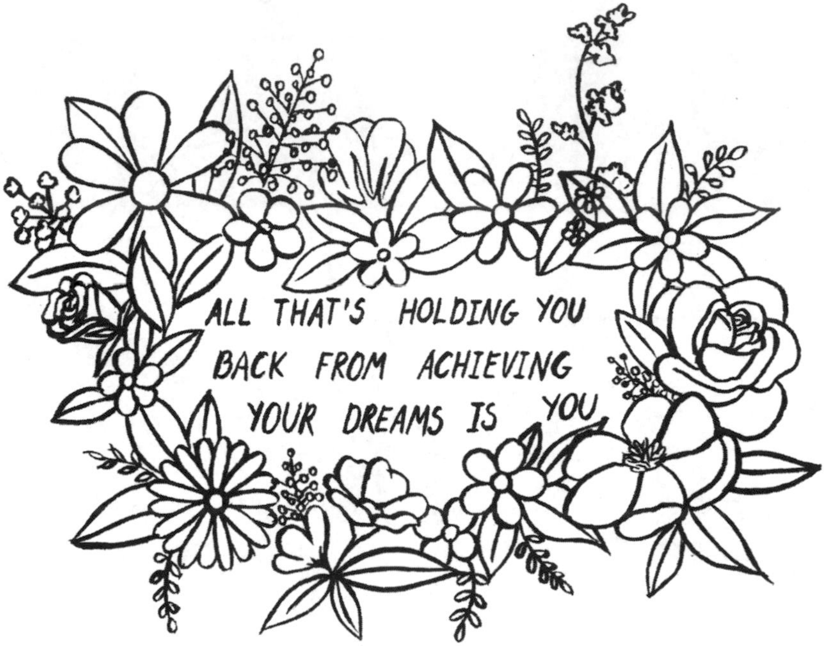
ALL THAT'S HOLDING YOU
BACK FROM ACHIEVING
YOUR DREAMS IS YOU

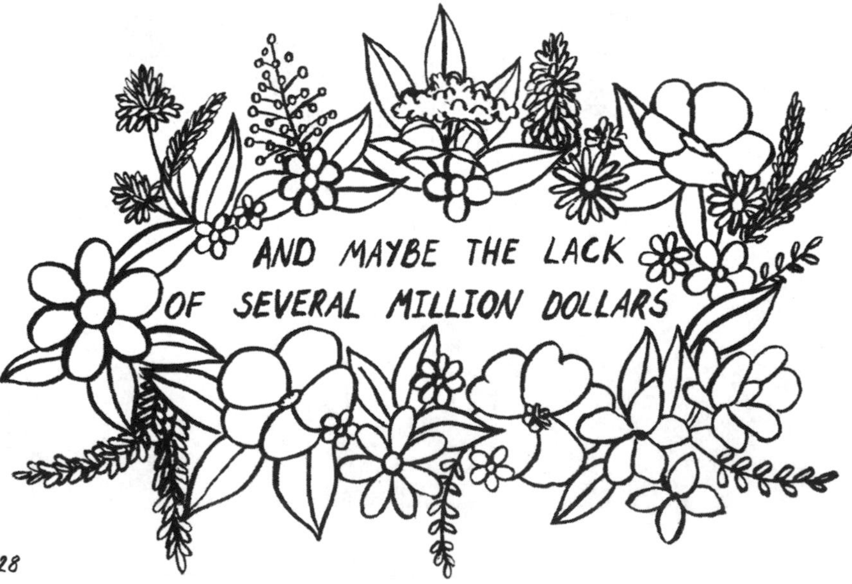
AND MAYBE THE LACK
OF SEVERAL MILLION DOLLARS

TOXIC WORKPLACE BINGO

"WE'RE LIKE FAMILY HERE"	FRENEMIES	SUNDAY NIGHT DREAD	EXPECTED TO WORK LATE OR SEEN AS LAZY	HIGH TURNOVER
ANY YELLING WHATSOEVER	BOSS HAS FAVORITES	DRAMATIC QUITTING FANTASIES	MALICIOUS GOSSIP	UNION-BUSTING
CONSTANT FEAR OF BEING PUNISHED OR FIRED	CRYING IN THE BATHROOM	FREE SPACE	BUYING WORKERS' LOYALTY WITH EXCESSIVE PERKS BUT NO CHANGES	BURN-OUT
PEOPLE SCARED TO QUESTION IDEAS	OPPORTUNITIES IMPEDED	PEOPLE REGULARLY FAKING "SICK DAYS"	IF THE BOSS IS IN A BAD MOOD, THEN EVERYONE HAS A BAD DAY	BLAMED FOR THINGS THAT WERE NOT YOUR FAULT
HAVING TO PLACATE YOUR BOSS'S EGO	SNIDE REMARKS	"PROMOTIONS" WITH MORE WORK BUT NOT PAY	DOING WORK ABOVE YOUR PAY GRADE	PASSIVE-AGGRESSION

COMPANIES PRETENDIING TO CARE
ABOUT YOUR MENTAL HEALTH

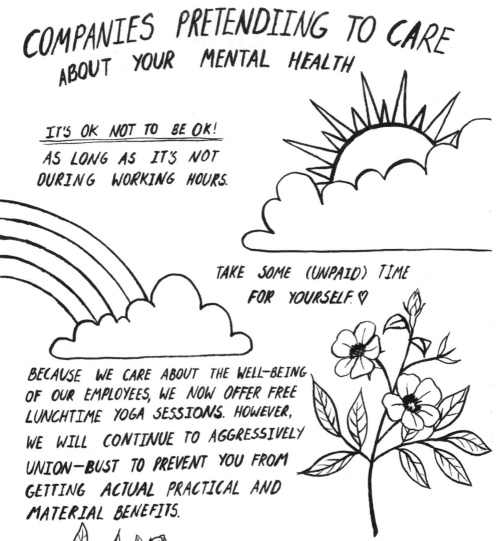

IT'S OK NOT TO BE OK!
AS LONG AS IT'S NOT
DURING WORKING HOURS.

TAKE SOME (UNPAID) TIME
FOR YOURSELF. ♡

BECAUSE WE CARE ABOUT THE WELL-BEING
OF OUR EMPLOYEES, WE NOW OFFER FREE
LUNCHTIME YOGA SESSIONS. HOWEVER,
WE WILL CONTINUE TO AGGRESSIVELY
UNION-BUST TO PREVENT YOU FROM
GETTING ACTUAL PRACTICAL AND
MATERIAL BENEFITS.

THERE IS NO SHAME IN
MENTAL ILLNESS!
HOWEVER, IF IT AFFECTS
YOUR PRODUCTIVITY, WE
WILL BE REPLACING YOU.

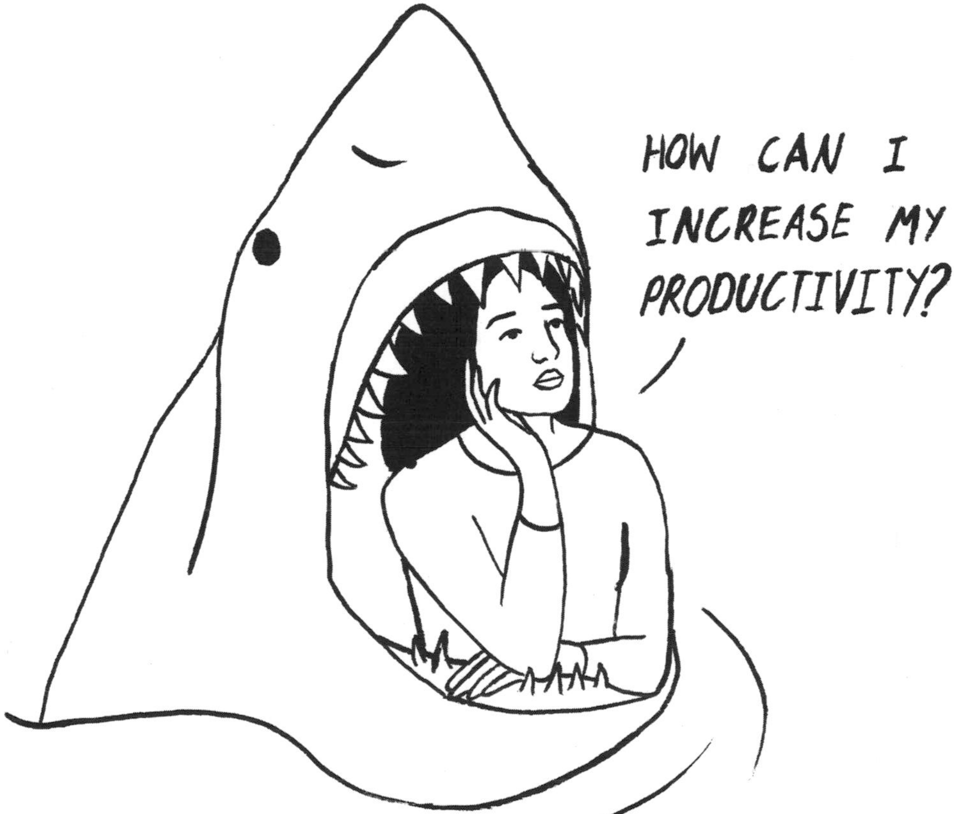
HOW CAN I INCREASE MY PRODUCTIVITY?

SO PEOPLE JUST WAKE UP AND
ARE IMMEDIATELY PRODUCTIVE?

YOU'RE TELLING ME THEY
SIMPLY OPEN THEIR EYES
AND START DOING TASKS?

WOW.

THAT'S CRAZY.

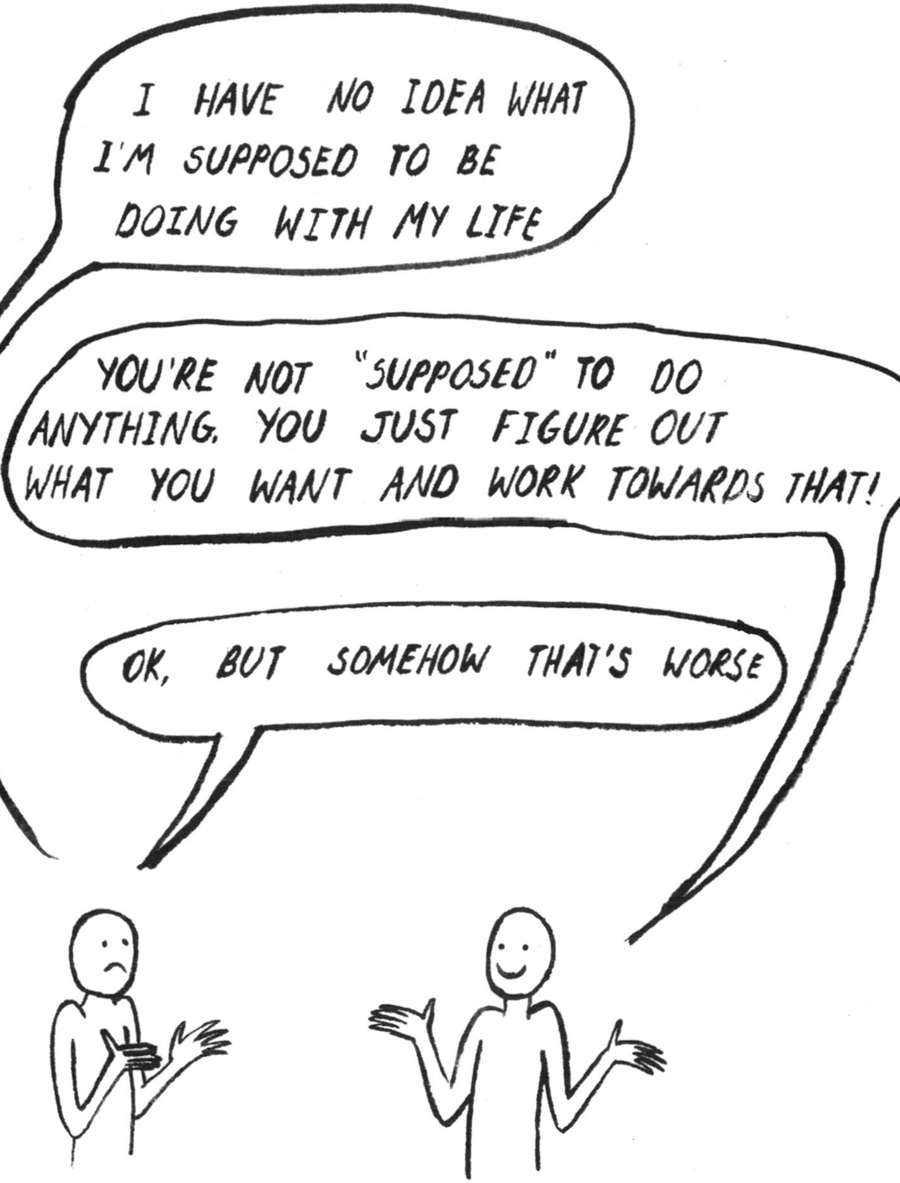
I HAVE NO IDEA WHAT I'M SUPPOSED TO BE DOING WITH MY LIFE
YOU'RE NOT "SUPPOSED" TO DO ANYTHING. YOU JUST FIGURE OUT WHAT YOU WANT AND WORK TOWARDS THAT!
OK, BUT SOMEHOW THAT'S WORSE

CORPORATE SNAKES AND LADDERS (MILLENNIAL AND GEN Z EDITION)

1
UNDEREMPLOYED AND OVERQUALIFIED
2
YOUR FIRST ENTRY-LEVEL JOB IN YOUR CHOSEN FIELD
YOU NEED 3-4 YEARS EXPERIENCE FOR THIS ROLE

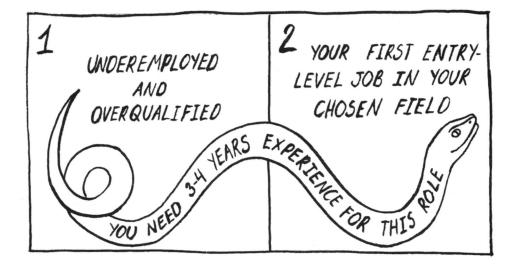

THESE IDEAS ARE TERRIBLE

NOT HAVING A JOB
IS THE WORST

HAVING A JOB
IS THE WORST

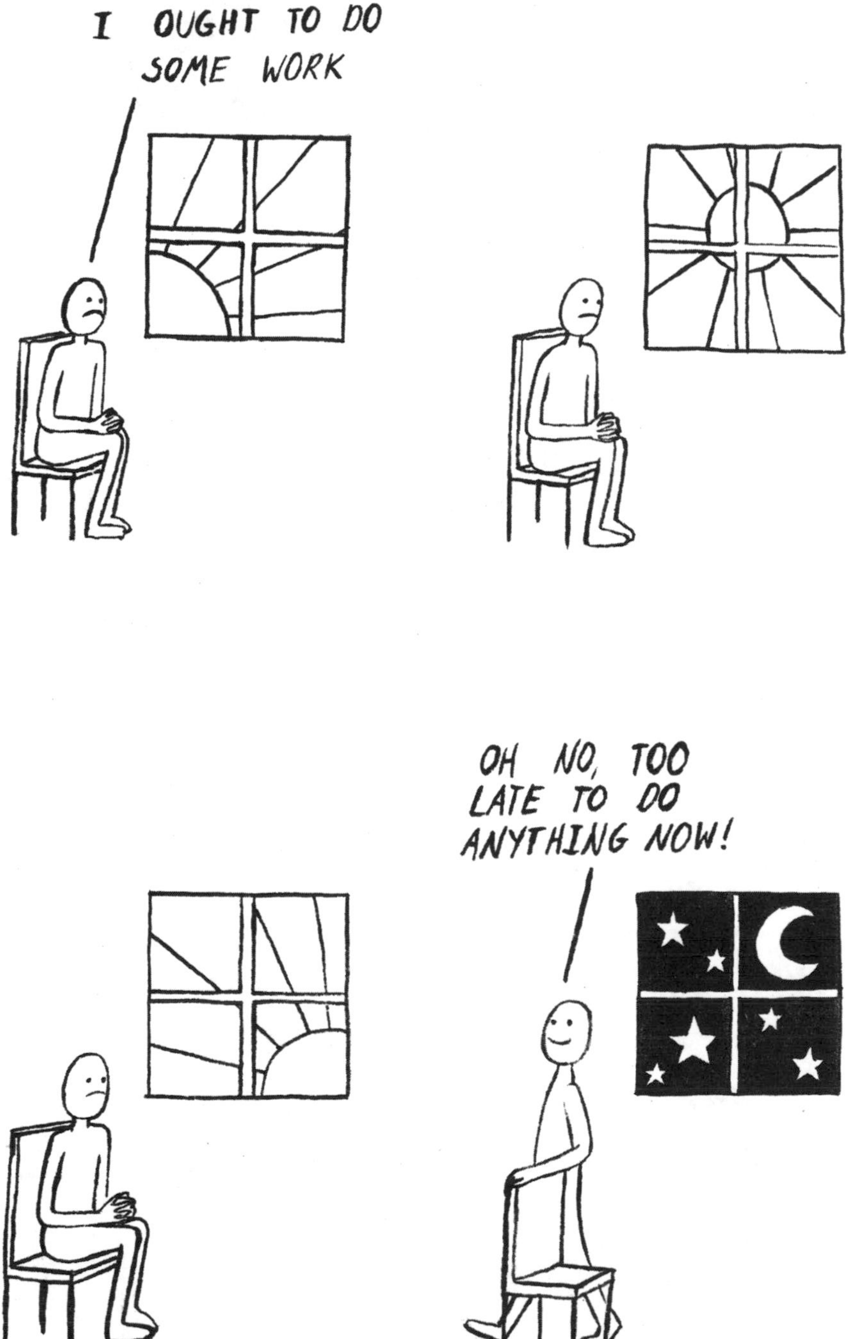
I OUGHT TO DO SOME WORK
OH NO, TOO LATE TO DO ANYTHING NOW!

A SIMPLE FLOWCHART TO FIGURE OUT IF YOU WILL ACHIEVE YOUR GOALS

DO YOU ACTUALLY DO THE WORK TOWARDS YOUR GOALS OR DO YOU JUST TALK ABOUT DOING THE WORK?
I DO THE WORK
I JUST TALK ABOUT DOING THE WORK
YOU MIGHT ACHIEVE YOUR GOALS
YOU WILL NOT ACHIEVE YOUR GOALS

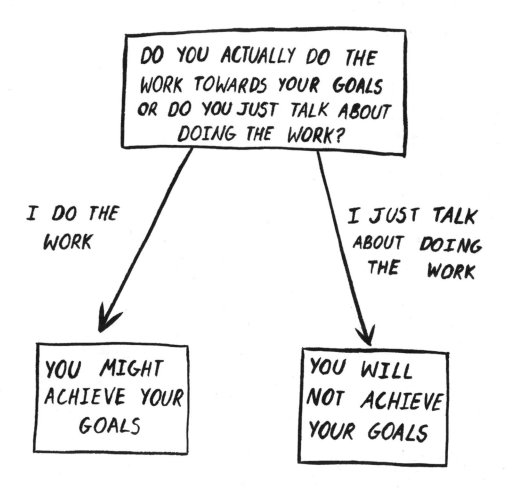

NON-CAPITALIST ALTERNATIVES TO LIFELONG AMBITIONS

1. WINNING THE LOVE AND RESPECT OF A MURDER OF CROWS AND EVENTUALLY TRAINING THEM TO ATTACK YOUR ENEMIES.

2. FINDING A FOUR-LEAF CLOVER. (THEY'RE FREE! YOU CAN JUST TAKE THEM, STRAIGHT FROM THE GROUND!)

3. AGING SIGNIFICANTLY BETTER THAN YOUR PEERS BY NEVER, EVER GOING OUT IN THE SUN.

4. TAKING CANDY FROM A BABY.

5. GROWING ALL THE FOOD YOU CONSUME, EVEN IF IT MEANS A DIET CONSISTING ENTIRELY OF POTATOES, BECAUSE YOU LIVE IN THE NORTHERN HEMISPHERE.

6. PERFECTING THE ART OF ACCURATELY IMITATING ALL BIRD SOUNDS.

7. MAKING A REALLY NICE PATCHWORK QUILT.

8. DOING A CARTWHEEL AT AGE 52.

9. EATING THE RICH.

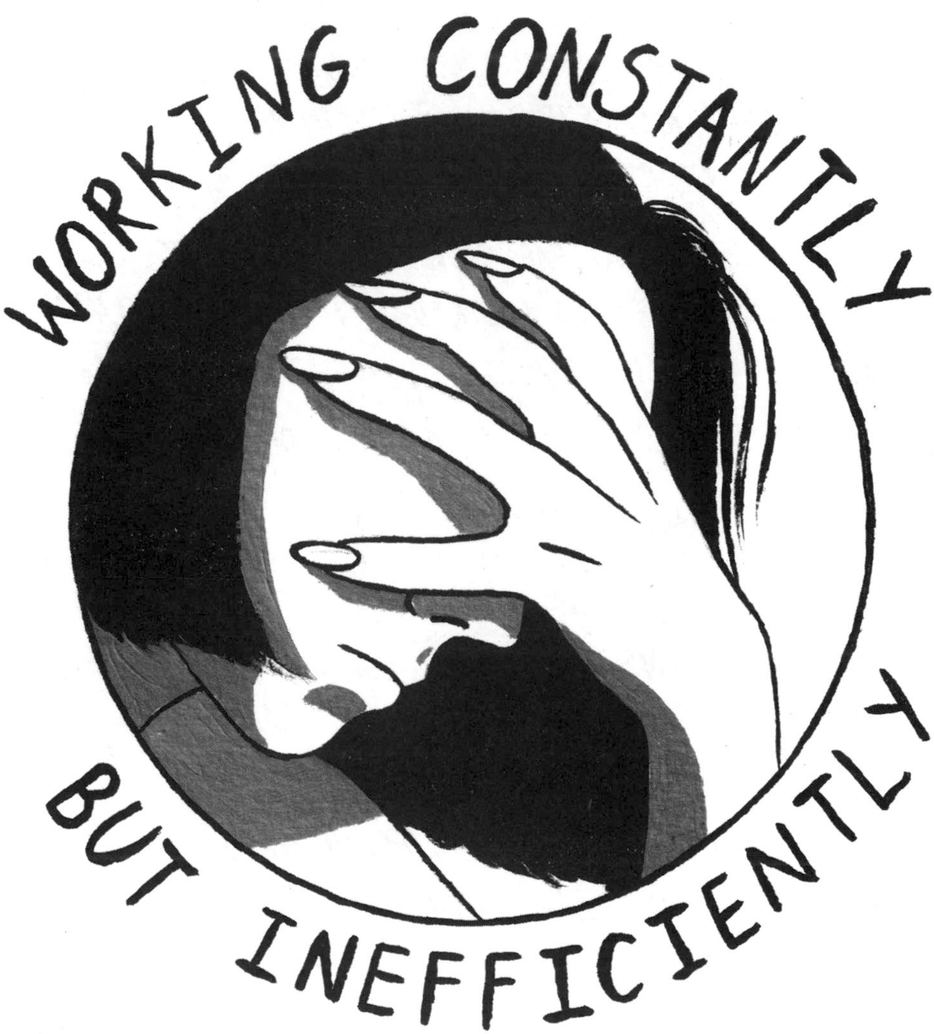
WORKING CONSTANTLY
BUT INEFFICIENTLY

I HAVE SO MUCH
TO DO TODAY

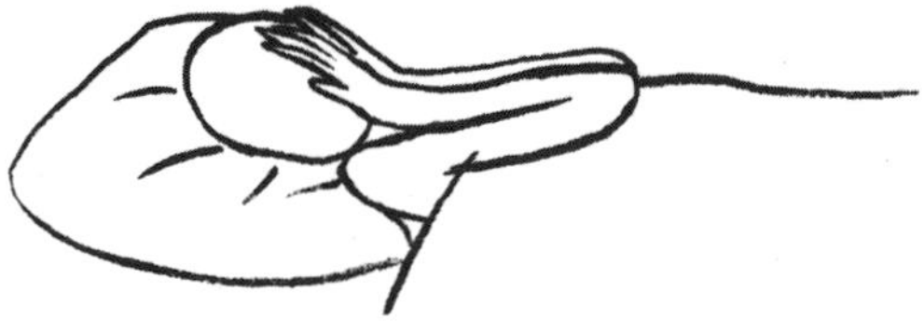

INSTEAD, I DID

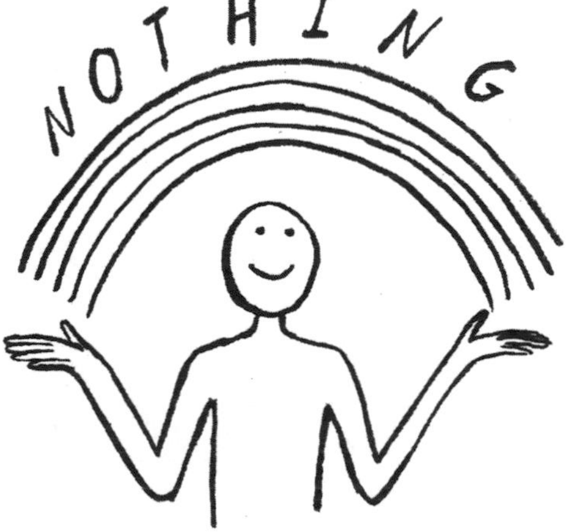
NOTHING

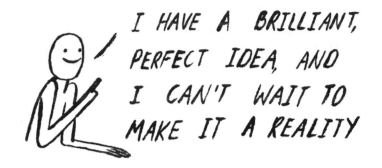

I HAVE A BRILLIANT, PERFECT IDEA, AND I CAN'T WAIT TO MAKE IT A REALITY

A FLAWED, YET STILL GOOD AND IMPRESSIVE END RESULT

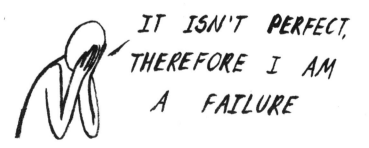

IT ISN'T **PERFECT**, THEREFORE I AM A FAILURE

TIME TO

NOT DO MYSELF ANY FAVORS

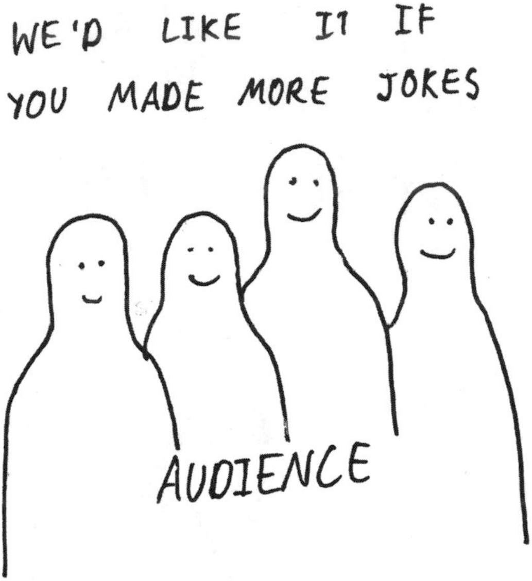
WE'D LIKE IT IF
YOU MADE MORE JOKES
AUDIENCE

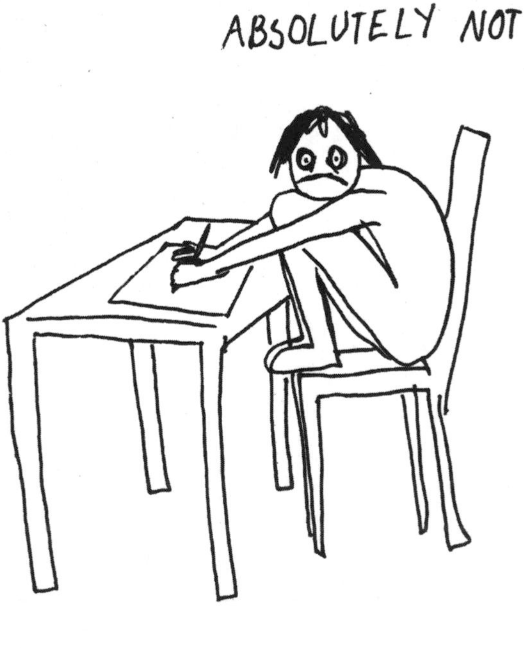
ABSOLUTELY NOT

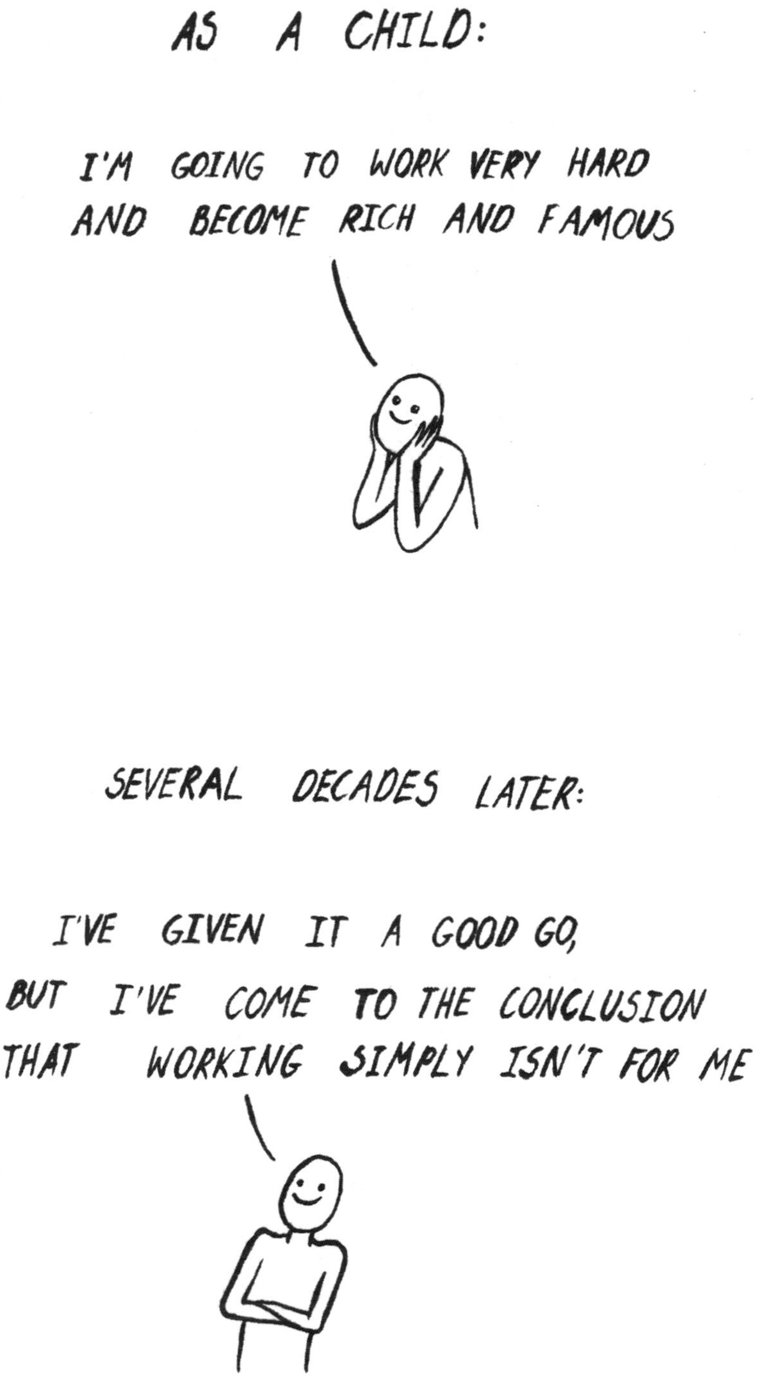
AS A CHILD:
I'M GOING TO WORK VERY HARD AND BECOME RICH AND FAMOUS
SEVERAL DECADES LATER:
I'VE GIVEN IT A GOOD GO, BUT I'VE COME TO THE CONCLUSION THAT WORKING SIMPLY ISN'T FOR ME

I HAVE JUST RECIEVED
AN EMAIL INFORMING ME
THAT I'VE JUST ACHIEVED
A MAJOR GOAL

OK, BACK TO
WORK

LAZINESS ISN'T A REAL CHARACTER TRAIT.

WHAT WE CONSIDER TO BE LAZINESS IS ACTUALLY SYMPTOMS OF BURNOUT, DISINTEREST, DEPRESSION, OR OTHER BARRIERS. NO ONE IS ACTUALLY, INHERENTLY LAZY.

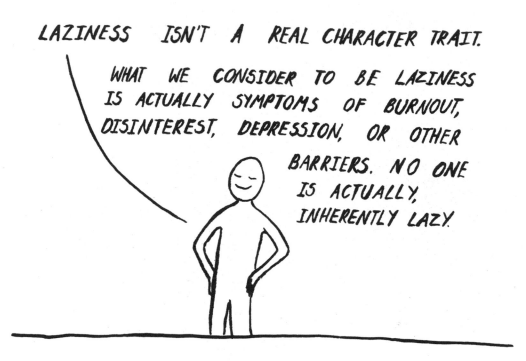

EXCEPT FOR ME. I'M THE EXCEPTION.

THE MOST EFFICIENT WAY TO CLEAN

STEP ONE:

HAVE A PRESSING TASK YOU ABSOLUTELY NEED TO DO.

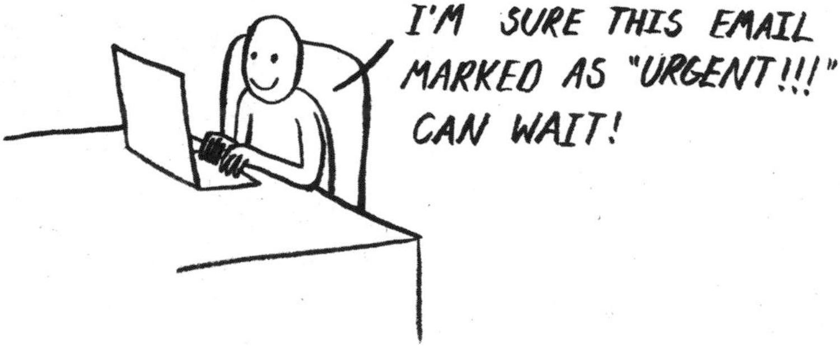
I'M SURE THIS EMAIL MARKED AS "URGENT!!!" CAN WAIT!

STEP TWO:

MANICALLY CLEAN YOUR ENTIRE LIVING SPACE AS A WAY OF PROCRASTINATING WHILE MAINTAINING A VENEER OF PRODUCTIVITY!

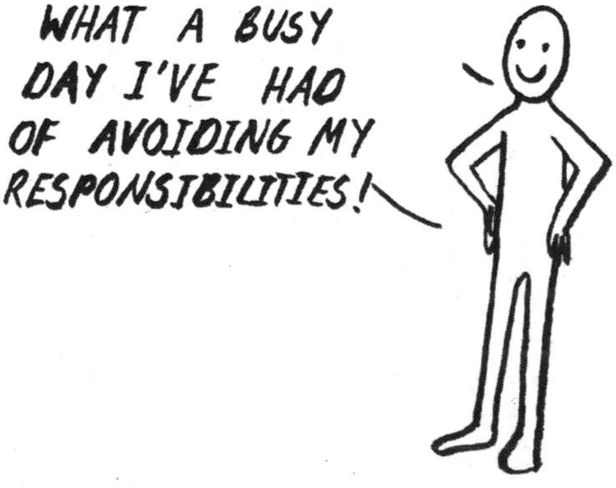
WHAT A BUSY DAY I'VE HAD OF AVOIDING MY RESPONSIBILITIES!

THE FIRST WORD YOU SEE
IS HOW YOU WILL SPEND TODAY PROCRASTINATING

```
E A T I N G A S L E E P I N G S O L
D S Z F L I N S T A G R A M M I N G
S T A R I N G I N T O S P A C E P T
F R P S A R G U I N G O N L I N E I
O C R Y I N G X F A R T I N G T G K
W J T P M S I S C R O L L I N G C T
C M N E T F L I X B I N G E A W D O
K A W I K I P E D I A H O L E Z X K
E X I S T E N T I A L C R I S I S B
H C M C O B J W A L K I N G O M P C
C B X W R F M E M E S J C A K G Y P
R E K L M N H E P A C W S H N J O O
Y F A E R B L T L X Q F T I D S U K
I E D R I N K I N G D G P W T H T L
N J C Q Z E P N S X P P U Q F L U N
G S E R V I N G L O O K S B J P B F
D T F H G S K M Y H V C R G K F E G
A E B L F O P D S N A L K I N G T Z
```

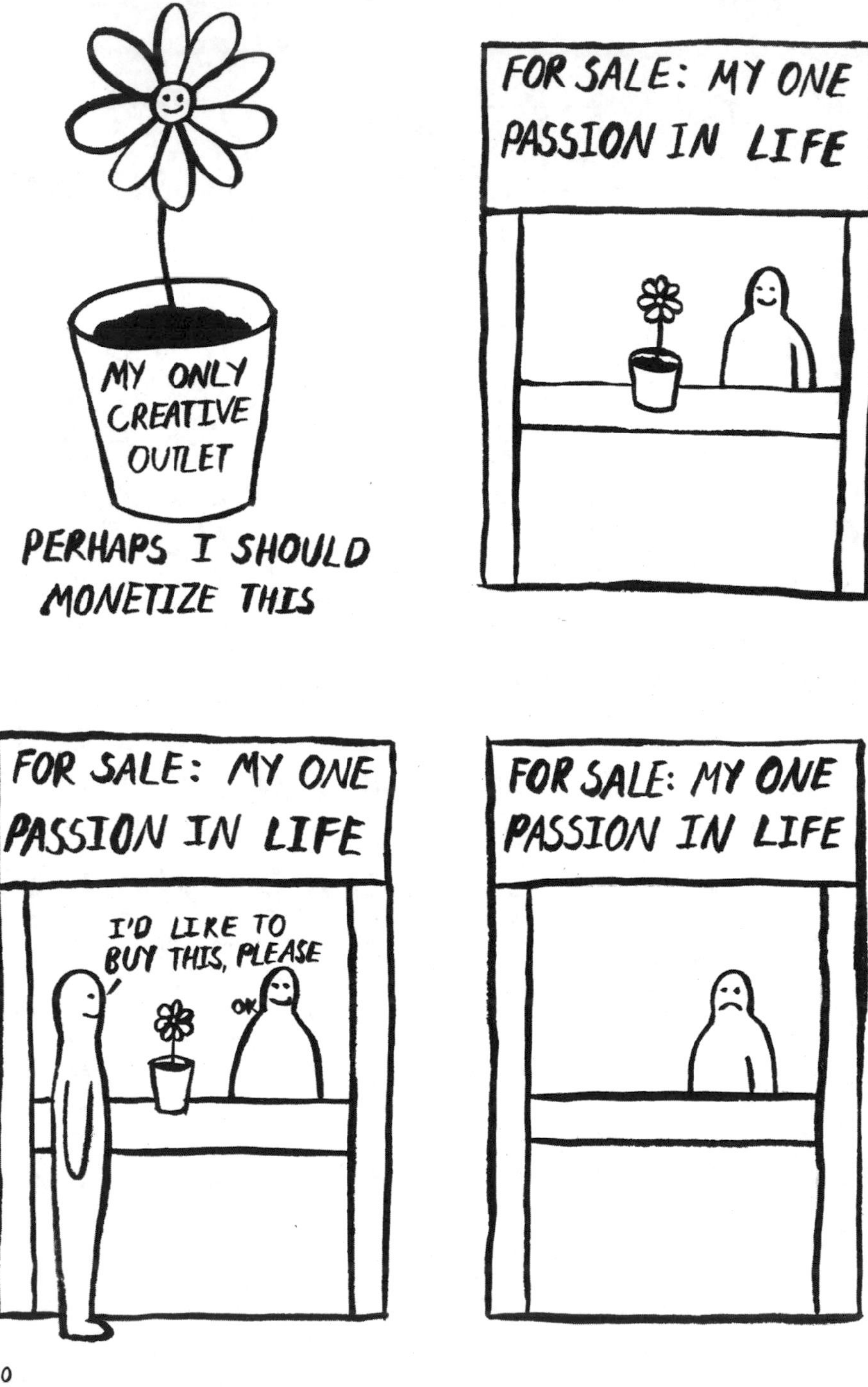
MY ONLY CREATIVE OUTLET
PERHAPS I SHOULD MONETIZE THIS
FOR SALE: MY ONE PASSION IN LIFE
FOR SALE: MY ONE PASSION IN LIFE
I'D LIKE TO BUY THIS, PLEASE
OK
FOR SALE: MY ONE PASSION IN LIFE

JUST BE KIND TO YOURSELF DURING THIS TIME. YOU **DON'T** HAVE TO BE PRODUCTIVE.

HMM... YES SHALL I SEE IF MY **LANDLORD** WILL ACCEPT MY RENT PAYMENT IN SELF-CARE AND BANANA BREAD THIS MONTH?

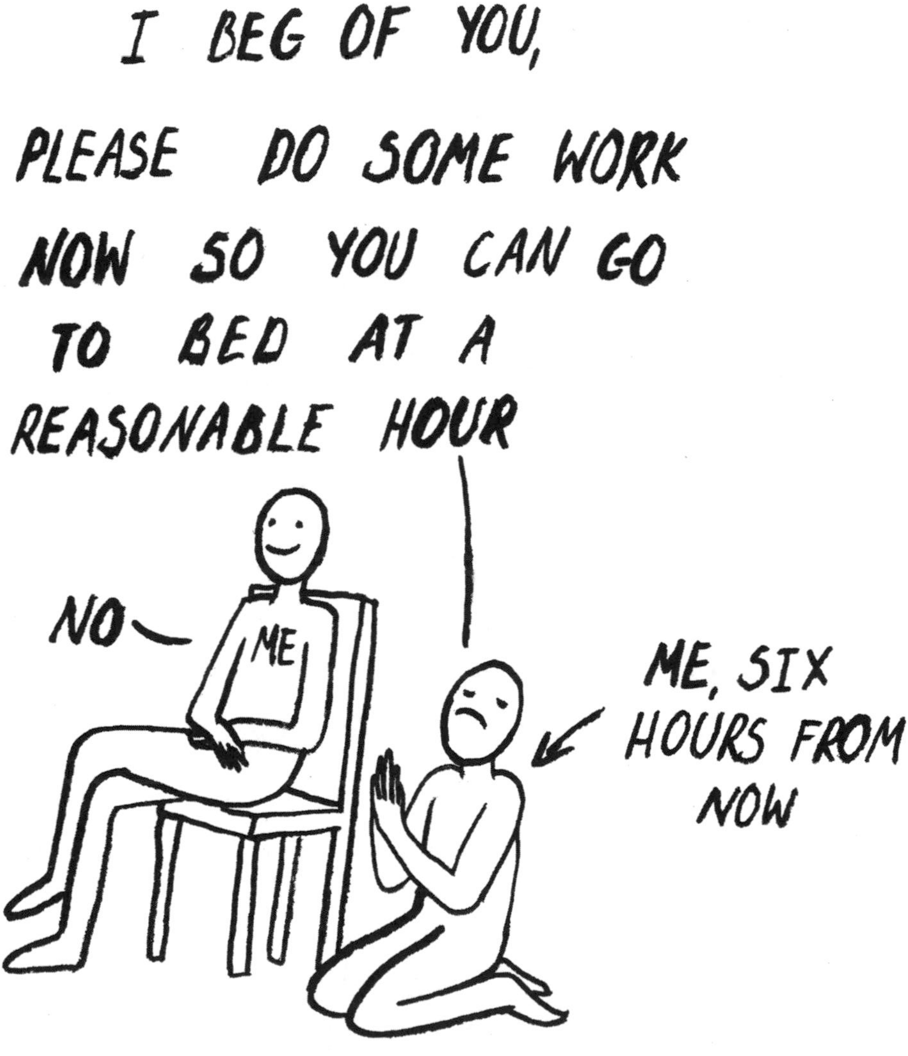
I BEG OF YOU,
PLEASE DO SOME WORK NOW SO YOU CAN GO TO BED AT A REASONABLE HOUR
NO
ME
ME, SIX HOURS FROM NOW

AT LAST!
MY GREATEST WORK IS COMPLETE

OK, I NEVER WANT TO LOOK AT IT AGAIN

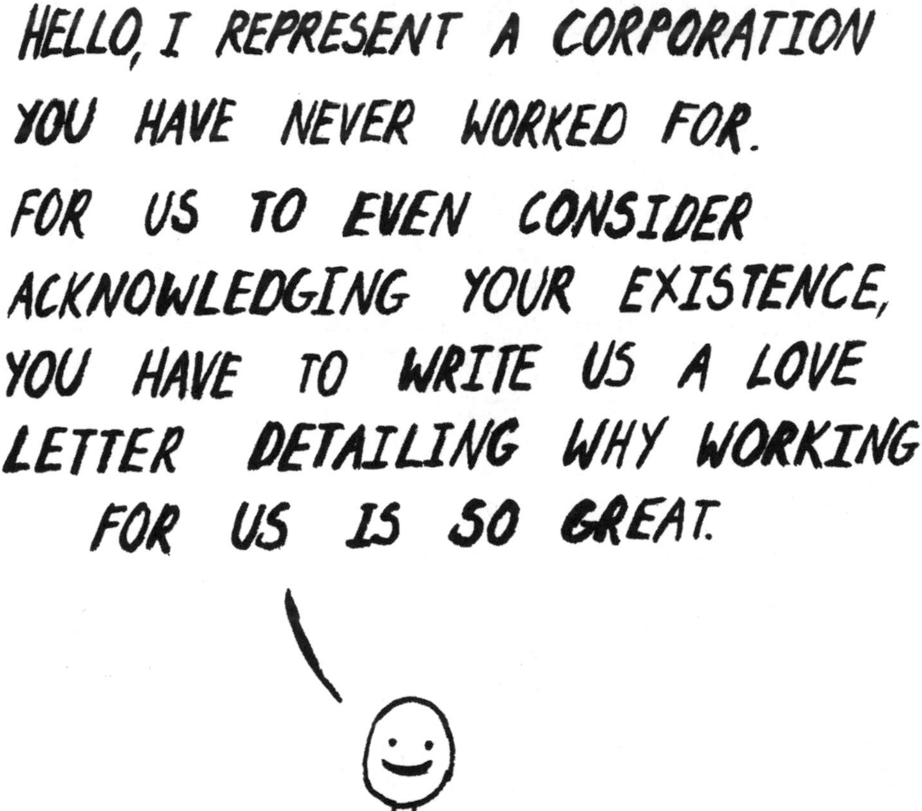

HELLO, I REPRESENT A CORPORATION YOU HAVE NEVER WORKED FOR. FOR US TO EVEN CONSIDER ACKNOWLEDGING YOUR EXISTENCE, YOU HAVE TO WRITE US A LOVE LETTER DETAILING WHY WORKING FOR US IS SO GREAT.

DO I ACTUALLY LIKE THIS JOB OR DO I JUST HATE APPLYING TO NEW ONES?

HOW PEOPLE THINK INSPIRATION WORKS:

EUREKA! I'VE JUST BEEN BLESSED WITH A BRILLIANT IDEA, ENTIRELY AT RANDOM!

HOW INSPIRATION ACTUALLY WORKS:

AFTER OBSESSING OVER THIS FOR WEEKS, NAY, MONTHS, AND TRYING HUNDREDS OF IDEAS, I'M SURE AT LEAST TWO OR THREE OF THEM ARE OK.

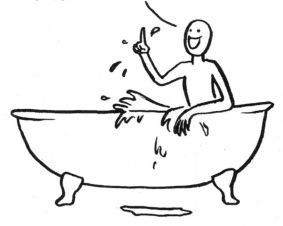

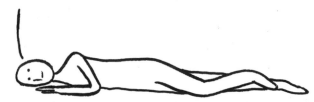

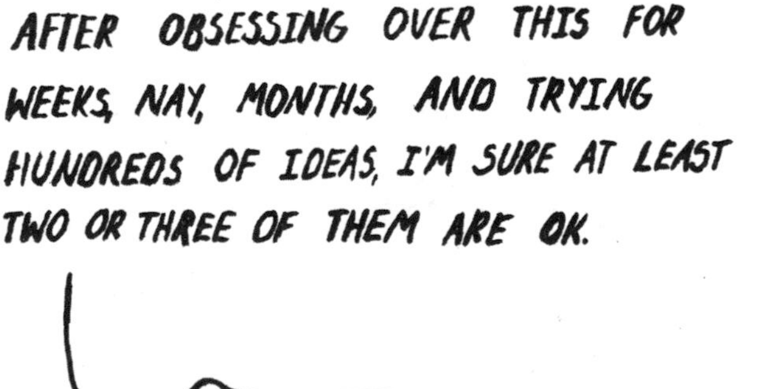

ASSERTIVE EMAIL PRACTICE

TO:

SUBJECT:

HELLO ———————,

_____
_____
_____
_____
_____
_____
_____

BEST,

_____

TRY FILLING THIS IN WITHOUT USING
ANY EXCLAMATION MARKS!!!

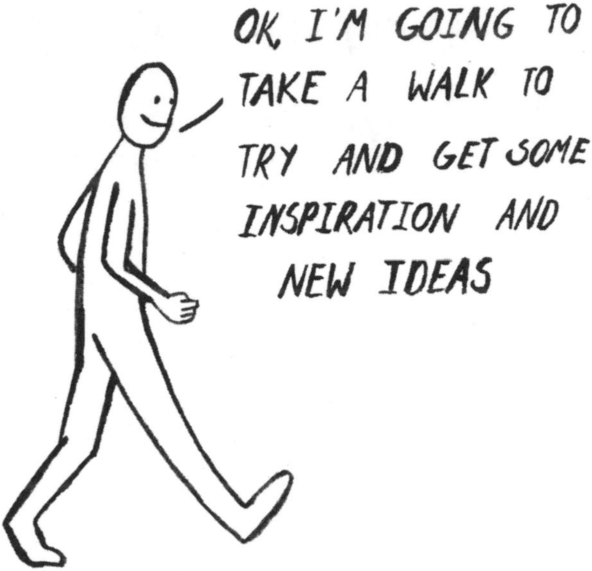
OK, I'M GOING TO TAKE A WALK TO TRY AND GET SOME INSPIRATION AND NEW IDEAS

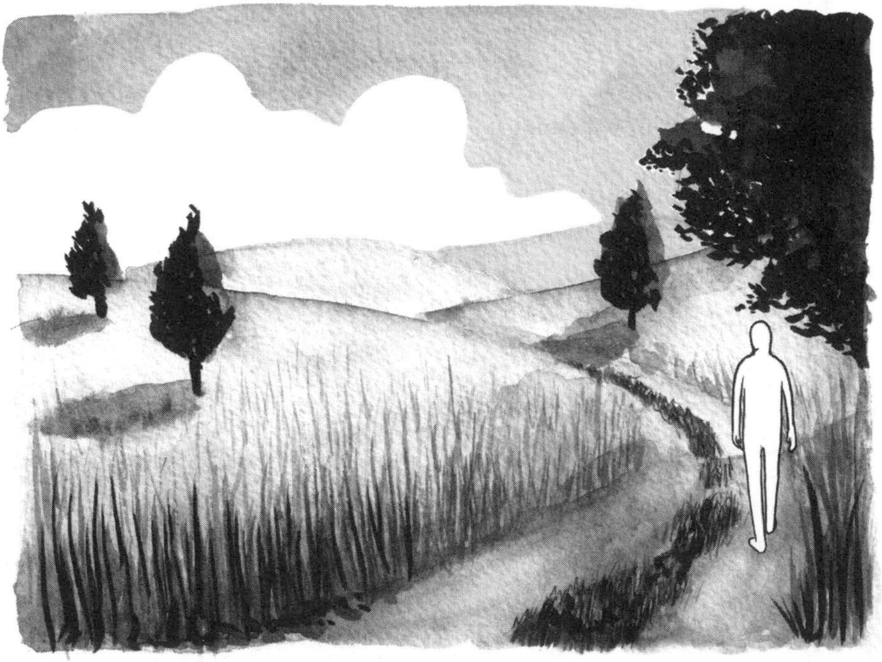

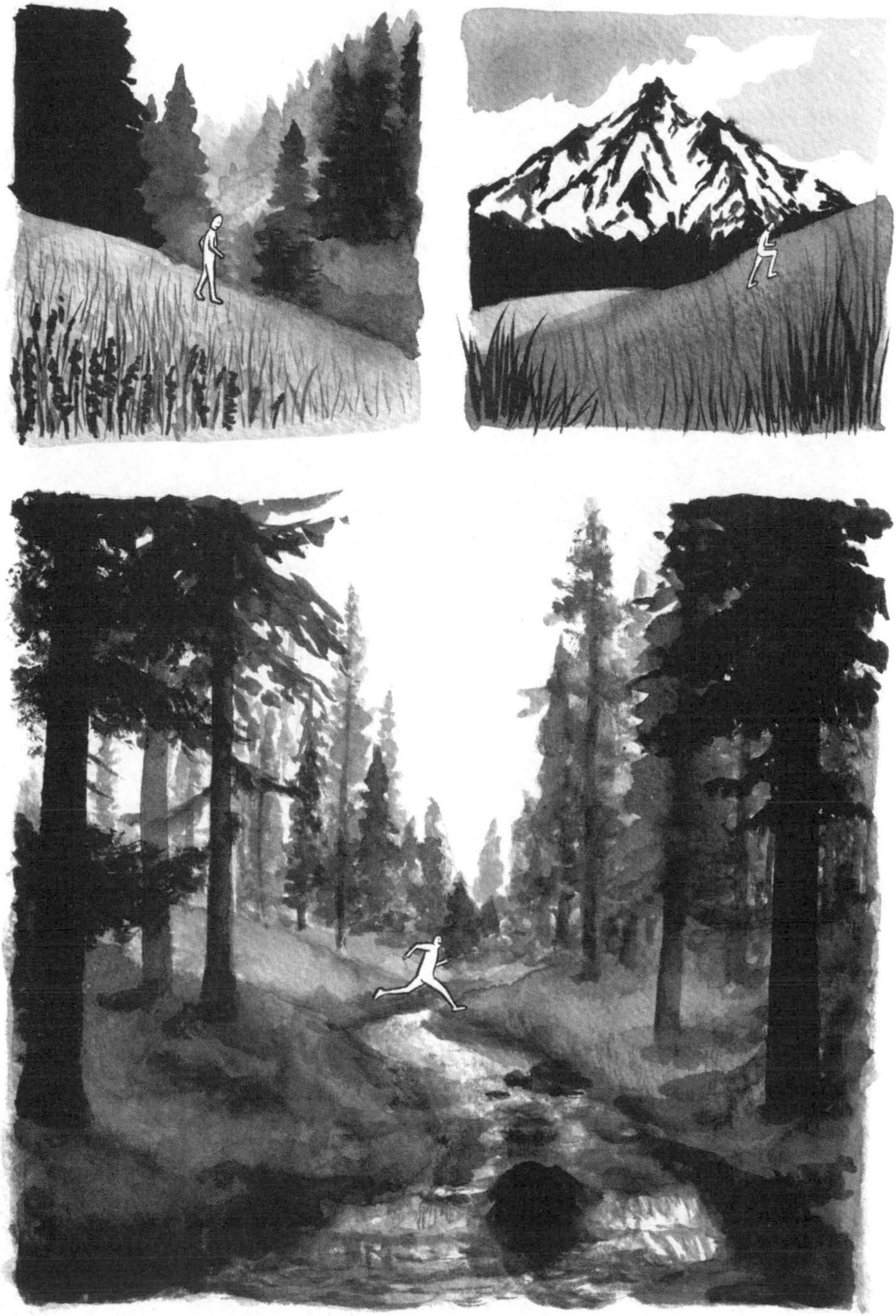

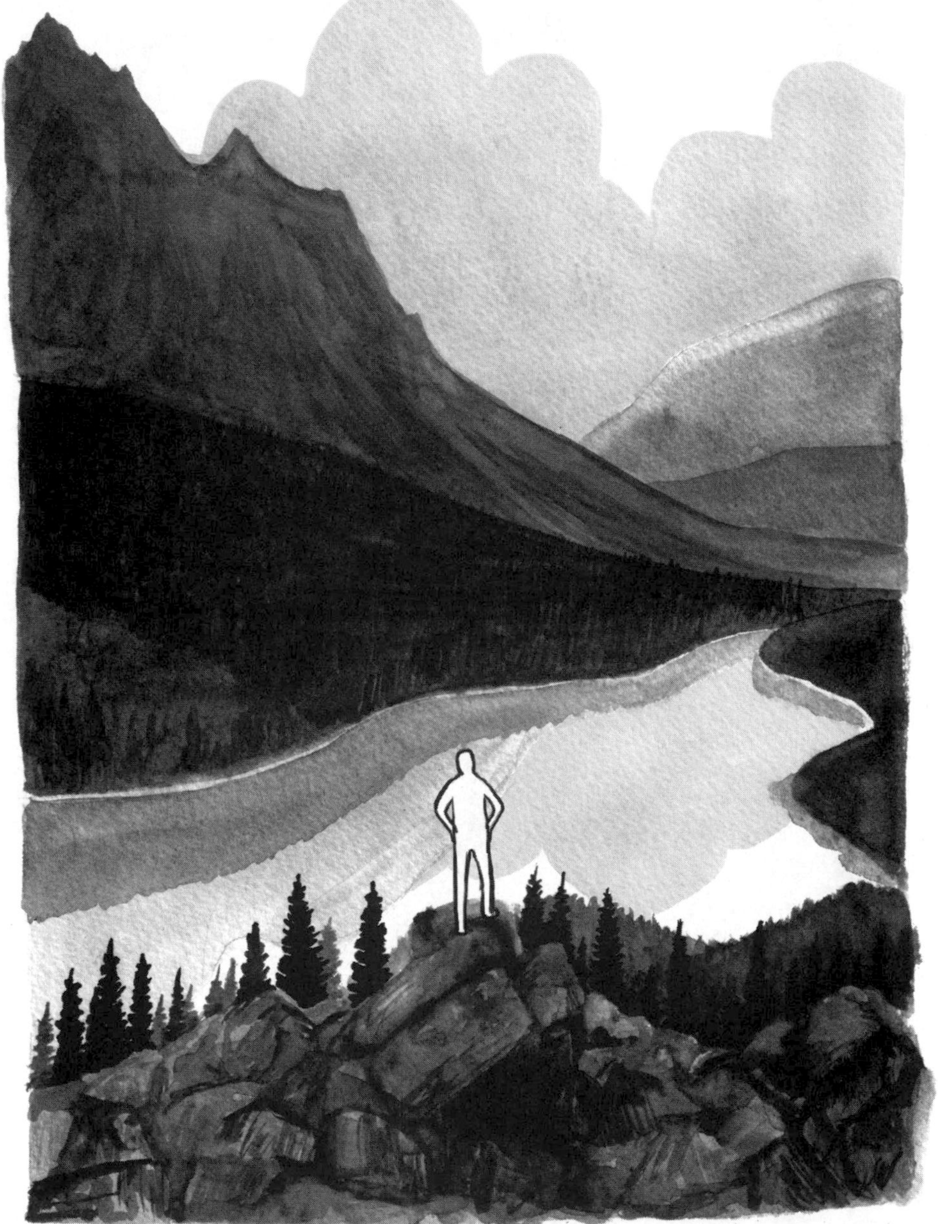

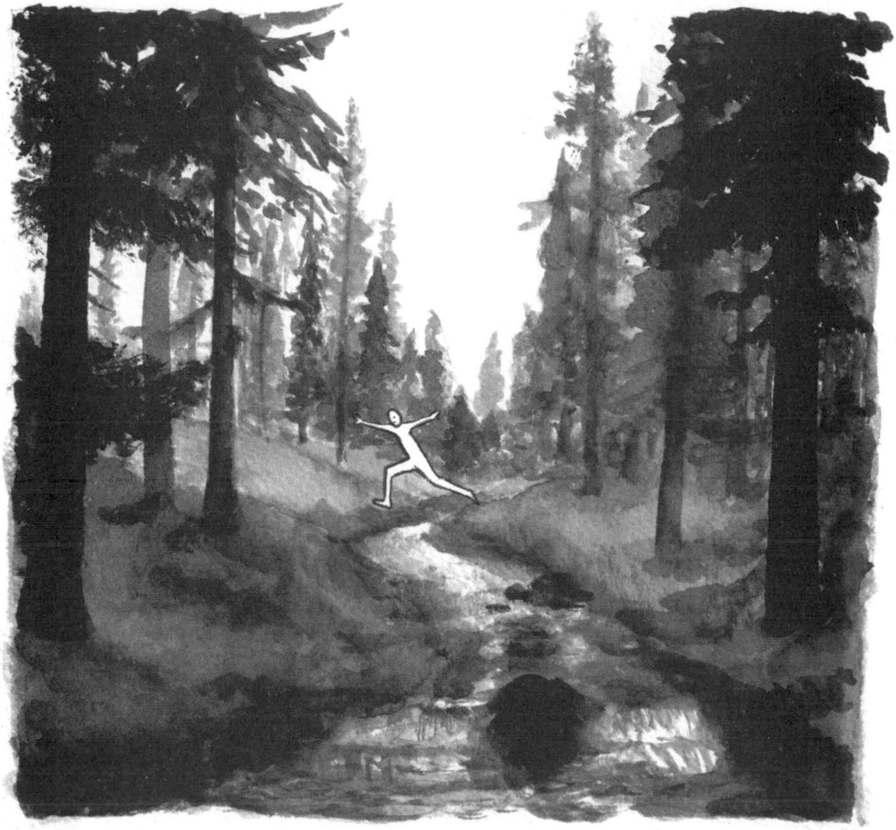

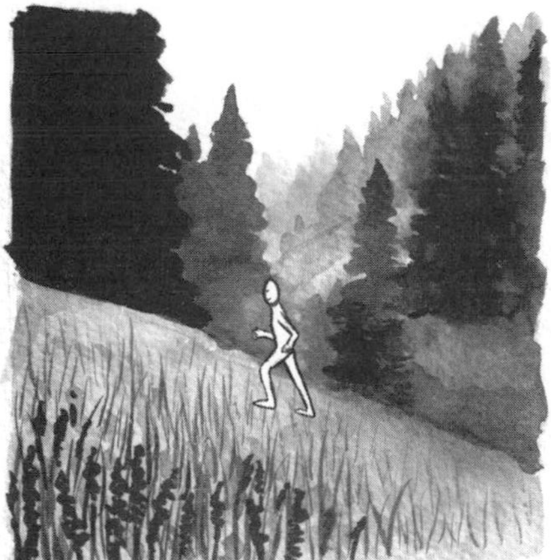

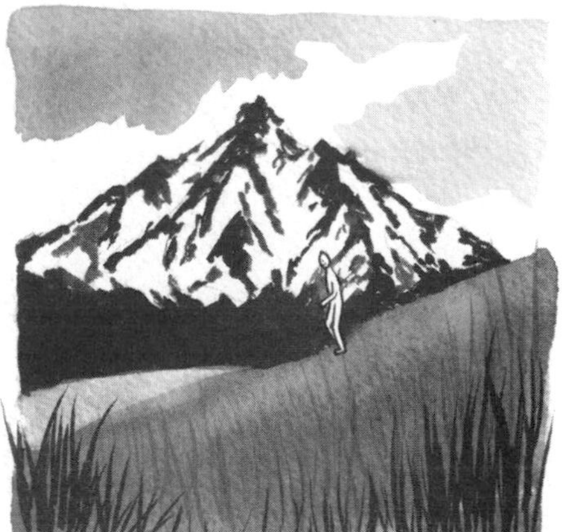

THAT WAS REFRESHING!

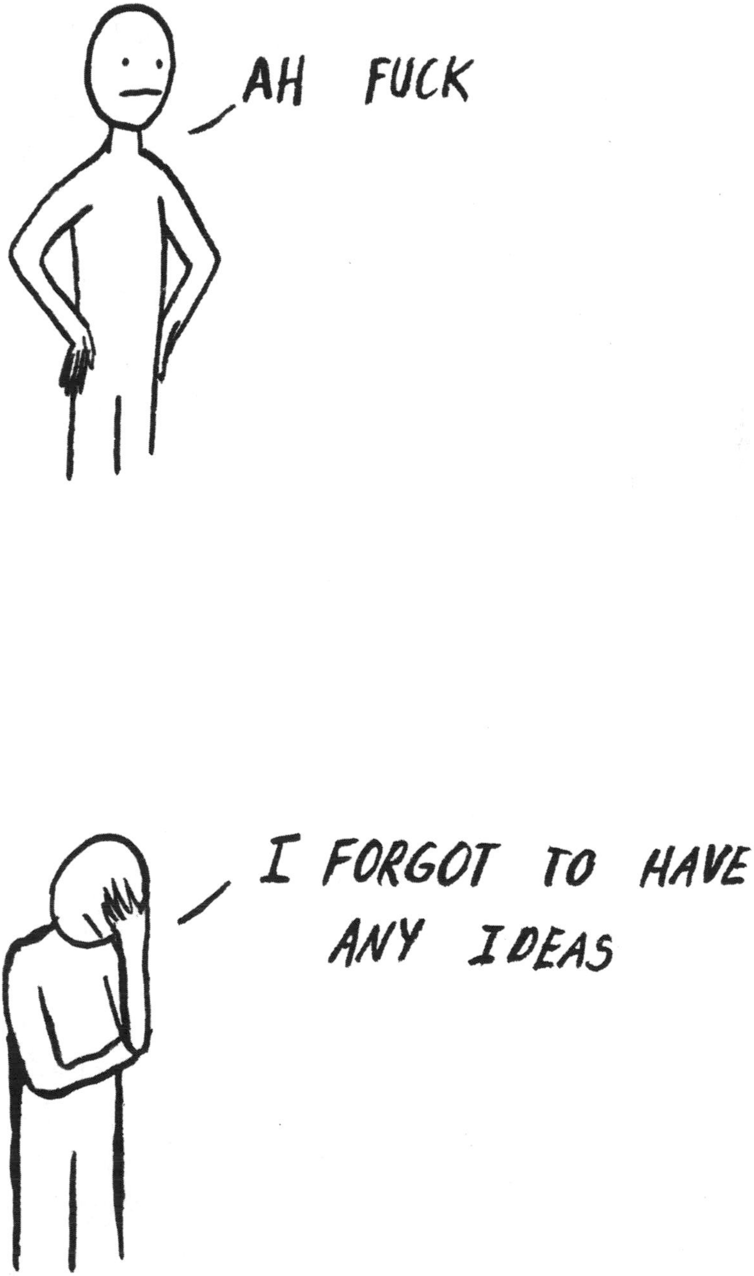
AH FUCK
I FORGOT TO HAVE ANY IDEAS

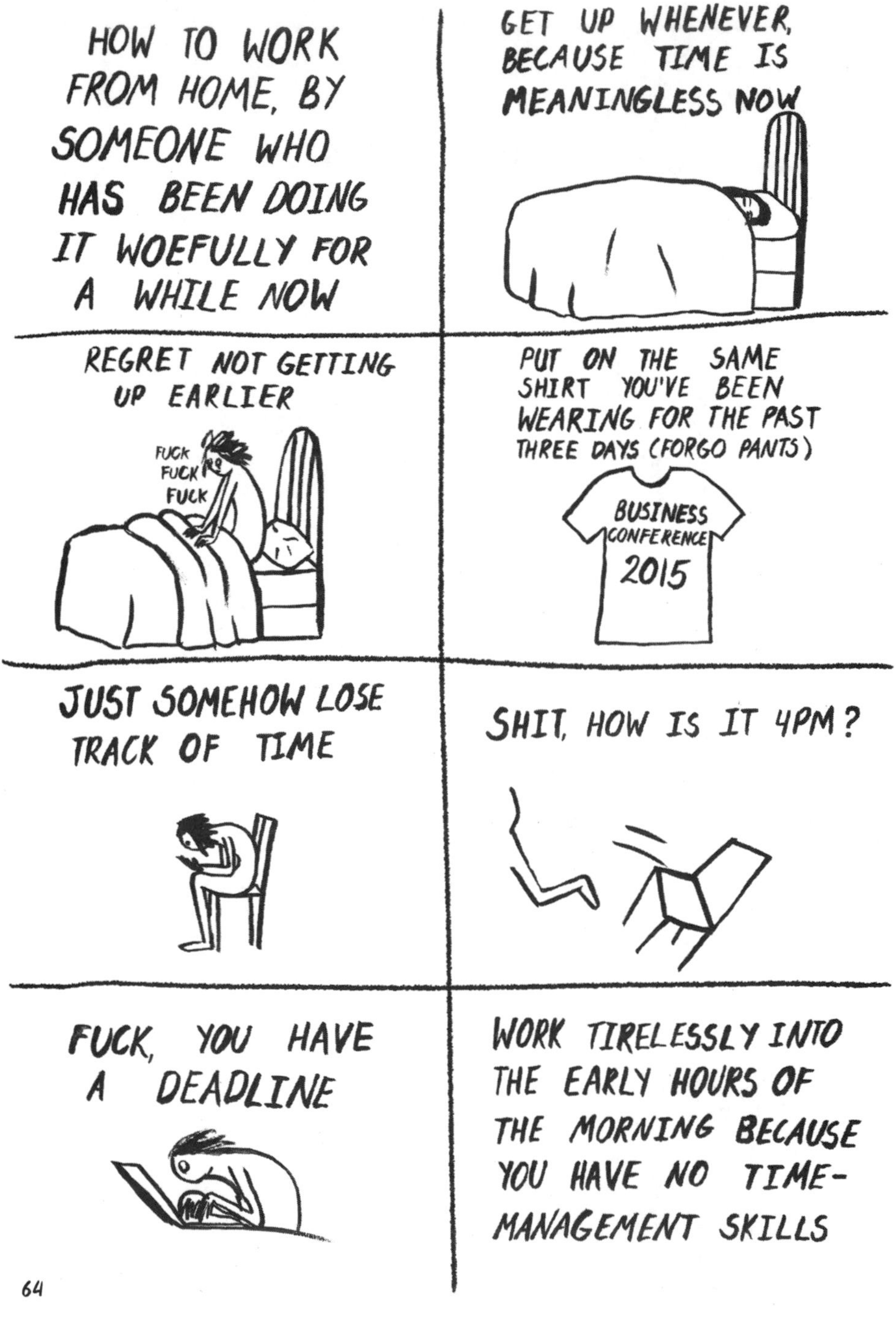
HOW TO WORK FROM HOME, BY SOMEONE WHO HAS BEEN DOING IT WOEFULLY FOR A WHILE NOW
GET UP WHENEVER, BECAUSE TIME IS MEANINGLESS NOW
REGRET NOT GETTING UP EARLIER
FUCK
FUCK
FUCK
PUT ON THE SAME SHIRT YOU'VE BEEN WEARING FOR THE PAST THREE DAYS (FORGO PANTS)
BUSINESS CONFERENCE 2015
JUST SOMEHOW LOSE TRACK OF TIME
SHIT, HOW IS IT 4PM?
FUCK, YOU HAVE A DEADLINE
WORK TIRELESSLY INTO THE EARLY HOURS OF THE MORNING BECAUSE YOU HAVE NO TIME-MANAGEMENT SKILLS

AWFUL AT LOVE

YOU'RE PROBABLY NOT UNLOVABLE, JUST A BIT DRAMATIC

Everyone feels like they're unequipped for love, or deeply unlucky, or always "attracting the wrong types of people," or worse—everyone *else* is attracted to the "wrong types of people," aka not you. In truth: Some people are just awful, and you may be one of them. Or you may be bad at telling awful people to get lost, so they stick around and waste your time just because they can.

Allow me to be briefly earnest—we often prefer to believe our own fictions rather than the reality of what is happening. We make up excuses for people's behavior. We read between the lines, when actually the lines very clearly spell out "I AM WASTING YOUR TIME" or form a perfect, giant red flag. Or, we create narratives where everyone else is the problem and take little accountability for our own actions.

This, I think, is the crux of it. It is all well and good to accept advice, but it is very, very hard to follow through with it. We bond with people, get addicted to the rush of endorphins they give us, and we so hope they can live up to the fantasy of them that we have built up in our heads that we overlook the red flags for far too long. Then, in our unhappy relationships, we ask, "How can I make them do this thing?" or "How can I get them to listen to me?" or "How can I get them to try more, love more, give more?"

Other times, we become so paralyzed by the fear of depending on someone and opening ourselves up to being hurt that we set impossible standards as an excuse to cut people off before they get too close. Then we can live in the comfortable, if lonely, idea that we just haven't found "the right one," rather than accepting that we're emotionally unavailable and unwilling to ever be vulnerable with someone else.

It is probably the most universal human experience to lay in bed late at night, convinced you're irrevocably unlovable, destined to die alone and to have never felt the warmth of human touch. It's so universal, in fact, that I'm fairly certain people have experienced this all while sharing a bed with someone who does, actually, love them. Fortunately for you, it takes a truly exceptionally awful person to actually be "unlovable," and you're almost definitely just being dramatic. Which is great, by the way, because this drama is precisely the inspiration for endless great works of art, and one small book of comics that you're holding right now.

There is no great key to "figuring out" love. It isn't a gift bestowed on only the most beautiful, kind, and deserving. Nor is it simply a biological function—not in the way we experience it, anyway.

What love *actually* is, is the world's richest resource for excruciatingly embarrassing moments that make for excellent punch lines.

OK, earnestness over.

HOW TO SHOW SOMEONE YOU'RE INTERESTED IN THEM:

IGNORE THEM.

HOW TO SHOW SOMEONE YOU'RE _NOT_ INTERESTED IN THEM:

ALSO IGNORE THEM.

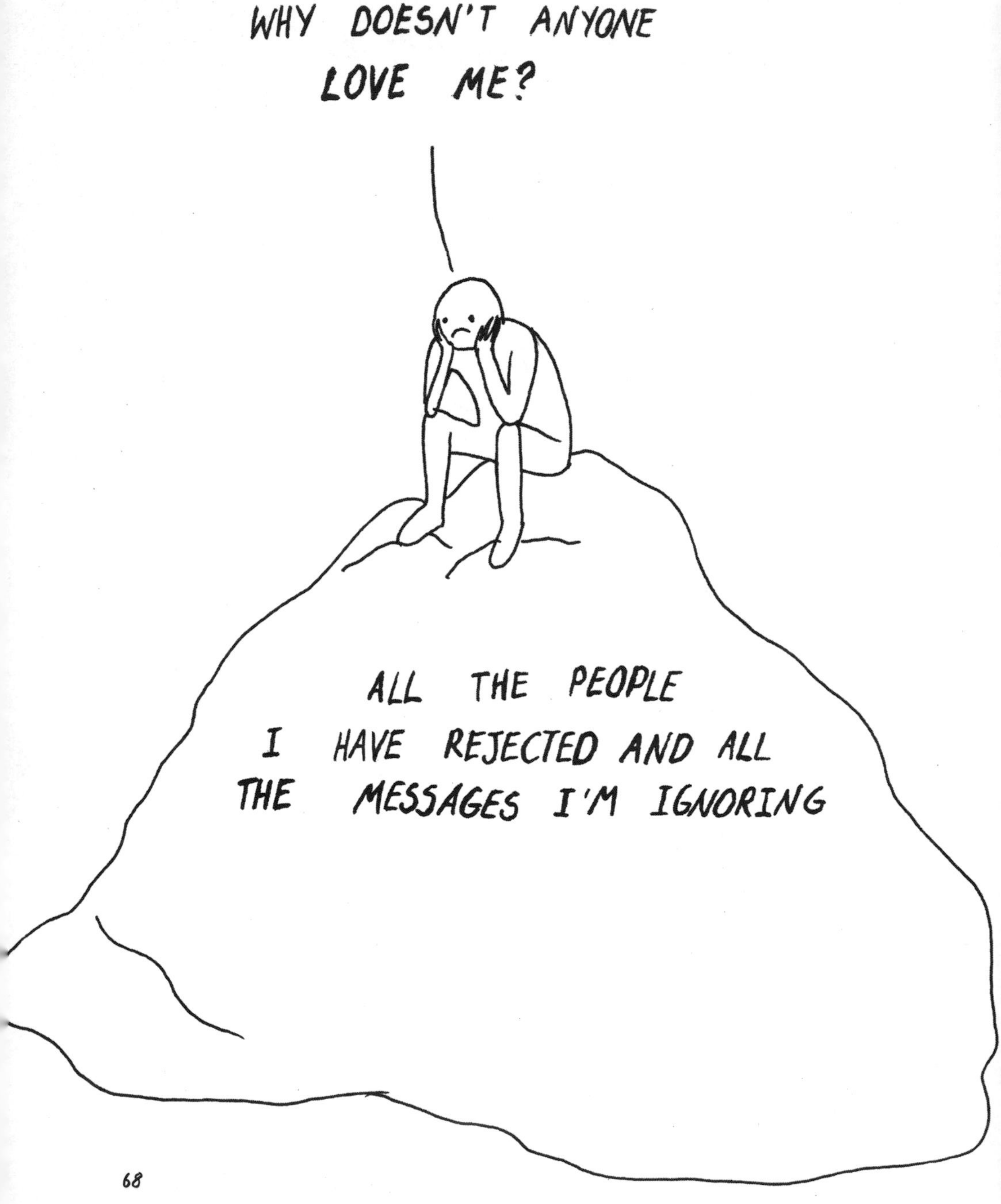
WHY DOESN'T ANYONE LOVE ME?
ALL THE PEOPLE I HAVE REJECTED AND ALL THE MESSAGES I'M IGNORING

STOP WORRYING IF YOU'LL DIE ALONE ≡ ♡

DIED SINGLE AND ALSO WAS MAULED BY A BEAR

START WORRYING ABOUT HOW YOU'LL DIE ♡

I WONDER IF MY
COMPLETE LACK OF SOCIAL LIFE
HAS ANYTHING TO DO
WITH MY INABILITY TO
RESPOND TO ANYTHING

DATING TODAY:

THE WAY THEY PUT ON THEIR COAT DOES NOT ALIGN WITH MY ROMANTIC VISION. THEY'RE NOT THE ONE.

DATING FOR OUR ANCESTORS, PROBABLY:

YOU ARE THE ONLY PERSON AROUND MY AGE WITHIN THREE MILES OF MY HOME (WHICH IS THE FURTHEST I'VE EVER TRAVELLED) I THINK IT'S LOVE.

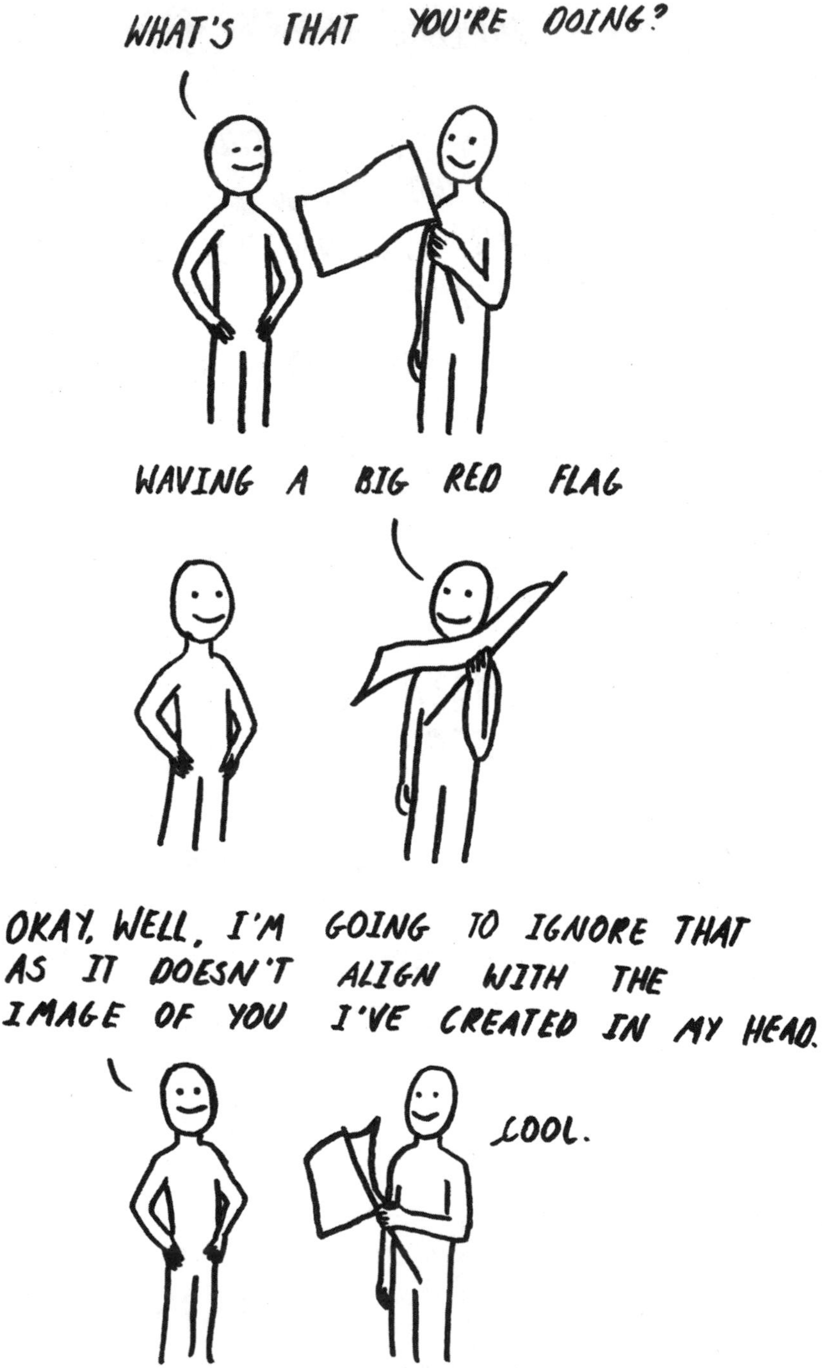
WHAT'S THAT YOU'RE DOING?
WAVING A BIG RED FLAG
OKAY, WELL, I'M GOING TO IGNORE THAT AS IT DOESN'T ALIGN WITH THE IMAGE OF YOU I'VE CREATED IN MY HEAD.
COOL.

ARE YOU READY FOR A NEW RELATIONSHIP?

1. **DOES** THE THOUGHT OF HAVING TO MEET AND INTEGRATE WITH **SOMEONE ELSE'S** FAMILY AND FRIEND **GROUP FILL YOU** WITH DREAD?   YES / NO

2. DO YOU **BELIEVE** THERE IS A CHANCE YOU MAY <u>NOT</u> BE THE HOTTEST PERSON ALIVE AND AN INCREDIBLE CATCH?   YES / NO

3. DO YOU THINK A NEW RELATIONSHIP WOULD FIX YOUR PROBLEMS AND MAKE YOU SO MUCH HAPPIER?   YES / NO

4. DO YOU STILL REGULARLY THINK ABOUT YOUR EX, EITHER WITH LONGING **OR** ANGER?   YES / NO

5. DOES THE IDEA OF DATING **FEEL** LIKE A CHORE **RATHER** THAN AN EXCITING PROSPECT ?   YES / NO

6. **ARE THERE** FRIENDS YOU NEGLECTED DURING YOUR LAST **RELATIONSHIP** THAT YOU HAVE YET TO RECONNECT **WITH?**   YES / NO

IF YOU MOSTLY ANSWERED "YES":

SORRY MY LOVE, BUT YOU ARE NOT READY TO DATE AGAIN. CONTINUE WORKING ON YOURSELF AND FIGURING OUT WHAT _YOU_ WANT OUT OF LIFE.

IF YOU MOSTLY ANSWERED "NO":

HELL YEAH! YOU ARE READY TO GET OUT THERE ONCE AGAIN AND VERY QUICKLY GROW DISILLUSIONED AND BITTER!

IF YOU ANSWERED A MIX OF BOTH:

I DON'T KNOW! I'M LITERALLY A BOOK, I CAN'T TELL YOU HOW TO LIVE YOUR LIFE.

74

THE BENEFITS OF BEING SINGLE

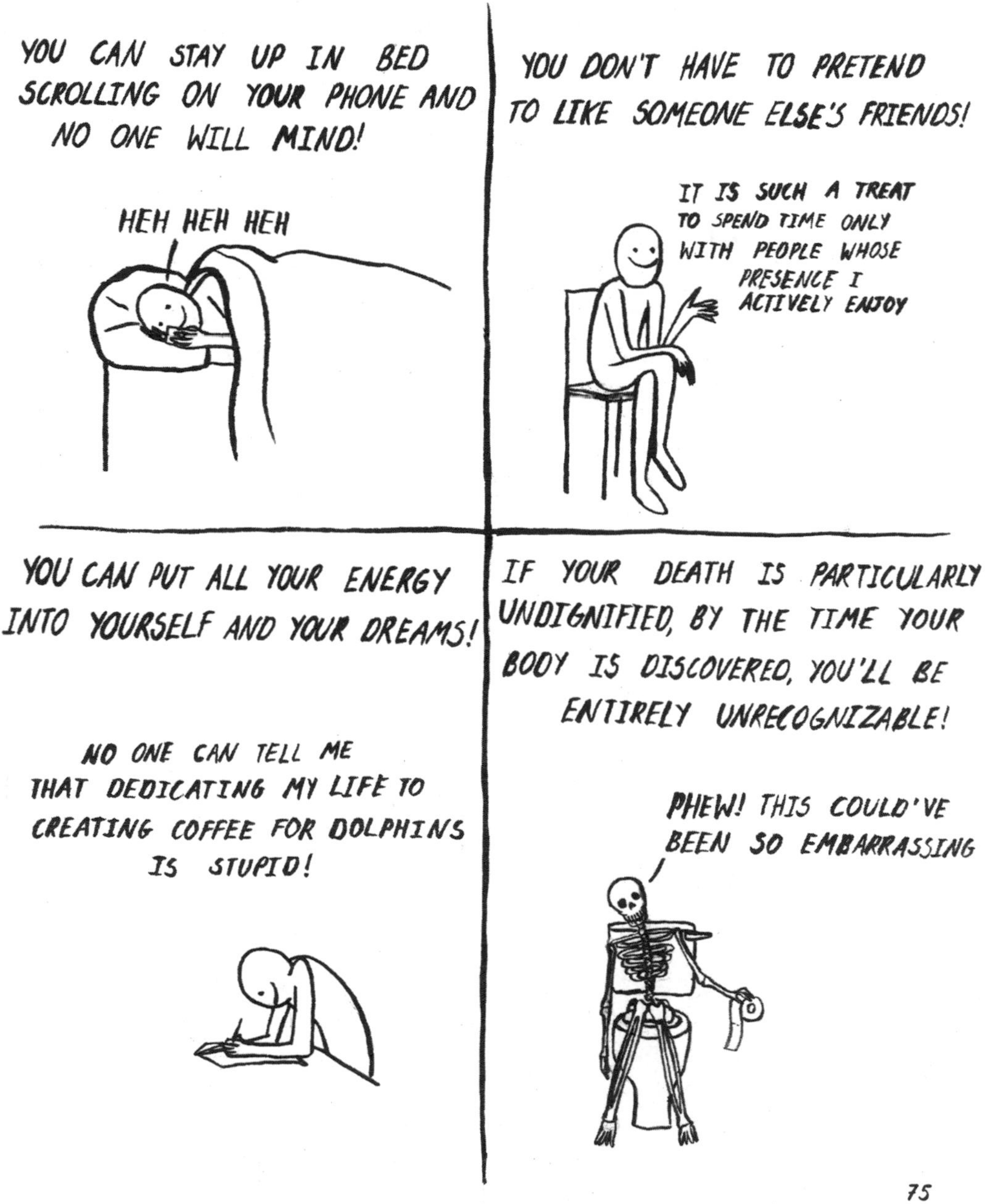
YOU CAN STAY UP IN BED SCROLLING ON YOUR PHONE AND NO ONE WILL MIND!
HEH HEH HEH
YOU DON'T HAVE TO PRETEND TO LIKE SOMEONE ELSE'S FRIENDS!
IT IS SUCH A TREAT TO SPEND TIME ONLY WITH PEOPLE WHOSE PRESENCE I ACTIVELY ENJOY
YOU CAN PUT ALL YOUR ENERGY INTO YOURSELF AND YOUR DREAMS!
NO ONE CAN TELL ME THAT DEDICATING MY LIFE TO CREATING COFFEE FOR DOLPHINS IS STUPID!
IF YOUR DEATH IS PARTICULARLY UNDIGNIFIED, BY THE TIME YOUR BODY IS DISCOVERED, YOU'LL BE ENTIRELY UNRECOGNIZABLE!
PHEW! THIS COULD'VE BEEN SO EMBARRASSING

SHOULD YOU GET BACK WITH YOUR EX?

A FLOWCHART

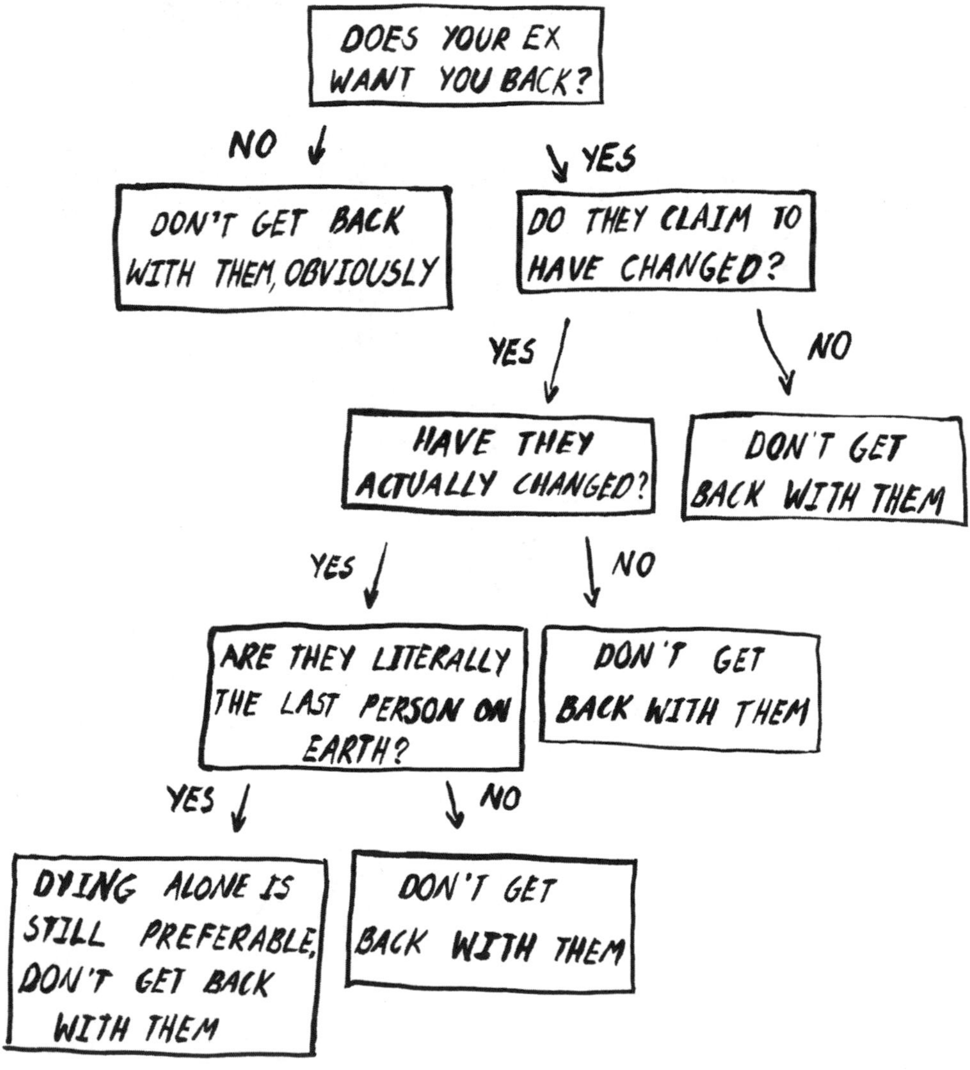
DOES YOUR EX WANT YOU BACK?
NO
DON'T GET BACK WITH THEM, OBVIOUSLY
YES
DO THEY CLAIM TO HAVE CHANGED?
YES
NO
HAVE THEY ACTUALLY CHANGED?
DON'T GET BACK WITH THEM
YES
NO
ARE THEY LITERALLY THE LAST PERSON ON EARTH?
DON'T GET BACK WITH THEM
YES
NO
DYING ALONE IS STILL PREFERABLE, DON'T GET BACK WITH THEM
DON'T GET BACK WITH THEM

IF YOU ARE LOOKING FOR SIGNS OF WHETHER OR NOT YOU SHOULD DUMP THEM, THEN YOU SHOULD PROBABLY

DUMP THEM

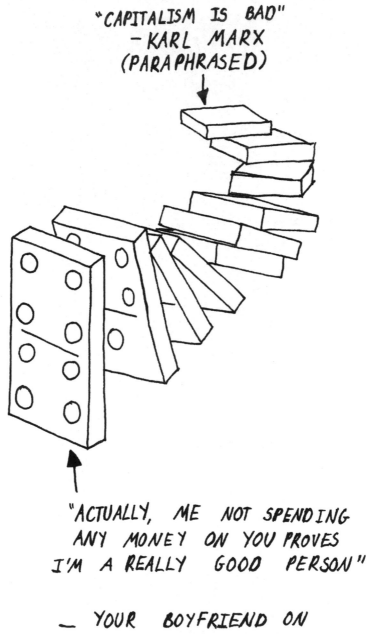

"CAPITALISM IS BAD"
— KARL MARX
(PARAPHRASED)

"ACTUALLY, ME NOT SPENDING
ANY MONEY ON YOU PROVES
I'M A REALLY GOOD PERSON"

— YOUR BOYFRIEND ON
VALENTINE'S DAY

PRACTICE TEXTING YOUR ♡ CRUSH ♡

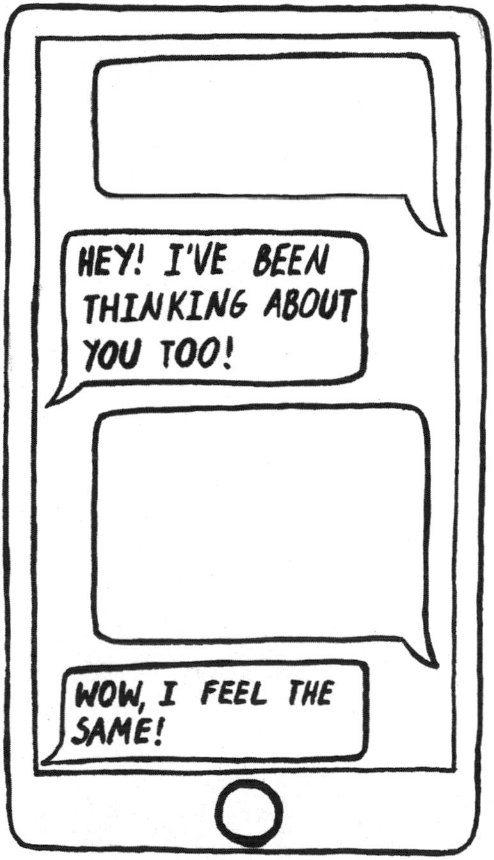
HEY! I'VE BEEN THINKING ABOUT YOU TOO!
WOW, I FEEL THE SAME!

FILL IN THE BLANKS

FUN WAYS TO FLIRT

GIVE THEM THE OL' BEDROOM EYES

THEN HIT 'EM WITH THE
KITCHEN LIPS

DO THE DISHES

FINALLY, WIN THEM OVER WITH A CLASSIC BATHROOM NOSE

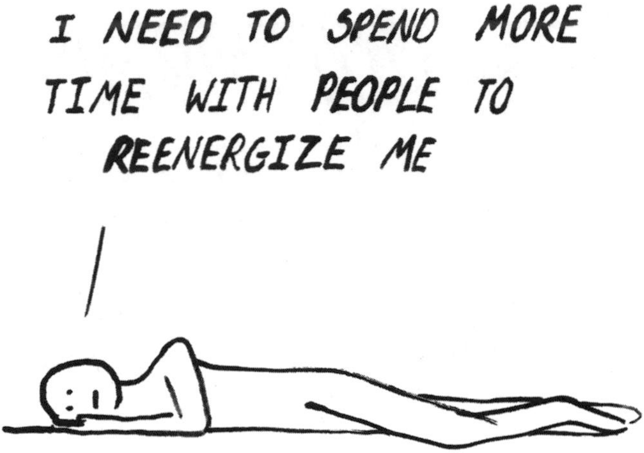
I NEED TO SPEND MORE TIME WITH PEOPLE TO REENERGIZE ME

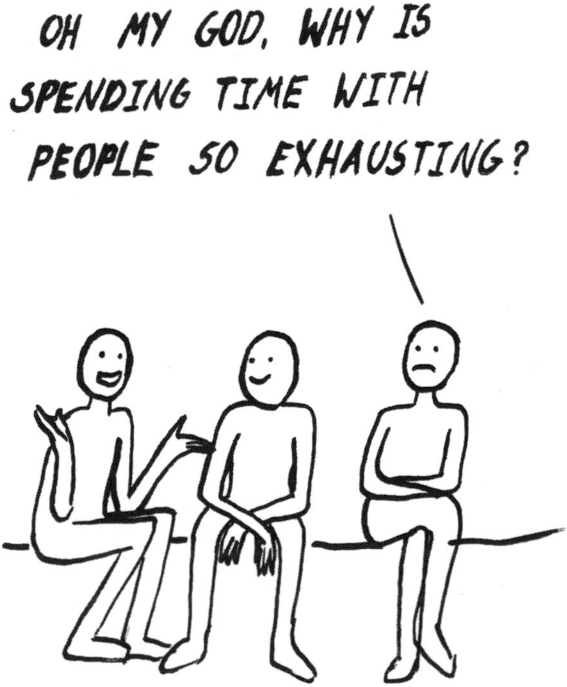
OH MY GOD, WHY IS SPENDING TIME WITH PEOPLE SO EXHAUSTING?

ARE THEY INTERESTED IN YOU?
(ACTUALLY)

A QUICK AND SIMPLE GUIDE

(CAN BE DONE AT ANY POINT DURING A RELATIONSHIP)

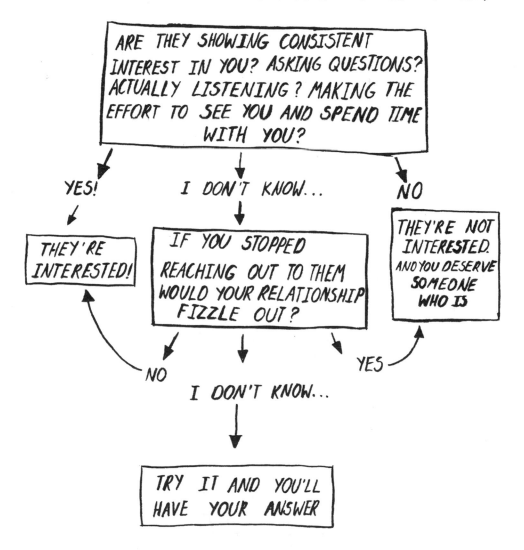

ARE THEY SHOWING CONSISTENT INTEREST IN YOU? ASKING QUESTIONS? ACTUALLY LISTENING? MAKING THE EFFORT TO SEE YOU AND SPEND TIME WITH YOU?

YES! → THEY'RE INTERESTED!

I DON'T KNOW... → IF YOU STOPPED REACHING OUT TO THEM WOULD YOUR RELATIONSHIP FIZZLE OUT?

NO → THEY'RE NOT INTERESTED. AND YOU DESERVE SOMEONE WHO IS

NO → THEY'RE INTERESTED!

YES → THEY'RE NOT INTERESTED.

I DON'T KNOW... → TRY IT AND YOU'LL HAVE YOUR ANSWER

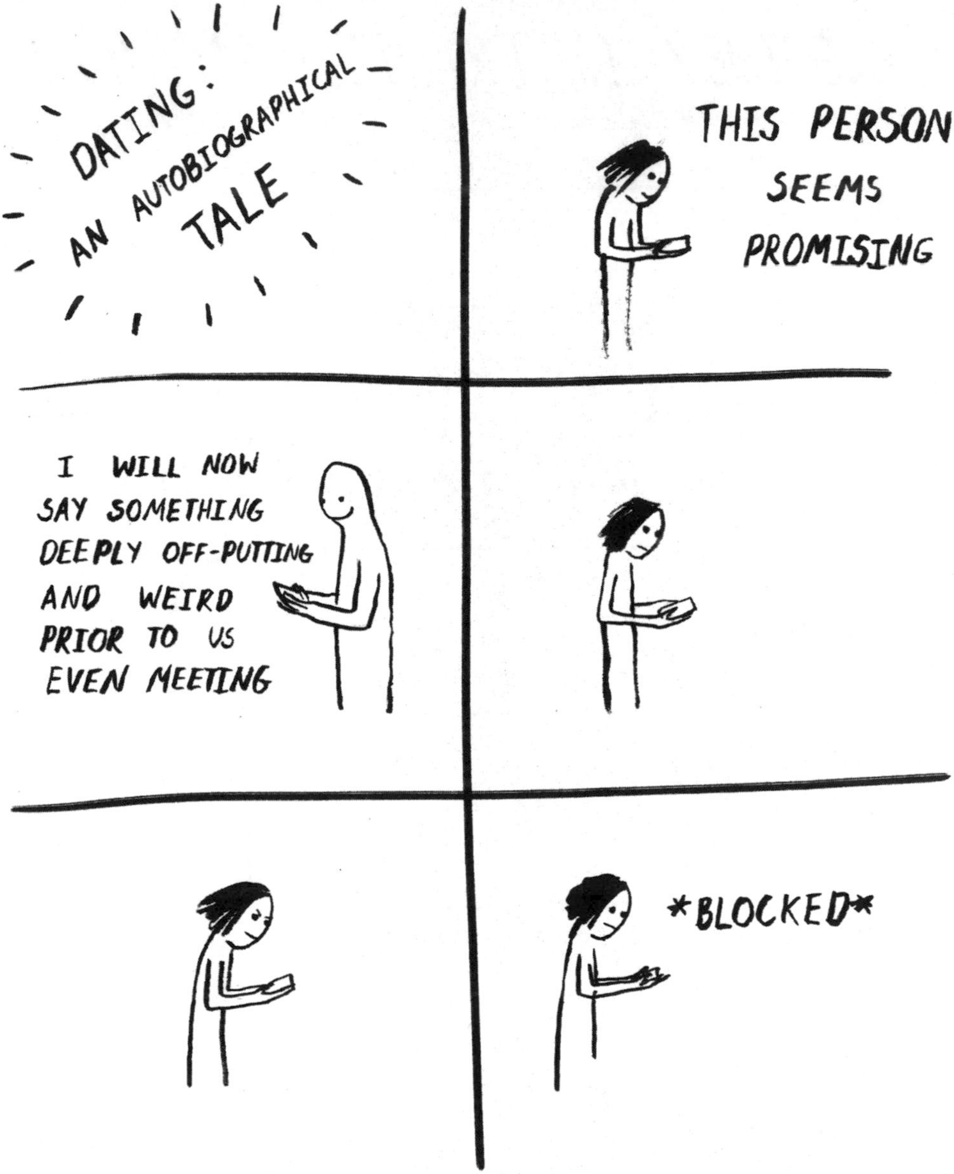
DATING: AN AUTOBIOGRAPHICAL TALE
THIS PERSON SEEMS PROMISING
I WILL NOW SAY SOMETHING DEEPLY OFF-PUTTING AND WEIRD PRIOR TO US EVEN MEETING
BLOCKED

THE END

PRACTICE SETTING BOUNDARIES

ANSWER ALL OF THESE LUDICROUS REQUESTS!

I DON'T FEEL LIKE WORKING TODAY, WILL YOU DO MY WORK FOR ME?

YOUR RESPONSE:

HEY, COULD YOU LISTEN TO ME COMPLAIN TO YOU FOR THREE HOURS, THEN COMPLETELY INVALIDATE YOUR FEELINGS?

YOUR RESPONSE:

WOULD YOU MIND TEACHING MY DOG TO SPEAK POLISH? OH, YOU DON'T SPEAK POLISH? NO WORRIES, YOU CAN LEARN.

YOUR RESPONSE:

IF YOU SAID NO TO ALL OF THESE, YOU

WIN THIS: - SELF-RESPECT -

"THEY'RE PROBABLY JUST BUSY"
AND OTHER LIES WE TELL OURSELVES

HE HASN'T TEXTED ME BACK IN DAYS... HE MUST JUST BE TOO BUSY. HE'S SUCH A HARD **WORKER!**♡

SHE NEVER MESSAGES ME FIRST AND HER REPLIES ARE ALWAYS CURT... SHE MUST LIKE ME SO MUCH THAT SHE GETS TOO SHY!

HE'S NEVER TAKEN ME OUT ON A DATE, SPENT ANY TIME WITH ME, TAKEN AN ACTIVE INTEREST IN ME AS A PERSON, OR EVEN ASKED ME A SINGLE QUESTION...

I JUST NEED TO TRY HARDER!

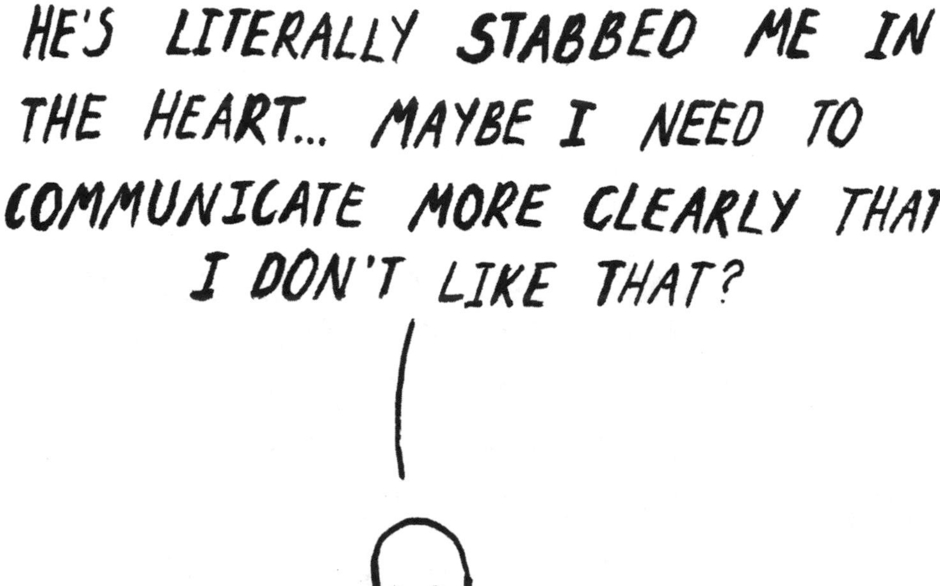
HE'S LITERALLY STABBED ME IN THE HEART... MAYBE I NEED TO COMMUNICATE MORE CLEARLY THAT I DON'T LIKE THAT?

LOVE

TIME
RESENTMENT

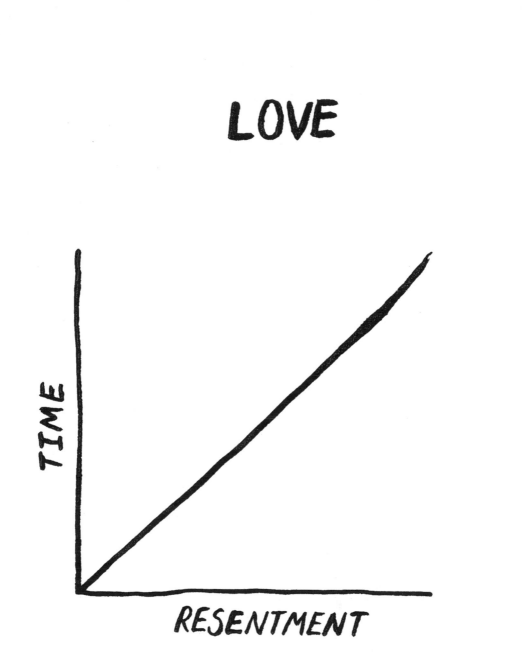

PEOPLE WHO ARE DEFINITELY OVERCOMPENSATING

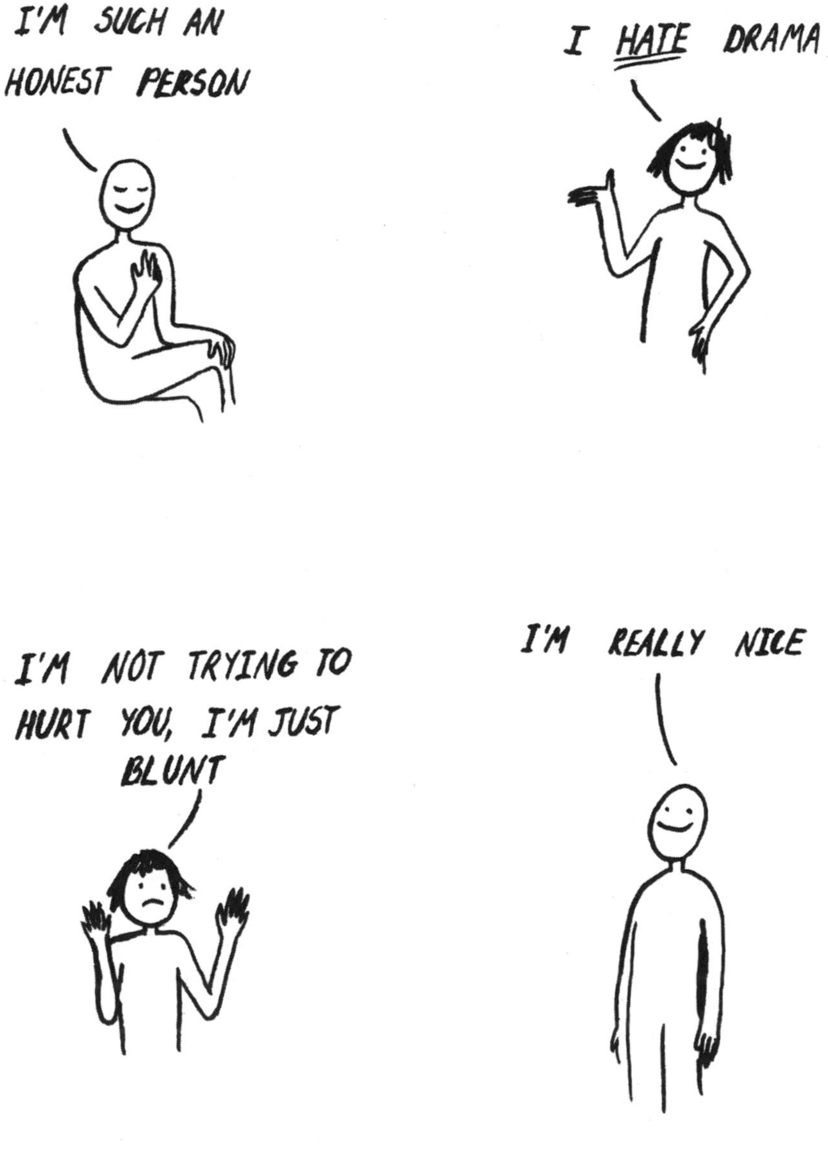
I'M SUCH AN HONEST PERSON
I HATE DRAMA
I'M NOT TRYING TO HURT YOU, I'M JUST BLUNT
I'M REALLY NICE

CREATE YOUR PERFECT* PERSON!

*OR AS CLOSE TO PERFECT AS REASONABLY POSSIBLE

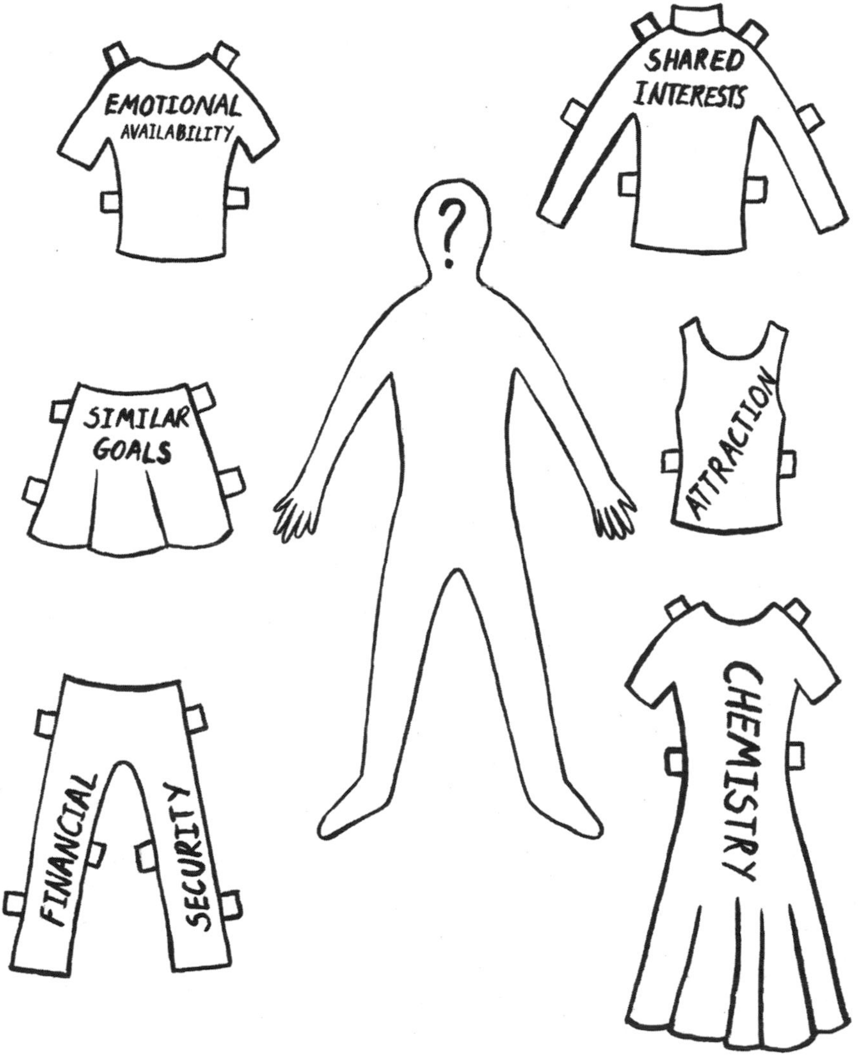
EMOTIONAL AVAILABILITY
SHARED INTERESTS
SIMILAR GOALS
ATTRACTION
FINANCIAL SECURITY
CHEMISTRY

HOW TO MAKE THE FIRST MOVE

1. THINK ABOUT THEM.

THEY SHOULD GET THE MESSAGE.

AND IF THEY CANNOT READ YOUR MIND TELEPATHICALLY, THEN MAYBE THEY'RE NOT THE ONE.

2. MAKE EYE CONTACT FOR 0.2 SECONDS,
THEN AVOID IT LIKE THE PLAGUE FOR
THE REST OF THE NIGHT.

OH GOD, THEY
SAW ME

PHEW! REALLY MADE YOURSELF VULNERABLE
THERE.

3. EXIST.

THIS ONE IS HARD TO DO, BUT IT'S A REALLY BOLD MOVE IF YOU THINK ABOUT IT.

I WANT TO FIND LOVE ORGANICALLY, I NO LONGER WANT TO DEPEND ON DATING APPS

EVERYONE IS SO DEPENDENT ON DATING APPS THAT FINDING LOVE ORGANICALLY FEELS IMPOSSIBLE

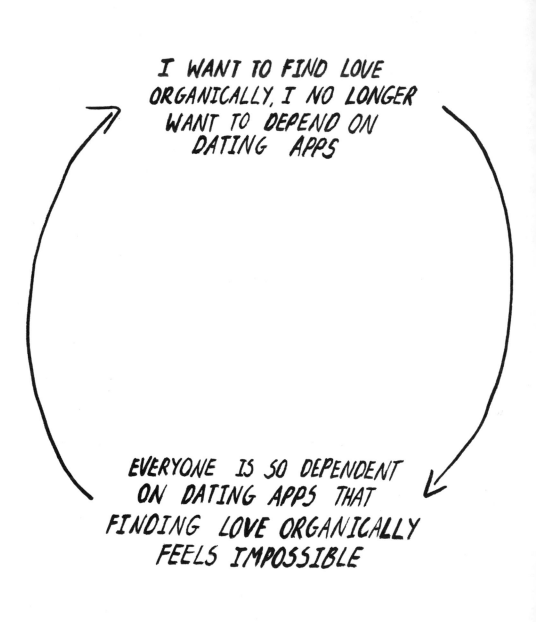

ARE YOU SICK AND TIRED OF GETTING YOUR HEART BROKEN?

WHY NOT TRY...

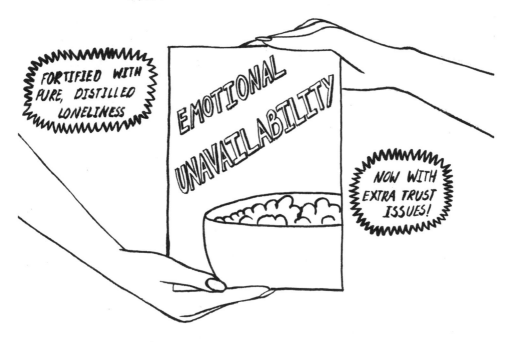

FORTIFIED WITH PURE, DISTILLED LONELINESS

EMOTIONAL UNAVAILABILITY

NOW WITH EXTRA TRUST ISSUES!

BENEFITS INCLUDE:

- DISAPPEARING FOREVER THE MOMENT YOU FEEL EVEN SLIGHTLY REJECTED!
- SABOTAGING ALL POTENTIAL RELATIONSHIPS TO CONFIRM YOUR CYNICAL WORLDVIEW!
- A COMPLEX SYSTEM OF DEFENSE MECHANISMS, INCLUDING THE ABILITY TO TURN EVERYTHING INTO A JOKE!

ME, AFTER I'VE SPENT HOURS GIVING MY FRIEND ADVICE THAT THEY COMPLETELY AGREE WITH, THEN PROCEED TO DO THE EXACT OPPOSITE OF WHAT I TOLD THEM TO DO:

ME AND MY FRIEND AFTER THEY'VE
SPENT HOURS GIVING ME ADVICE THAT
I GRACIOUSLY ACCEPTED, THEN PROMPTLY IGNORED:

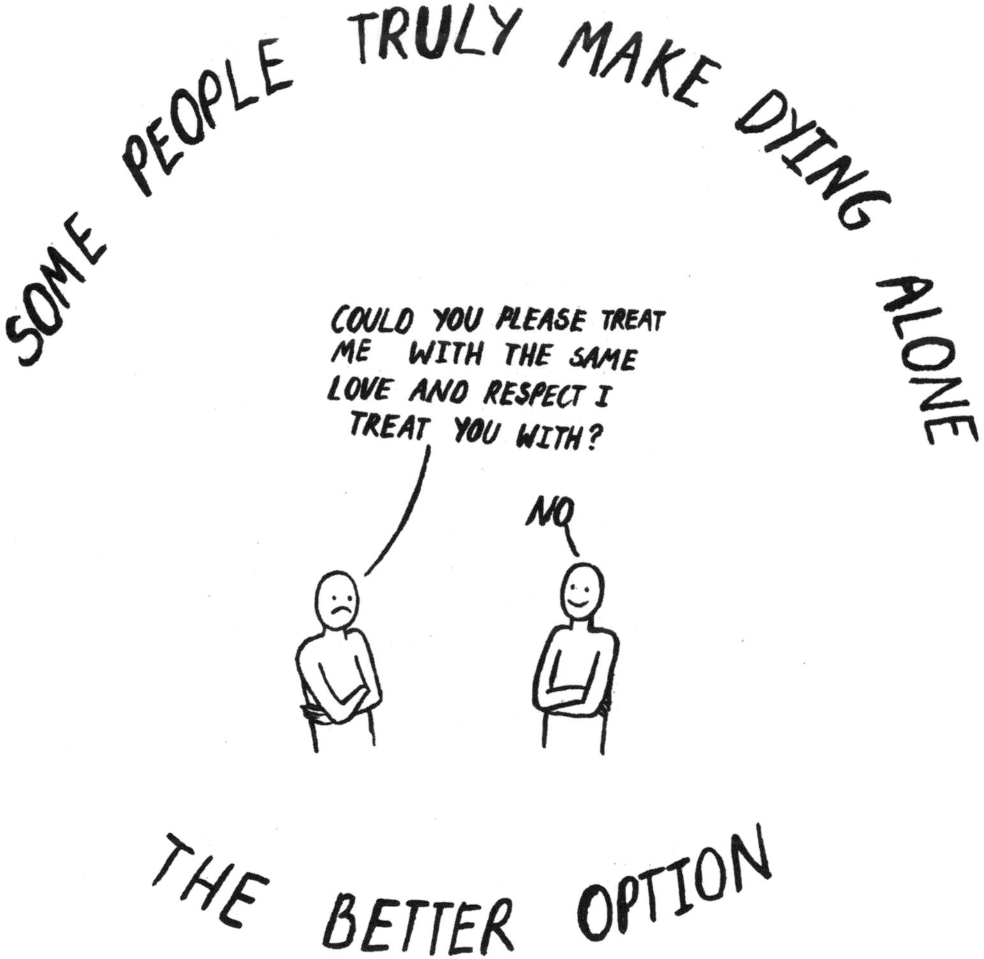
SOME PEOPLE TRULY MAKE DYING ALONE
COULD YOU PLEASE TREAT ME WITH THE SAME LOVE AND RESPECT I TREAT YOU WITH?
NO
THE BETTER OPTION

PRE-MADE LOVE NOTES FOR YOUR BEAU, JUST FILL IN THE BLANKS!

I MISS THE WAY YOUR BEAUTIFUL_____ WOULD GENTLY_____ MY_____

I WOULD _____ _____ _____ FOR YOU.

YOU ARE THE_____ _____ OF MY_____

YOUR LAUGH IS LIKE _____ TO ME, YOUR SMILE IS LIKE _____, AND YOUR_____ IS LIKE _____

YOUR ASS IS_____ _____ _____

YOUR EYES ARE LIKE THE _____, YOUR _____ IS LIKE THE _____, AND YOUR _____ IS COMPARABLE TO NOTHING ELSE.

I HAVE NEVER_____ _____ ANYONE QUITE LIKE YOU.

I LOVE IT WHEN YOU _____ MY _____ AND I_____ YOUR_____

MY BELOVED, I CAN'T WAIT TO _____ YOUR LITTLE_____. THEN, I WILL _____ YOUR _____ RAVENOUSLY. THEN WE WILL_____ _____ ALL NIGHT LONG.

COMMON DATING MISTAKES

AND WHAT TO DO INSTEAD!

COMMON DATING MISTAKE #1
REVEALING TOO MUCH, TOO SOON

I WET MY BED UNTIL I WAS 26 AND I'M NOT SURE THAT I CAN TELL THE TIME

INSTEAD, TRY THIS!

DON'T REVEAL ANYTHING AT ALL! WHY DO THEY WANT TO KNOW YOUR LAST NAME? WHO GAVE THEM THE RIGHT TO ASK YOU WHAT YOUR FAVORITE COLOR IS?!

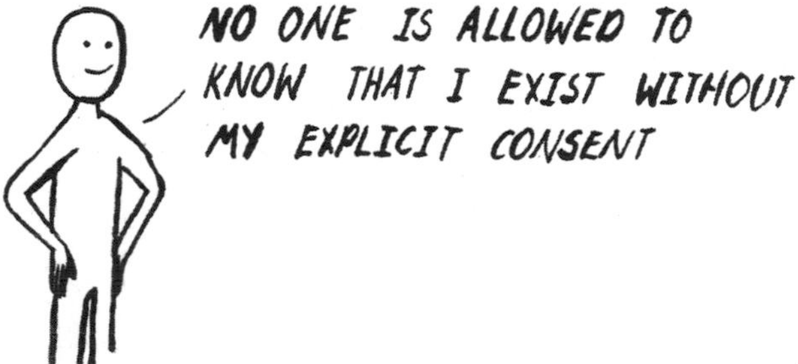

NO ONE IS ALLOWED TO KNOW THAT I EXIST WITHOUT MY EXPLICIT CONSENT

COMMON DATING MISTAKE #2

COMMITTING FAR TOO QUICKLY

YOU DON'T EVEN KNOW THIS PERSON—DON'T RISK COMMITTING TO SOMEONE WHO IS BAD FOR YOU, JUST FOR THE CHANCE OF HAVING A WHIRLWIND ROMANCE. IF THEY'RE SERIOUS, THEY'LL TAKE THEIR TIME.

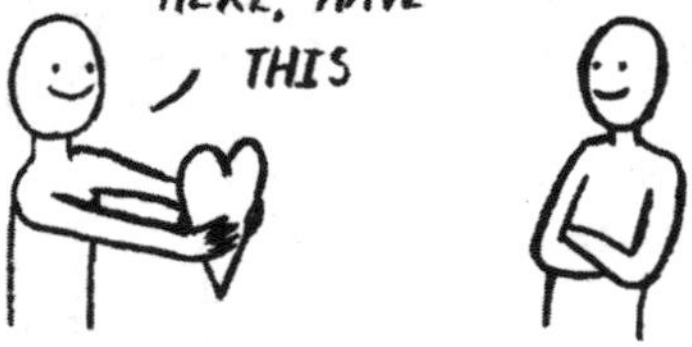
HERE, HAVE THIS

INSTEAD, TRY THIS!

NEVER COMMITTING, EVER! PREEMPTIVELY BREAK YOUR OWN HEART, BABY!

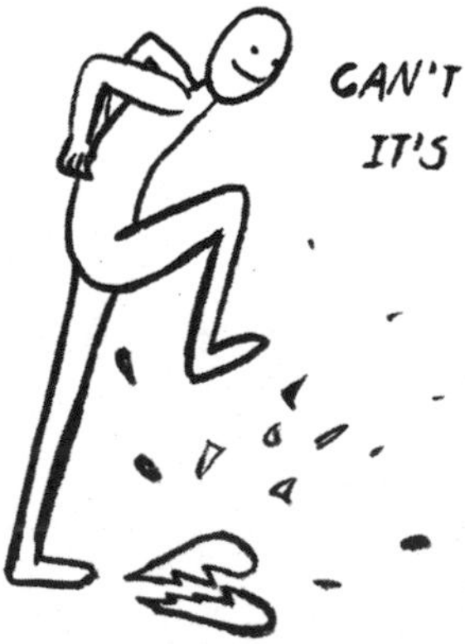
CAN'T BREAK IT IF IT'S ALREADY BROKEN!

COMMON DATING MISTAKE #3

THINKING YOU CAN CHANGE SOMEONE

NO AMOUNT OF COMMUNICATING WILL MAKE SOMEONE RESPECT YOU OR TREAT YOU THE WAY YOU WANT TO BE TREATED IF THEY DON'T WANT TO DO THAT.

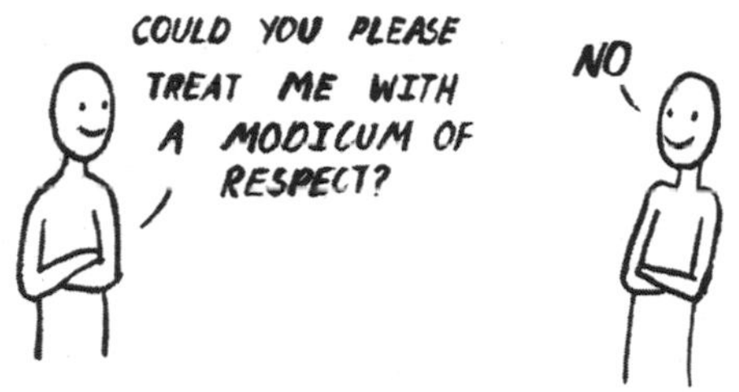
COULD YOU PLEASE TREAT ME WITH A MODICUM OF RESPECT?
NO

INSTEAD, TRY THIS!

JUST GIVE UP!

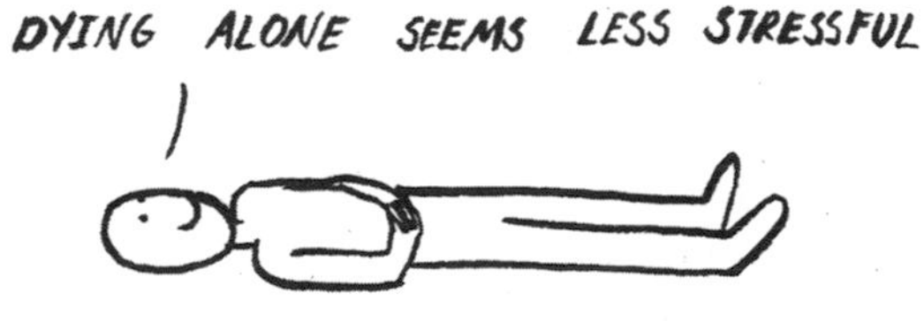
DYING ALONE SEEMS LESS STRESSFUL

EVERYONE IS AWFUL,

AND DON'T YOU FORGET IT!

ARE THEY ANNOYING, OR ARE YOU ACTUALLY THE PROBLEM?

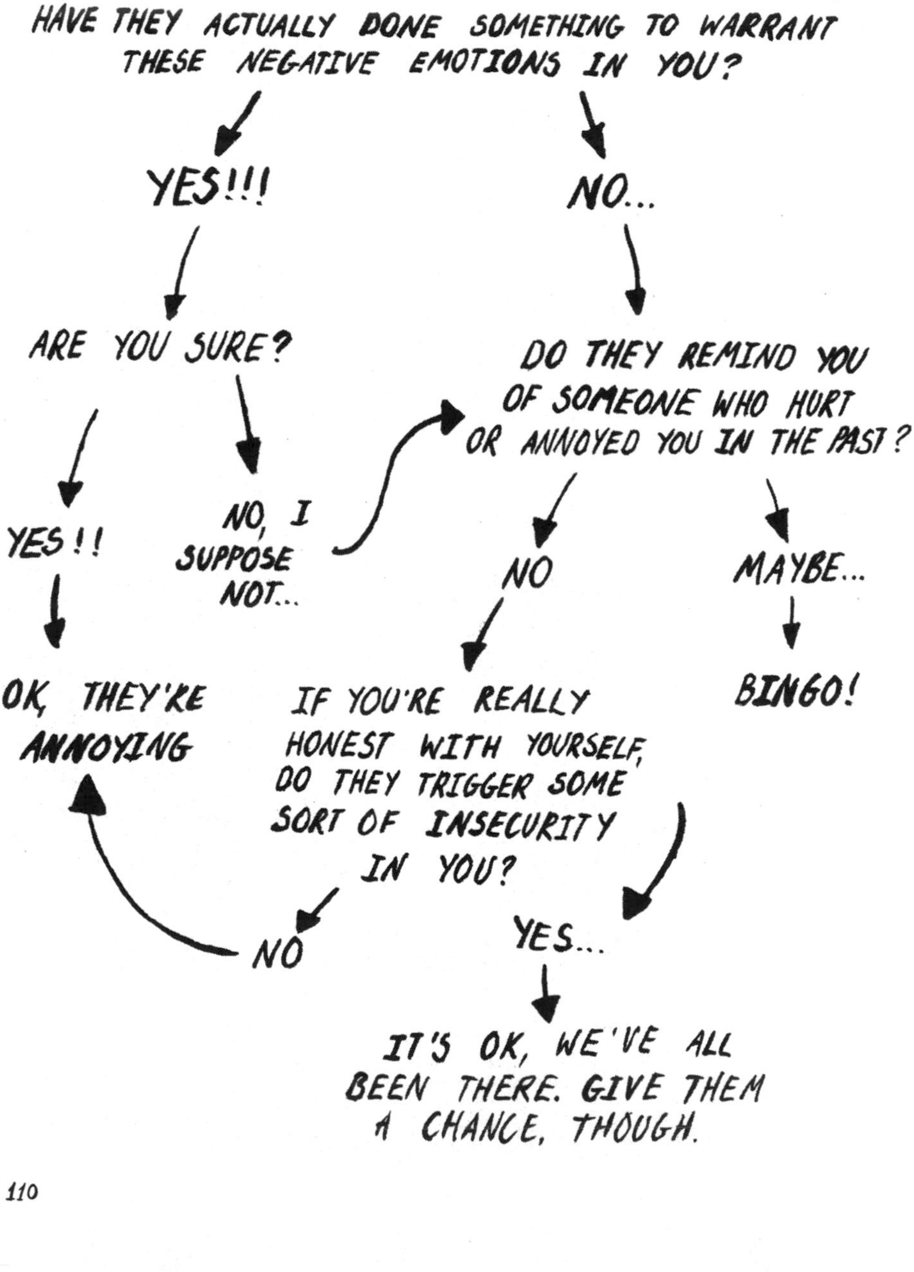

HAVE THEY ACTUALLY DONE SOMETHING TO WARRANT THESE NEGATIVE EMOTIONS IN YOU?
YES!!!
NO...
ARE YOU SURE?
YES!!
NO, I SUPPOSE NOT...
OK, THEY'RE ANNOYING
DO THEY REMIND YOU OF SOMEONE WHO HURT OR ANNOYED YOU IN THE PAST?
NO
MAYBE...
BINGO!
IF YOU'RE REALLY HONEST WITH YOURSELF, DO THEY TRIGGER SOME SORT OF INSECURITY IN YOU?
NO
YES...
IT'S OK, WE'VE ALL BEEN THERE. GIVE THEM A CHANCE, THOUGH.

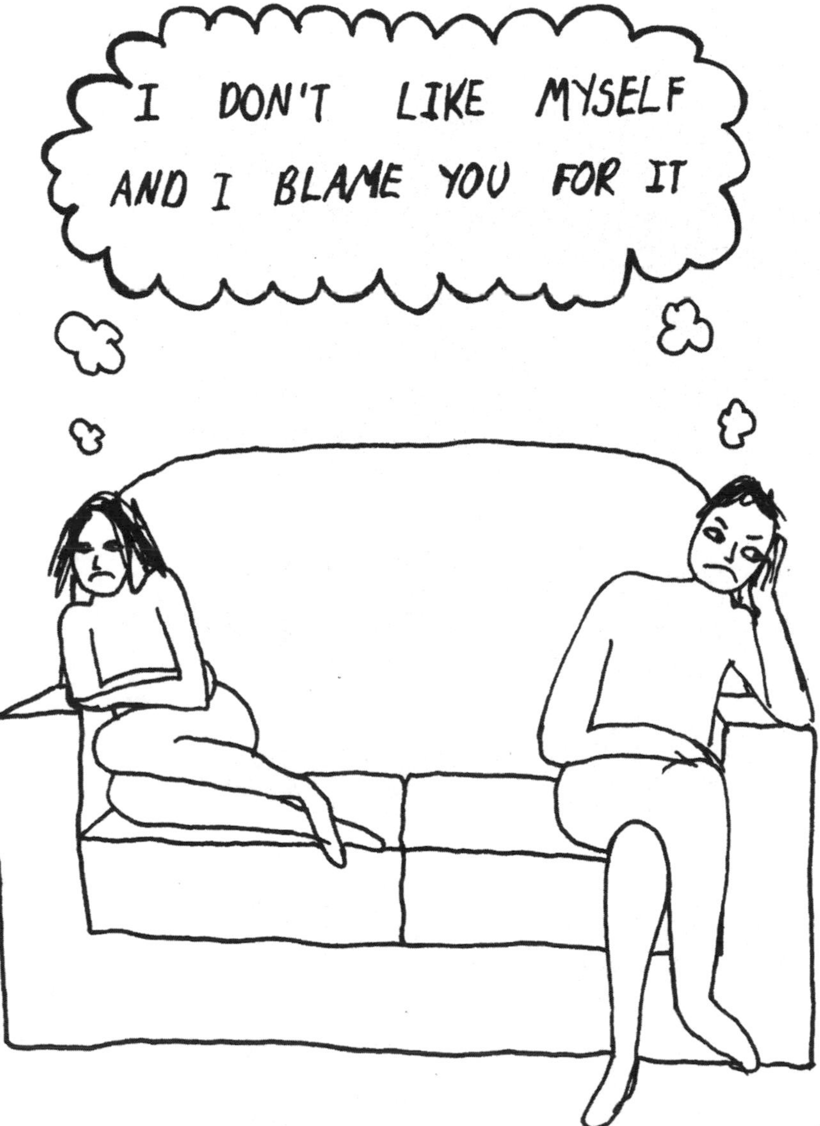
I DON'T LIKE MYSELF
AND I BLAME YOU FOR IT

BAD DATE BINGO

TAKE THIS WITH YOU NEXT TIME YOU
GO ON A DATE, AND IF IT'S AWFUL, AT
LEAST YOU'LL HAVE SOMETHING TO DO!

BAD BREATH	THEY "FORGET" THEIR WALLET	ZERO QUESTIONS ABOUT YOU	AGONIZING AWKWARD SILENCE	ONLY TALK ABOUT THEIR EX
RUDE TO THE WAITER	CATFISH	NO CONCEPT OF PERSONAL SPACE	BAD KISSER	CLEARLY UNSHOWERED
ALREADY DRUNK	SOBER, BUT YOU'RE DRUNK	FREE SPACE	TOO HORNY	NOT EVEN SLIGHTLY HORNY
CLEARLY NOT INTO YOU	WAY TOO INTO YOU	TEXTING AS YOU'RE TALKING	NEGGING	CREEPY
ZERO EYE CONTACT	4" SHORTER THAN ADVERTISED	DOESN'T GET YOUR JOKES	TURNS OUT YOU'RE DISTANTLY RELATED	A SMALL FIRE IS SET

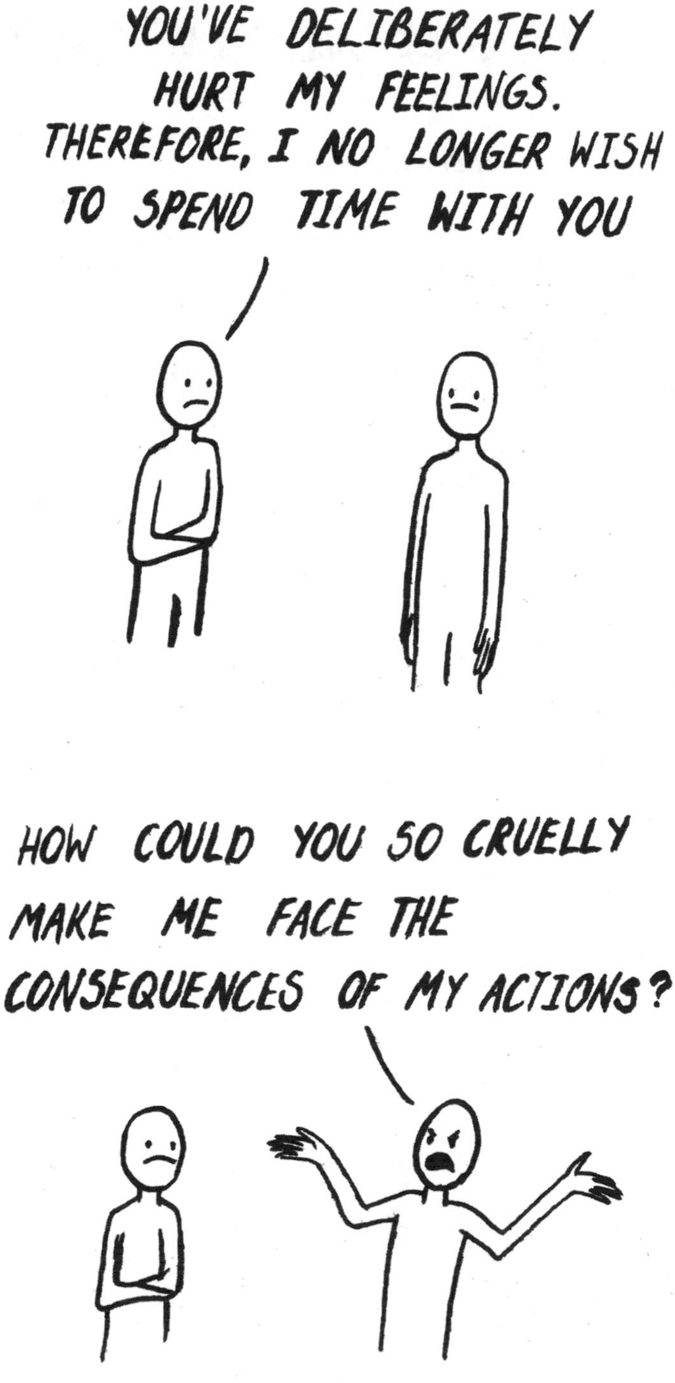
YOU'VE DELIBERATELY HURT MY FEELINGS. THEREFORE, I NO LONGER WISH TO SPEND TIME WITH YOU
HOW COULD YOU SO CRUELLY MAKE ME FACE THE CONSEQUENCES OF MY ACTIONS?

DO YOU STRUGGLE ACCEPTING COMPLIMENTS?

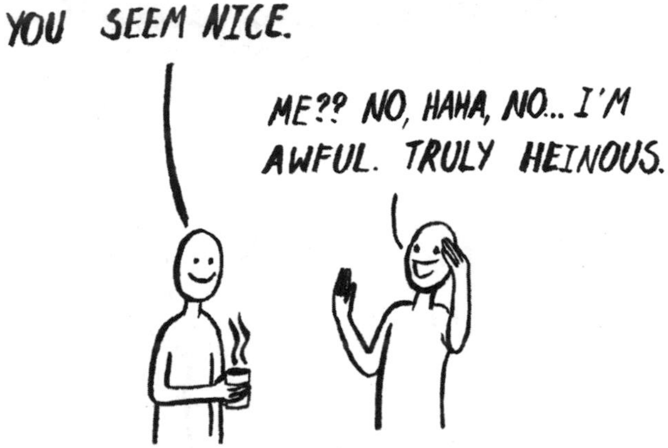
YOU SEEM NICE.
ME?? NO, HAHA, NO... I'M AWFUL. TRULY HEINOUS.

THEN TRY THIS!

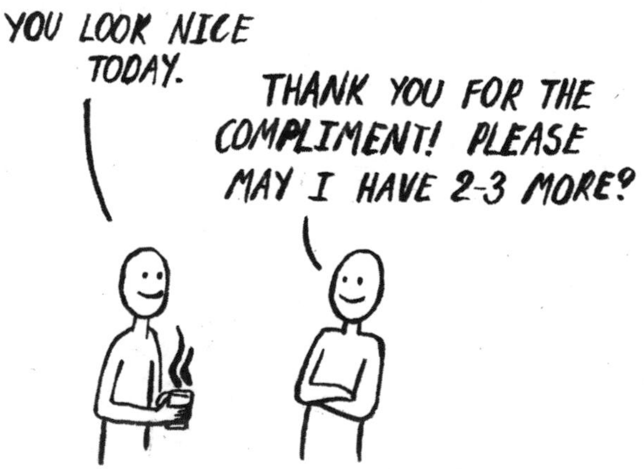
YOU LOOK NICE TODAY.
THANK YOU FOR THE COMPLIMENT! PLEASE MAY I HAVE 2-3 MORE?

OH GOD,
WHAT IF I END UP
ALONE FOREVER

I'LL NEVER HAVE TO
SHARE A BED OR A ROOM

WHENEVER I AM ON A DATE, I WONDER, DO ANIMALS EXPERIENCE THE DEEP EMBARRASSMENT THAT WE DO DURING THEIR MATING RITUALS?

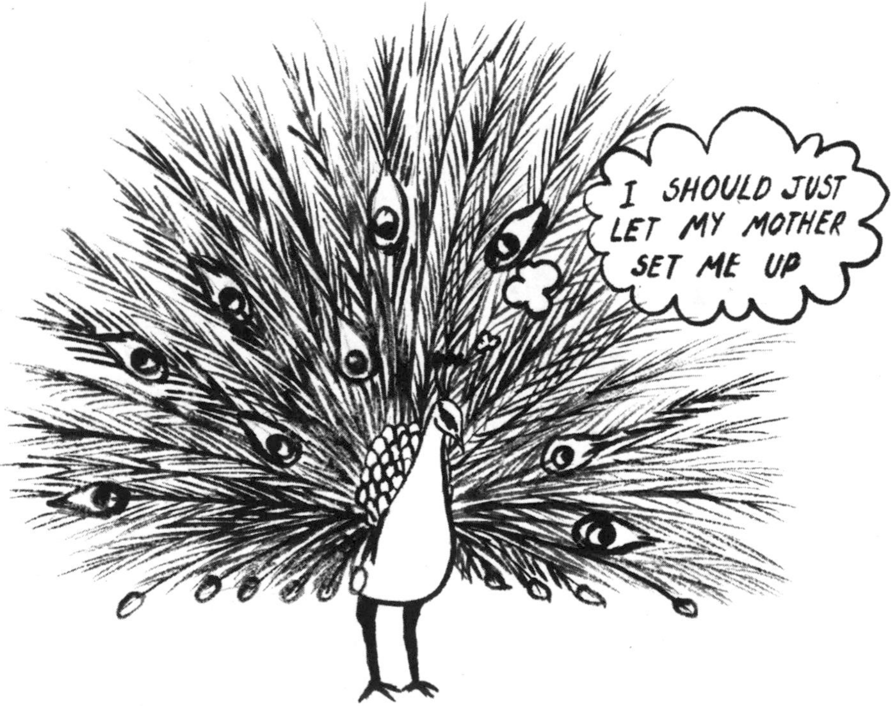
I SHOULD JUST LET MY MOTHER SET ME UP

WHEN I'VE BEEN INVITED:

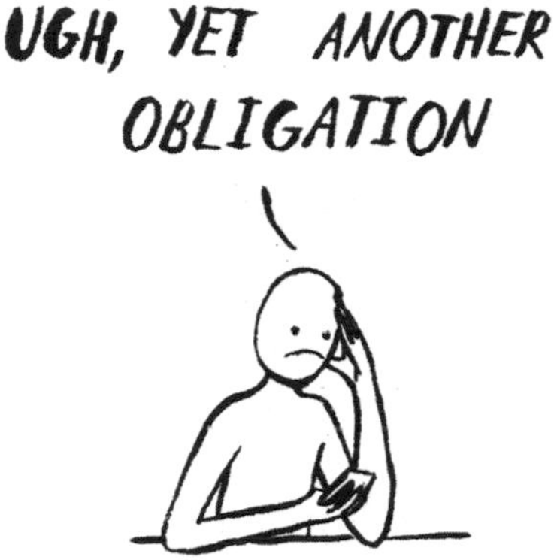
UGH, YET ANOTHER OBLIGATION

WHEN I HAVEN'T BEEN INVITED:

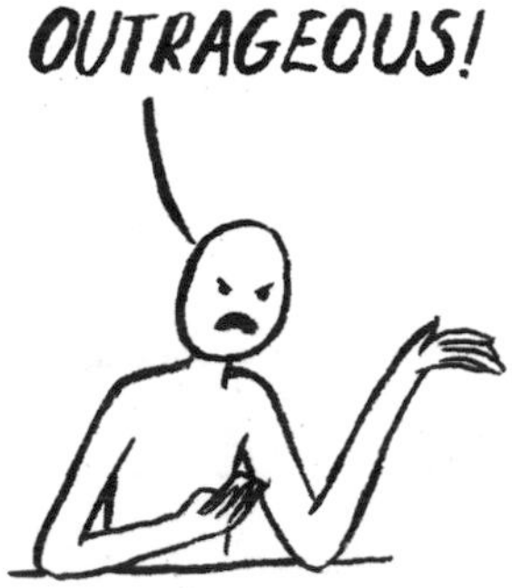
OUTRAGEOUS!

ARE YOUR STANDARDS TOO LOW?
A QUICK TEST!

HOW CAN YOU TELL THAT SOMEONE IS KIND?

HOW CAN YOU TELL THAT SOMEONE IS SUPPORTIVE?

HOW CAN YOU TELL THAT SOMEONE ISN'T BIGOTED?

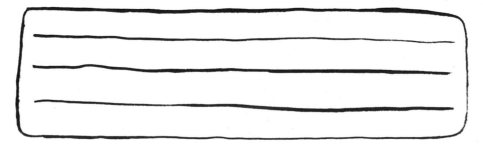

IF YOU SAID:

1. BECAUSE THEY WOULD NEVER DO ANYTHING TO HURT ME.
2. THEY WOULD NEVER TRY TO STOP ME FROM PURSUING MY DREAMS.
3. BECAUSE THEY NEVER SAY ANYTHING BIGOTED.

THEN YOUR STANDARDS ARE TOO LOW!

THE ABSENCE OF A NEGATIVE TRAIT IS NOT PROOF OF THE PRESENCE OF THE OPPOSITE, POSITIVE TRAIT.

THE ABSENCE OF CRUELTY IS NOT KINDNESS.
THE ABSENCE OF UNDERMINING IS NOT SUPPORT.
THE ABSENCE OF HATE IS NOT LOVE.

TO BE KIND, SOMEONE NEEDS TO:

NEVER BE CRUEL AND ACTIVELY DO KIND THINGS FOR YOU

NEVER BE CRUEL → THIS WITHOUT THE SECOND PART IS INDIFFERENCE

ACTIVELY DO KIND THINGS FOR YOU → THIS WITHOUT THE FIRST PART IS MANIPULATION

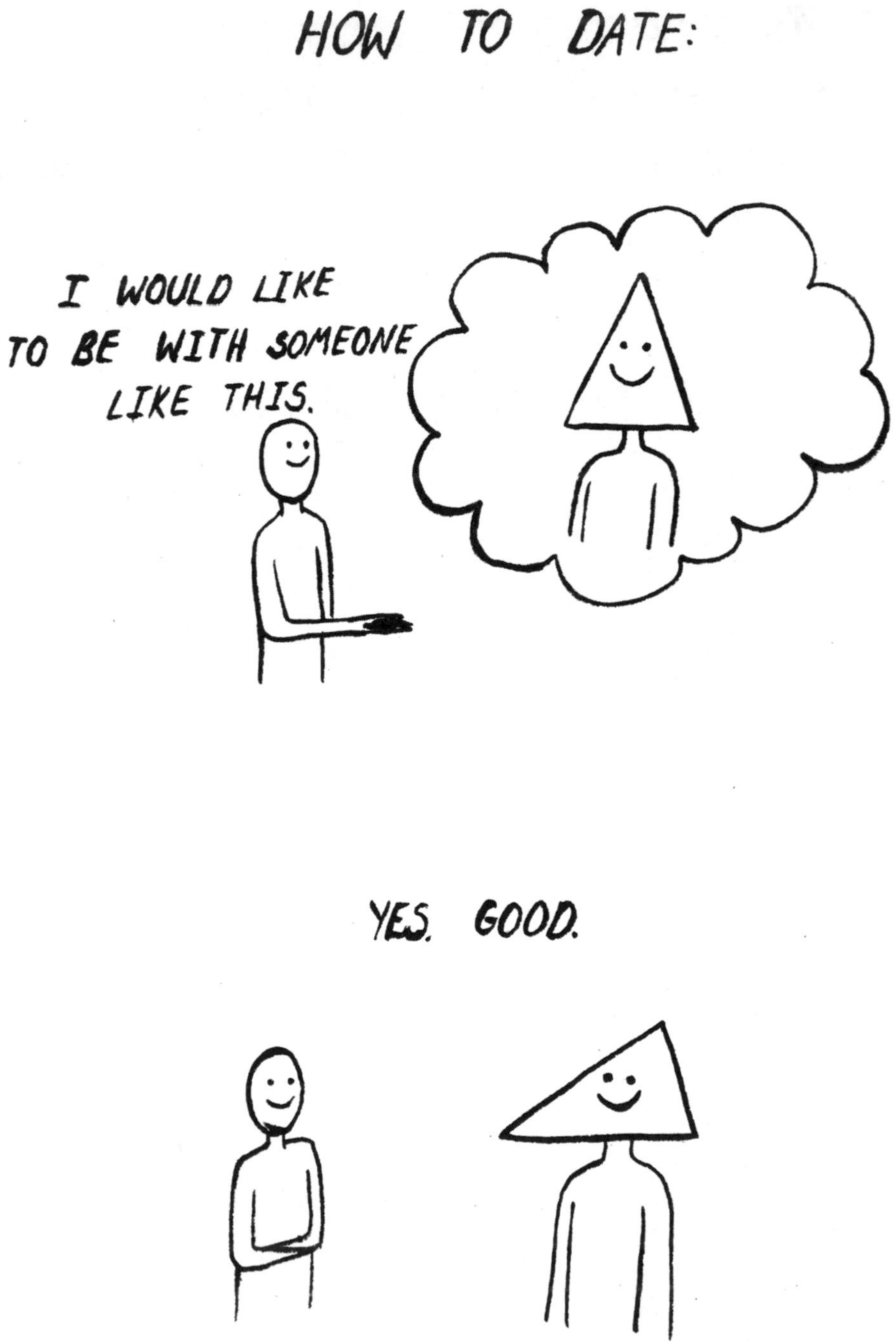
HOW TO DATE:
I WOULD LIKE TO BE WITH SOMEONE LIKE THIS.
YES. GOOD.

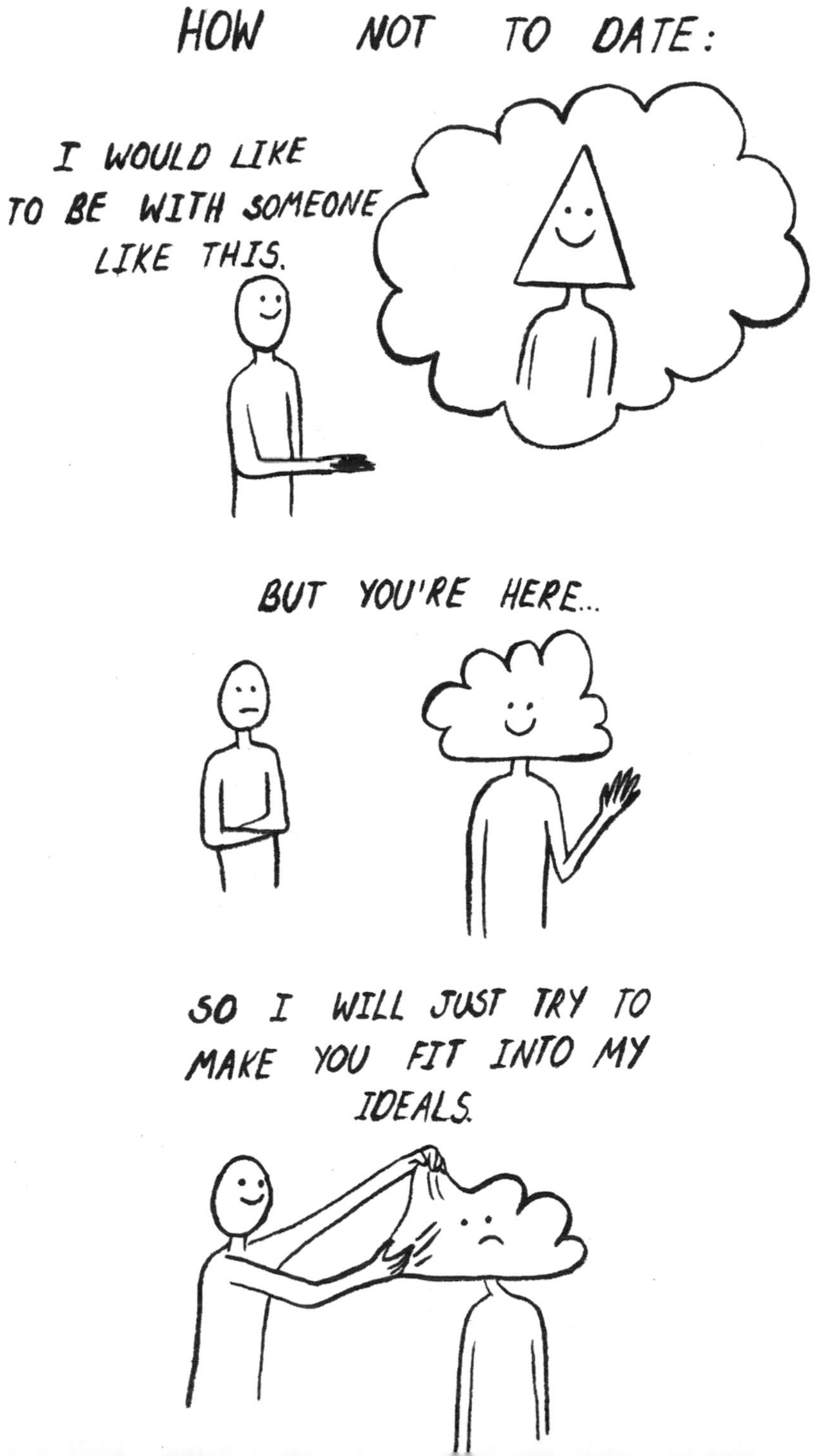
HOW NOT TO DATE:
I WOULD LIKE TO BE WITH SOMEONE LIKE THIS.
BUT YOU'RE HERE...
SO I WILL JUST TRY TO MAKE YOU FIT INTO MY IDEALS.

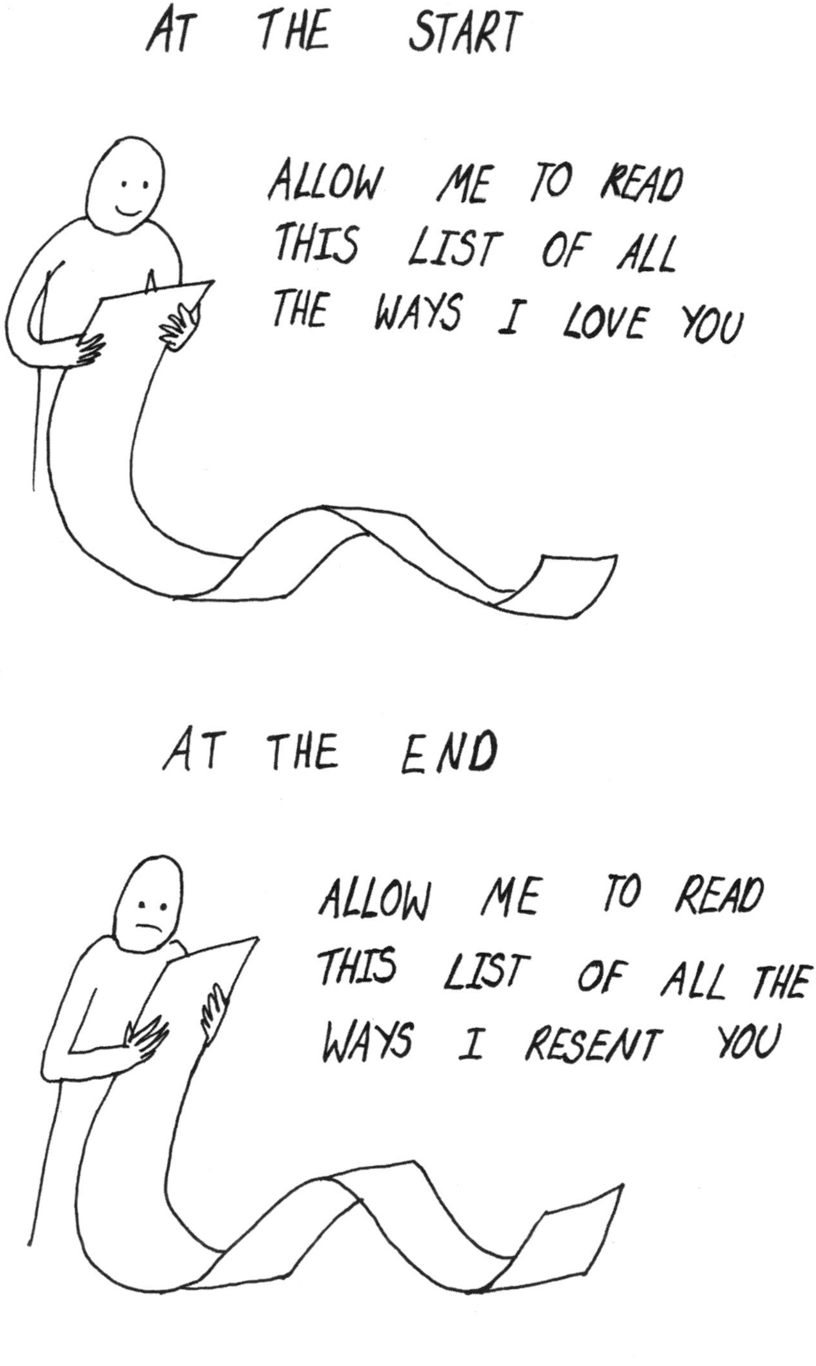
AT THE START
ALLOW ME TO READ THIS LIST OF ALL THE WAYS I LOVE YOU
AT THE END
ALLOW ME TO READ THIS LIST OF ALL THE WAYS I RESENT YOU

SURE, HAVING HIGH STANDARDS AND STRONG BOUNDARIES IS GREAT FOR MY MENTAL HEALTH, BUT AT WHAT COST?

FLOURISHING IS SO BORING SOMETIMES

WHAT'S YOUR LOVE LANGUAGE?

WHICH OF THE FIVE MAJOR WAYS TO EXPRESS LOVE IS YOUR WAY?

ACTS OF SERVICE	QUALITY TIME
SMALL OR BIG ACTIONS TO HELP YOU.	UNDIVIDED ATTENTION AND FULL PRESENCE.
GIFTS	PHYSICAL TOUCH
VISUAL SYMBOLS OF LOVE — NOT NECESSARILY EXPENSIVE.	HUGS, KISSING, HOLDING HANDS, SEX.
WORDS OF AFFIRMATION	
COMPLIMENTS, VERBAL ENCOURAGEMENT, "I LOVE YOU."	

1. WHICH OF THESE WOULD MAKE YOU HAPPIEST?

A) YOUR PARTNER RANDOMLY SURPRISING YOU WITH A SMALL THOUGHTFUL GIFT, "JUST BECAUSE."

B) YOUR PARTNER TAKING THE INITIATIVE TO COMPLETE A TASK AROUND THE HOUSE, JUST TO BENEFIT YOU.

C) YOUR PARTNER CUDDLING YOU FOR HALF AN HOUR.

D) YOUR PARTNER GIVING YOU A RANDOM BUT VERY SINCERE AND SPECIFIC COMPLIMENT.

E) YOUR PARTNER TAKING A WHOLE DAY OFF JUST SO YOU CAN SPEND IT TOGETHER.

2. WHICH OF THESE THINGS DO YOU NEED FOR A GOOD BIRTHDAY?

A) THOUGHTFUL GIFTS FROM YOUR LOVED ONES.
B) HELP IN ORGANIZING AND PLANNING THE DAY, OR SOMEONE ELSE DOING IT ALL ENTIRELY.
C) LOTS OF LOVE AND AFFECTION FROM EVERYONE.
D) THOUGHTFUL WORDS SPOKEN ABOUT YOU ON THE DAY.
E) ALL YOUR CLOSEST ONES BEING THERE AT THE PARTY.

3. WHICH OF THESE SMALL THINGS WOULD YOU APPRECIATE THE MOST FROM YOUR PARTNER?

A) A SURPRISE TREAT FROM THE COFFEE SHOP.
B) THEM DOING A TASK YOU'VE BEEN PUTTING OFF.
C) A HUG.
D) A RANDOM SWEET TEXT FROM YOUR LOVE IN THE MIDDLE OF THE NIGHT.
E) AN EVENING TOGETHER, WITH ALL SCREENS BANNED FOR THE DURATION.

RESULTS ON THE NEXT PAGE!

IF YOU ANSWERED MOSTLY A'S
(OR B'S, C'S, D'S, OR E'S)
THEN YOUR LOVE LANGUAGE IS...

ALL OF THEM

THOUGH LOVE LANGUAGES CAN BE USEFUL TOOLS IN EXPLAINING WHAT YOU NEED FROM A PARTNER, DIVIDING THEM INTO CATEGORIES CAN ALSO BE USED AS A MANIPULATIVE WAY OF LOWERING YOUR STANDARDS AND MAKING YOU FEEL LIKE YOU CAN ONLY HAVE YOUR NEEDS PARTIALLY MET. IT IS NOT UNREASONABLE TO EXPECT YOUR PARTNER TO GIVE YOU THOUGHTFUL GIFTS, SAY KIND WORDS, BE PHYSICALLY AFFECTIONATE, BE HELPFUL, AND BE PRESENT.

IN A HEALTHY RELATIONSHIP, ALL PARTIES SHOULD BE BOTH ABLE AND WILLING TO DO ALL THE ABOVE.

THINGS TO TELL
YOURSELF WHEN YOU
DON'T WANT TO ADMIT
THAT YOU'RE WASTING
YOUR TIME

HAHA! THEY'RE GOING TO FEEL _SOO_ SILLY WHEN THEY REALIZE THEY FORGOT TO TEXT ME BACK 268 DAYS AGO!

I'M SURE IF I CONTINUE TO
BEND OVER BACKWARDS, THEY'LL EVENTUALLY
NOTICE AND APPRECIATE ME

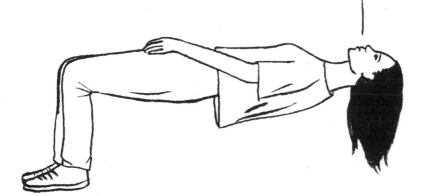

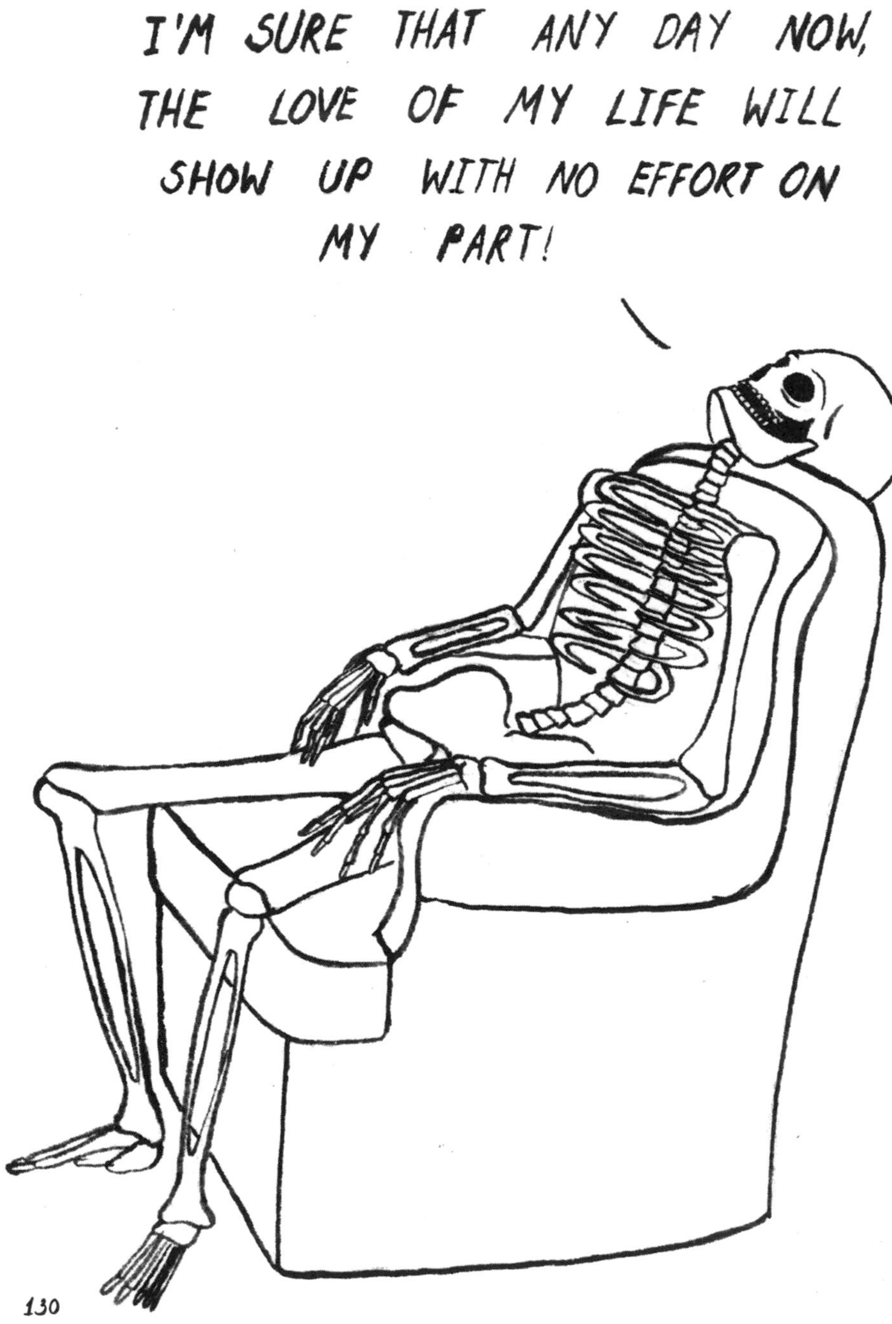
I'M SURE THAT ANY DAY NOW, THE LOVE OF MY LIFE WILL SHOW UP WITH NO EFFORT ON MY PART!

SOME PEOPLE ARE JUST AWFUL

AND YOU MAY BE ONE OF THEM

AWFUL AT LIFE

IT'S ACTUALLY VERY NORMAL
TO FEEL AWFUL MUCH OF THE TIME

I keep feeling like I need to tie this whole book up with some sage wisdom or an answer, but that (a) would not be the point and (b) would be a massive lie. If there were some correct way to live life, one of the ancient Greeks would have figured it out ages ago and we'd all be living perfect lives with flying cars by now. The reality is that, no matter how much we want it to be, life isn't a game to be won after completing a series of tasks and goals successfully. There is no clear "meaning" or truth, or a little pop-up message to tell you you're on the right path or have completed something successfully.

There are no definitive "stages" in life, and the milestones we set for ourselves are meaningless in the grand scheme of things. People are neither mostly good nor mostly bad—but your opinion on this is a reflection of you and your experiences more than anything else. There is no guidebook to make everything easier. All we can do is our best, and frankly, we barely even do that.

I concede that it would be much more beautiful and satisfying if what united us all was some divine purpose, something big and grand like art or love.

In reality, what unites us is the relentless mundanity of life. The irrational anger we feel when someone is walking exactly the same pace as you, instead of having the decency to slow down or speed up and overtake you. The absolute bliss of going to bed knowing you don't have to wake up early the next day. The embarrassment of having pushed a "pull" door.

That, and of course, the occasional terrifying pangs of not knowing what on earth we're doing.

Yet there's something incredibly reassuring about this fact. Very few of us will know what it feels like to be filthy rich, or to create a great work of art, or to invent something that changes the course of history. But every single last one of us knows the annoyance of running out of toilet paper and realizing it too late. Or the awkwardness of having asked someone to repeat something one too many times, so you just laugh and pretend to have heard them when you haven't. Or the sting of your first romantic rejection. We are all living the same lives when you look at the slightly awful parts.

I think we would all benefit from recognizing that feeling slightly underwhelmed is just the human condition. Because we have big brains full of fantasy and grand ambitions, but we are in dumb monkey bodies that just want to eat and sleep all day.

And that is why we are all awful at life.

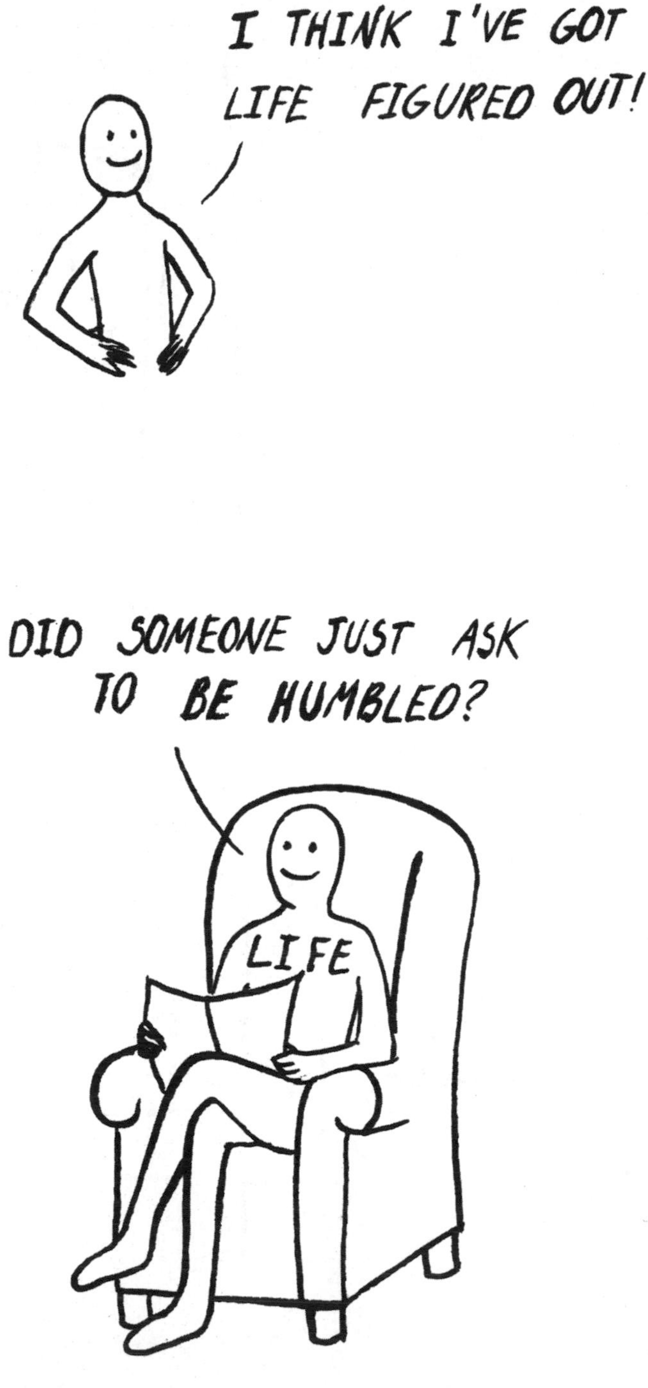
I THINK I'VE GOT LIFE FIGURED OUT!
DID SOMEONE JUST ASK TO BE HUMBLED?
LIFE

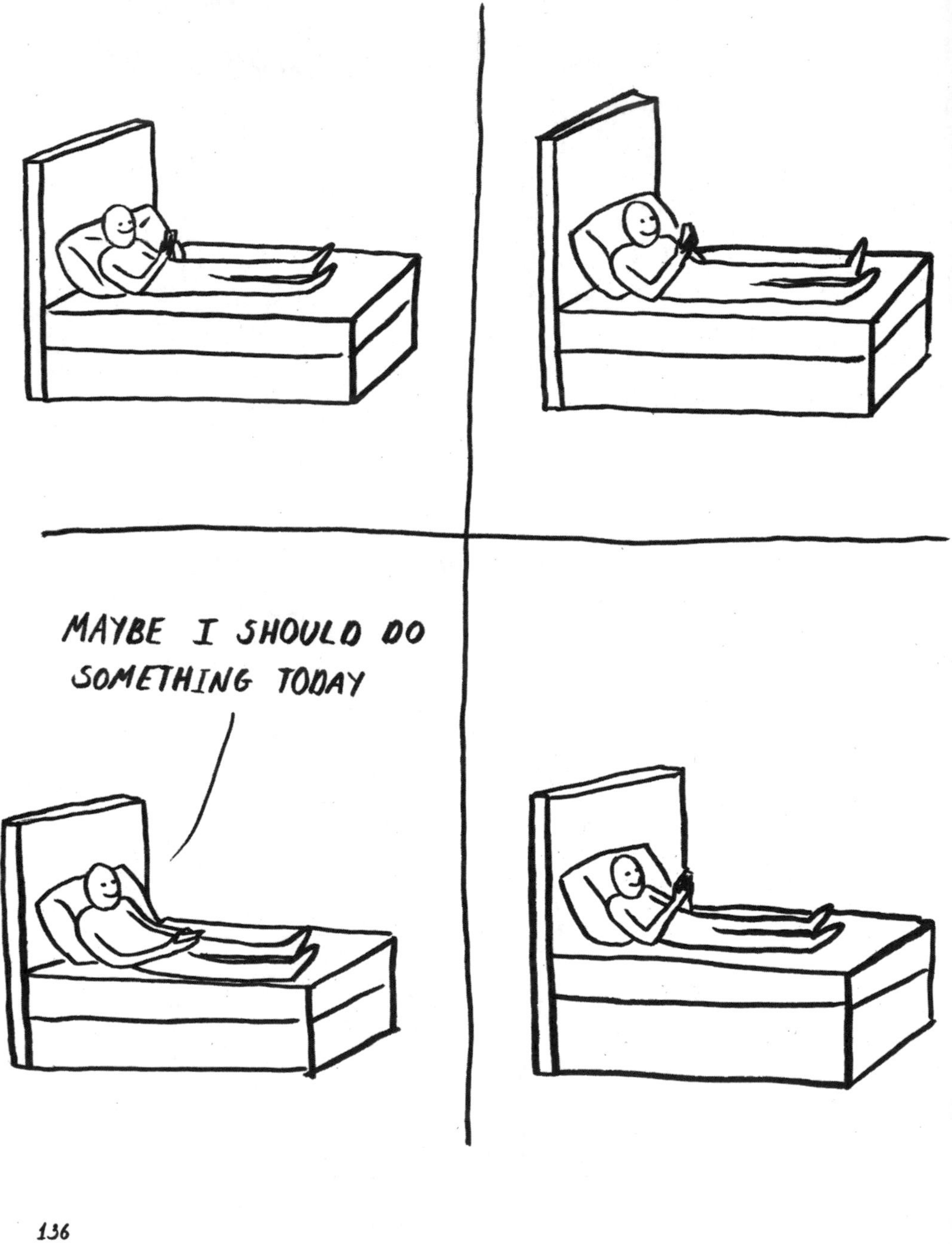
MAYBE I SHOULD DO SOMETHING TODAY

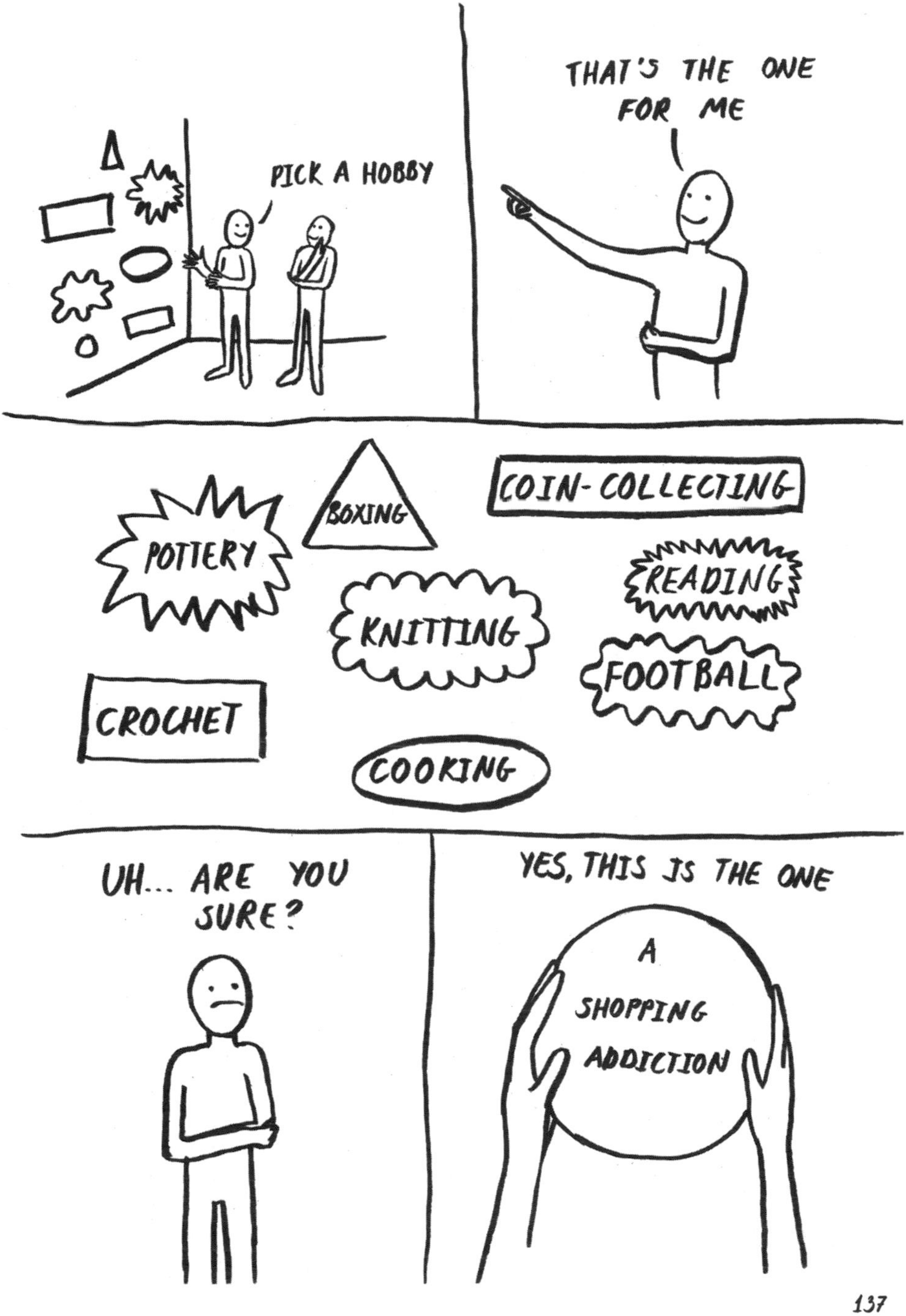
PICK A HOBBY
THAT'S THE ONE FOR ME
POTTERY
BOXING
COIN-COLLECTING
READING
KNITTING
FOOTBALL
CROCHET
COOKING
UH... ARE YOU SURE?
YES, THIS IS THE ONE
A SHOPPING ADDICTION

I LIKE BEING KIND TO MYSELF

YOU LOOK
BEAUTIFUL TODAY

SHE'S A CYNIC, THOUGH

THIS IS
DUMB

I'VE NEVER HAD AN ORIGINAL THOUGHT

I'VE NEVER HAD AN ORIGINAL THOUGHT BECAUSE THE HUMAN EXPERIENCE IS A UNIVERSAL ONE, AND WE ARE ALL MORE SIMILAR THAN WE THINK.

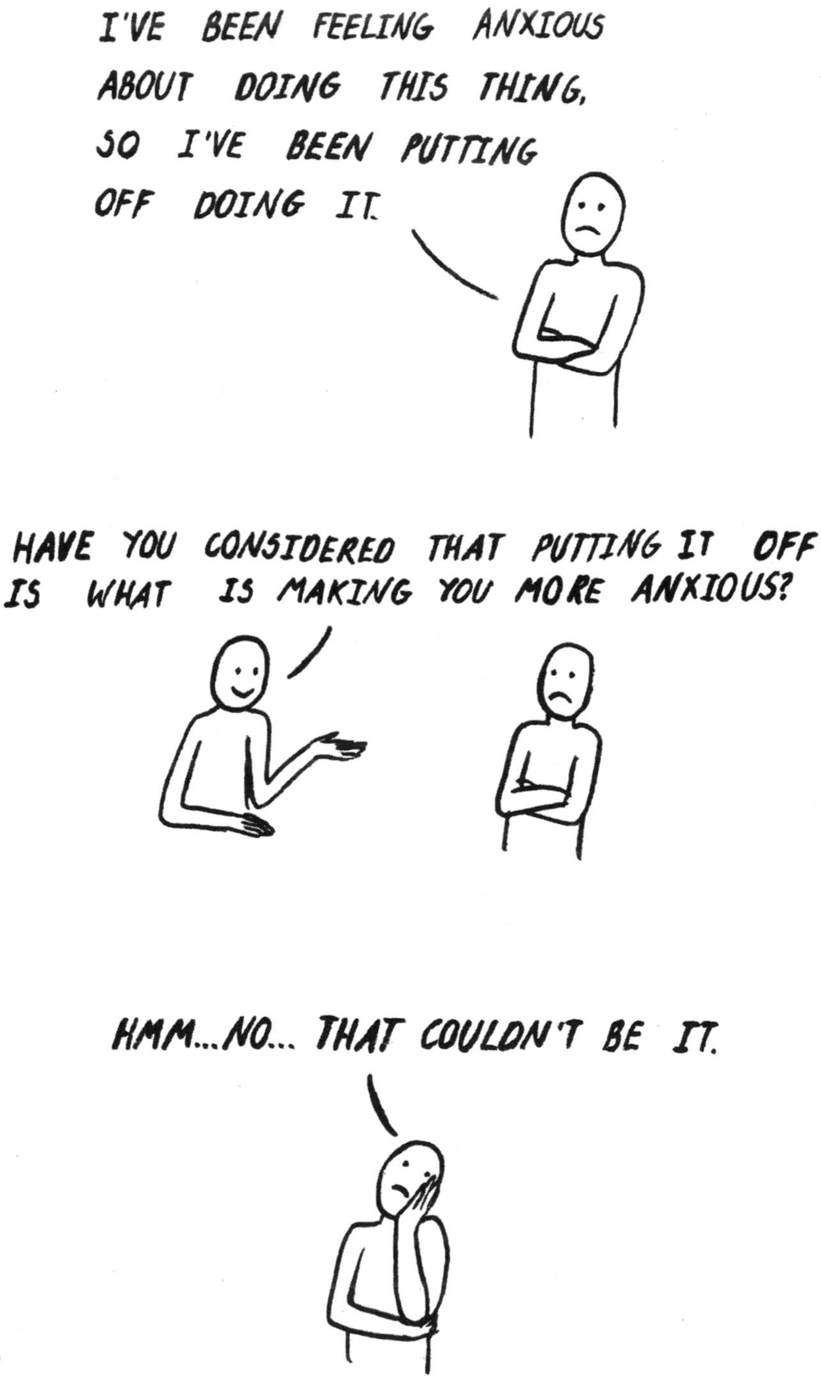
I'VE BEEN FEELING ANXIOUS ABOUT DOING THIS THING, SO I'VE BEEN PUTTING OFF DOING IT.
HAVE YOU CONSIDERED THAT PUTTING IT OFF IS WHAT IS MAKING YOU MORE ANXIOUS?
HMM...NO... THAT COULDN'T BE IT.

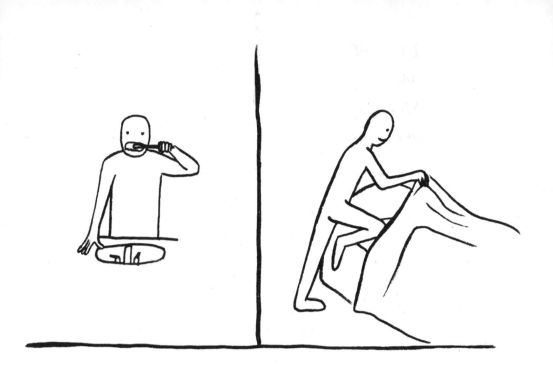

I ABSOLUTELY CANNOT WAIT FOR TOMORROW

WHEN I GET TO EAT AGAIN

I AM IN CONTROL OF MY OWN DESTINY

I AM IN CONTROL OF MY OWN DESTINY

IT'S OK TO NOT BE
OK SOMETIMES

BUT PLEASE KEEP IT TO
YOURSELF BECAUSE I
HAVE MY OWN SHIT
TO WORRY ABOUT

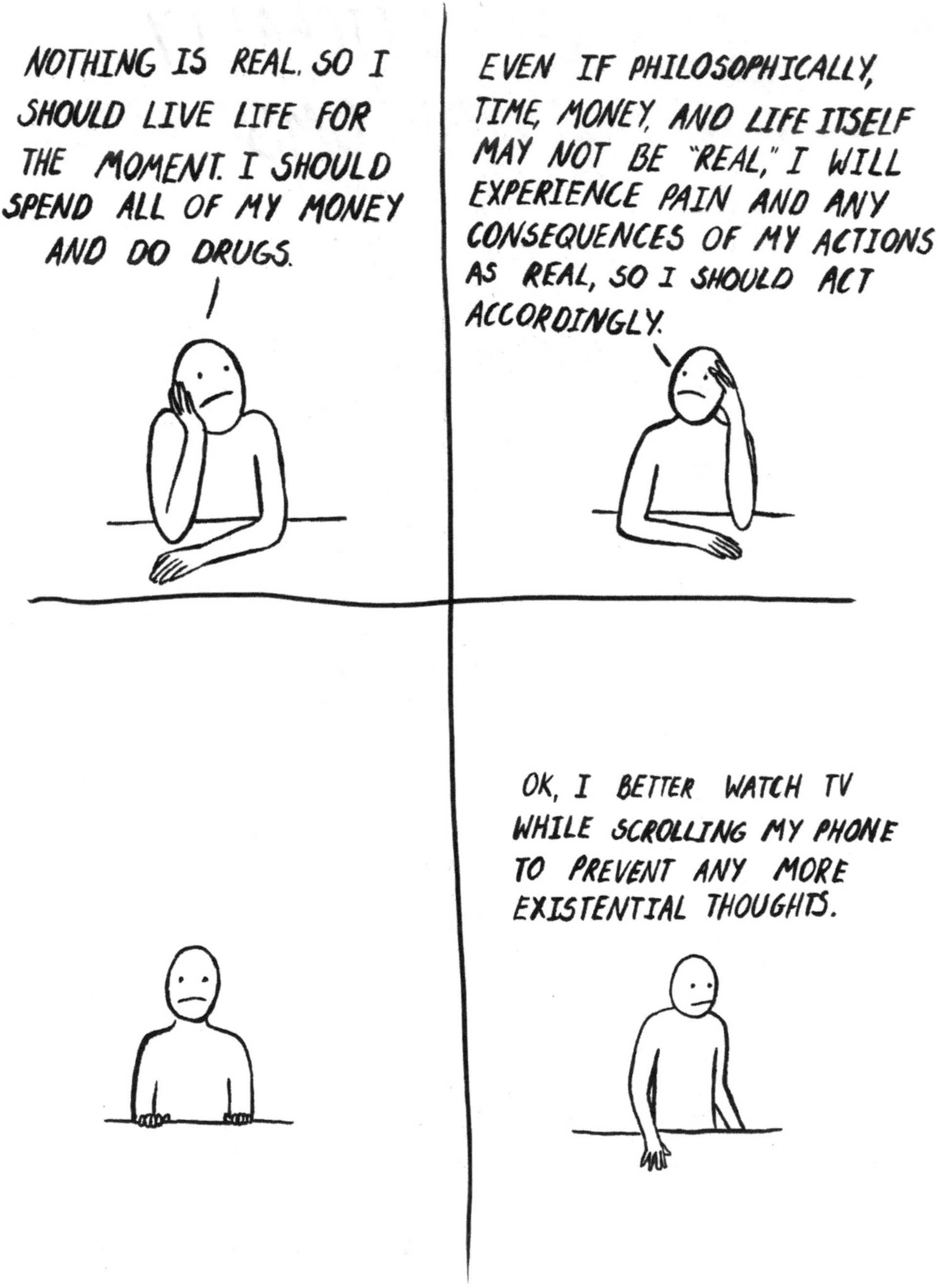
NOTHING IS REAL, SO I SHOULD LIVE LIFE FOR THE MOMENT. I SHOULD SPEND ALL OF MY MONEY AND DO DRUGS.
EVEN IF PHILOSOPHICALLY, TIME, MONEY, AND LIFE ITSELF MAY NOT BE "REAL," I WILL EXPERIENCE PAIN AND ANY CONSEQUENCES OF MY ACTIONS AS REAL, SO I SHOULD ACT ACCORDINGLY.
OK, I BETTER WATCH TV WHILE SCROLLING MY PHONE TO PREVENT ANY MORE EXISTENTIAL THOUGHTS.

GOOGLING LITERALLY ANY SYMPTOMS

DO YOU HAVE A MINOR AILMENT?
YES
NO
YOU'RE PREGNANT
NO I'M NOT
YOU HAVE CANCER
NO I DON'T

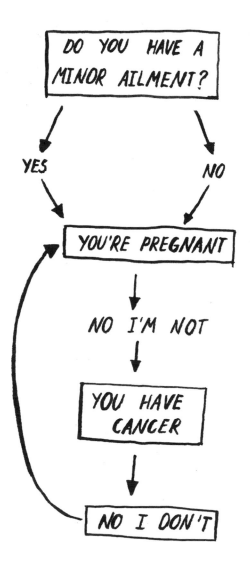

NO ONE UNDERSTANDS
THE DEMONS I'M BATTLING

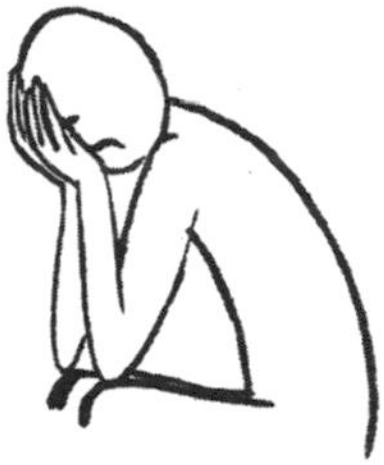

THE DEMONS IN QUESTION:

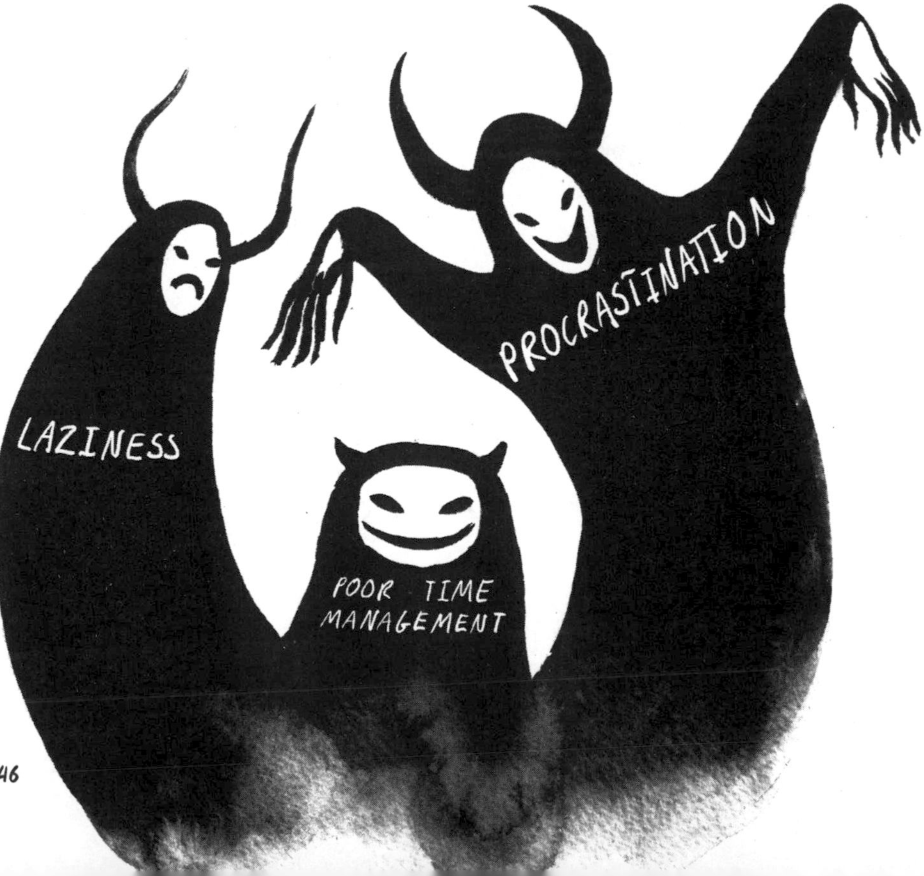
PROCRASTINATION
LAZINESS
POOR TIME MANAGEMENT

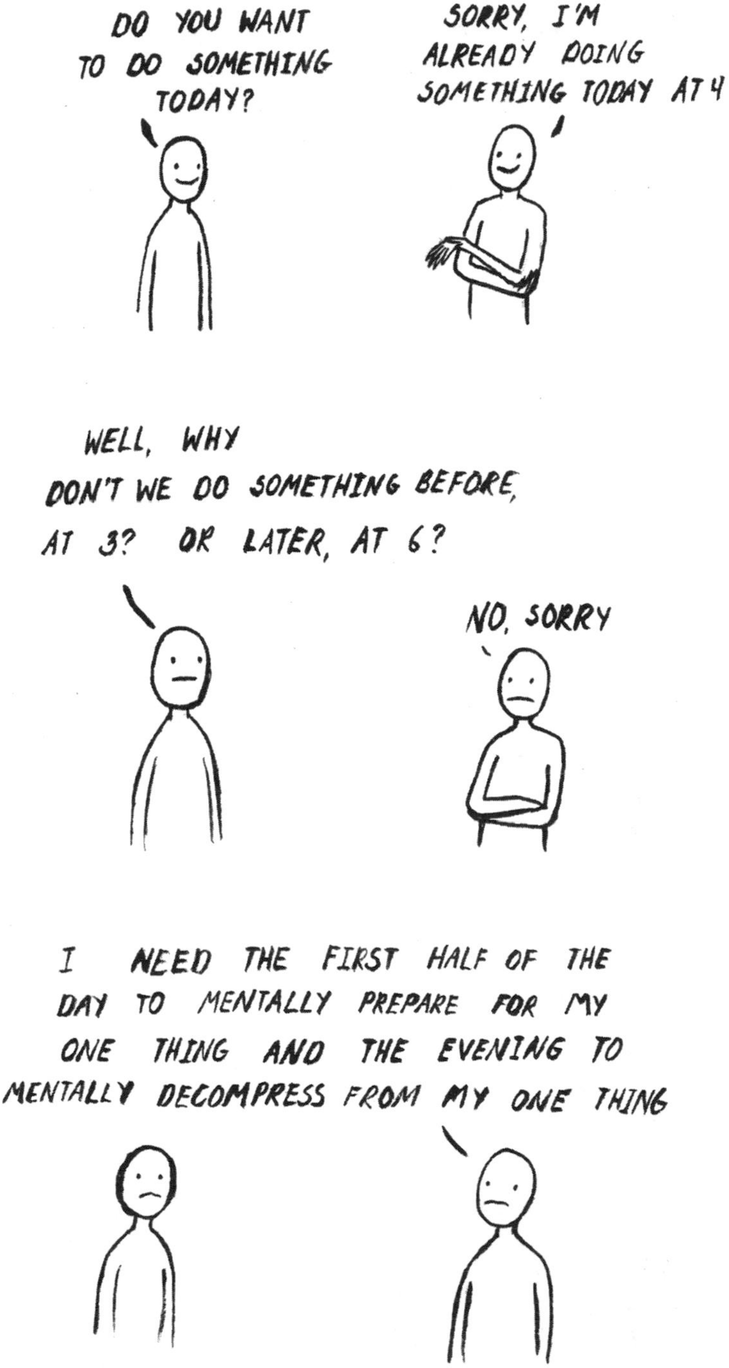

DO YOU WANT TO DO SOMETHING TODAY?
SORRY, I'M ALREADY DOING SOMETHING TODAY AT 4
WELL, WHY DON'T WE DO SOMETHING BEFORE, AT 3? OR LATER, AT 6?
NO, SORRY
I NEED THE FIRST HALF OF THE DAY TO MENTALLY PREPARE FOR MY ONE THING AND THE EVENING TO MENTALLY DECOMPRESS FROM MY ONE THING

I SHOULD PROBABLY TRY TO
FIX MY SLEEP SCHEDULE

BY NOT SLEEPING AT ALL AND
MAKING IT SIGNIFICANTLY WORSE

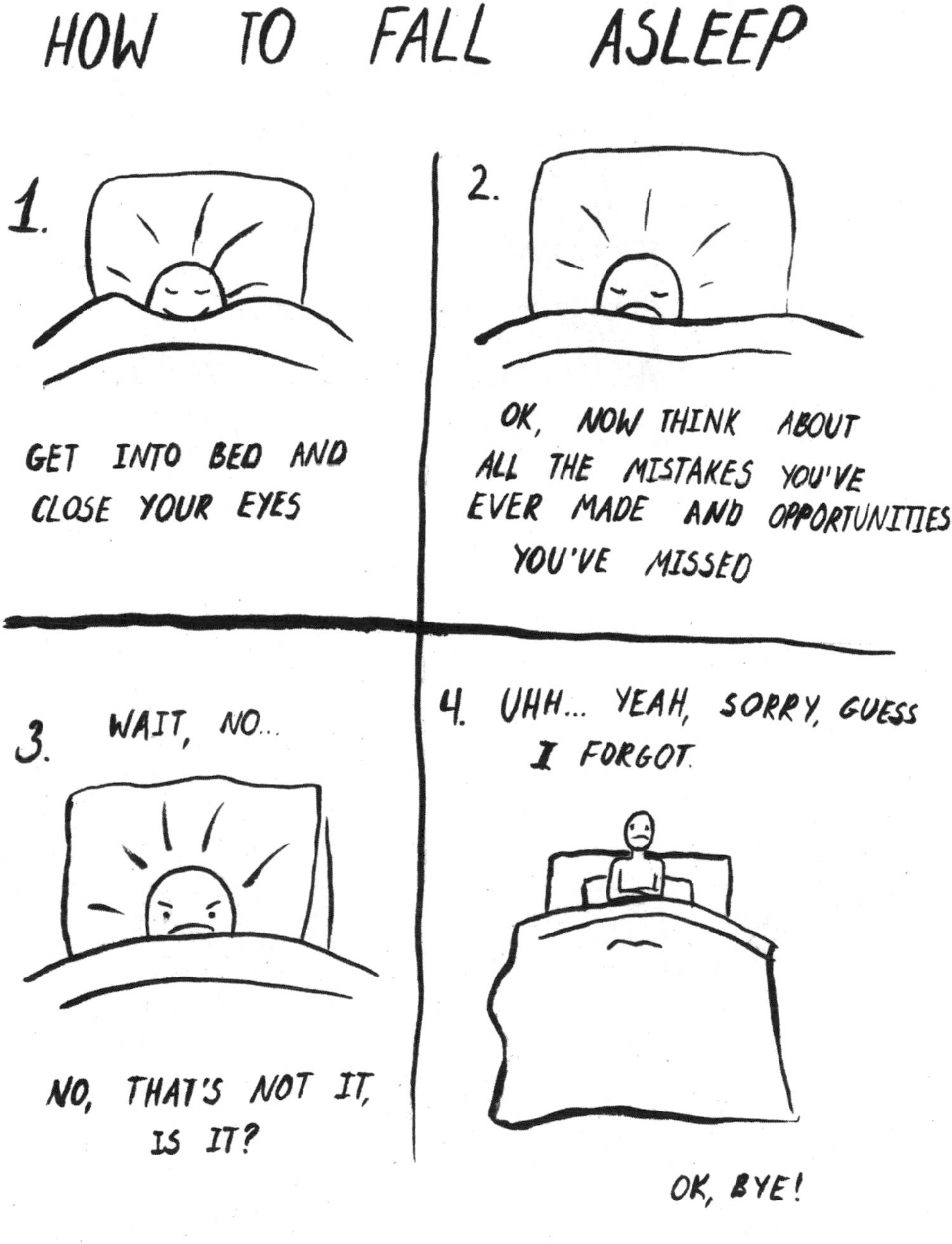
HOW TO FALL ASLEEP
1.
GET INTO BED AND CLOSE YOUR EYES
2.
OK, NOW THINK ABOUT ALL THE MISTAKES YOU'VE EVER MADE AND OPPORTUNITIES YOU'VE MISSED
3.
WAIT, NO...
NO, THAT'S NOT IT, IS IT?
4.
UHH... YEAH, SORRY, GUESS I FORGOT.
OK, BYE!

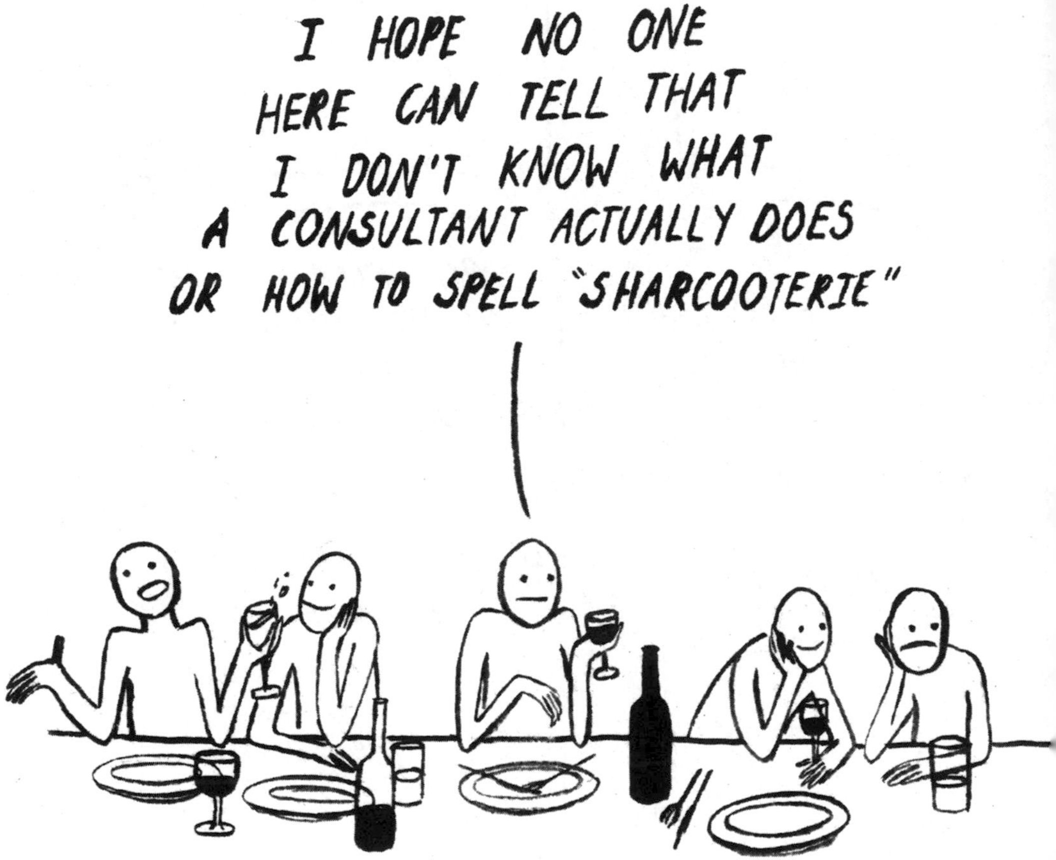
I HOPE NO ONE HERE CAN TELL THAT I DON'T KNOW WHAT A CONSULTANT ACTUALLY DOES OR HOW TO SPELL "SHARCOOTERIE"

AS A TEEN:

I'M A FREETHINKER. MY TASTES ARE NICHE AND REFINED. MY THOUGHTS CANNOT BE INFLUENCED BY THE MEDIA, ADS, OR PEER PRESSURE.

AS AN ADULT:

MY SILLY LITTLE LIFE HAS BEEN ENTIRELY INFLUENCED BY PROPOGANDA AND OTHER PEOPLE'S OPINIONS.

TIME TO GO
TO SLEEP

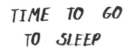

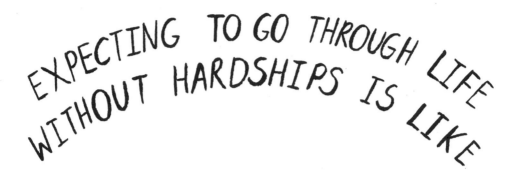

EXPECTING TO GO THROUGH LIFE WITHOUT HARDSHIPS IS LIKE

DOWNING FIVE CUPS OF **COFFEE** IN THE SPACE **OF** TWO **HOURS** AND NOT EXPECTING TO DO A MASSIVE TURD **SHORTLY AFTER**.

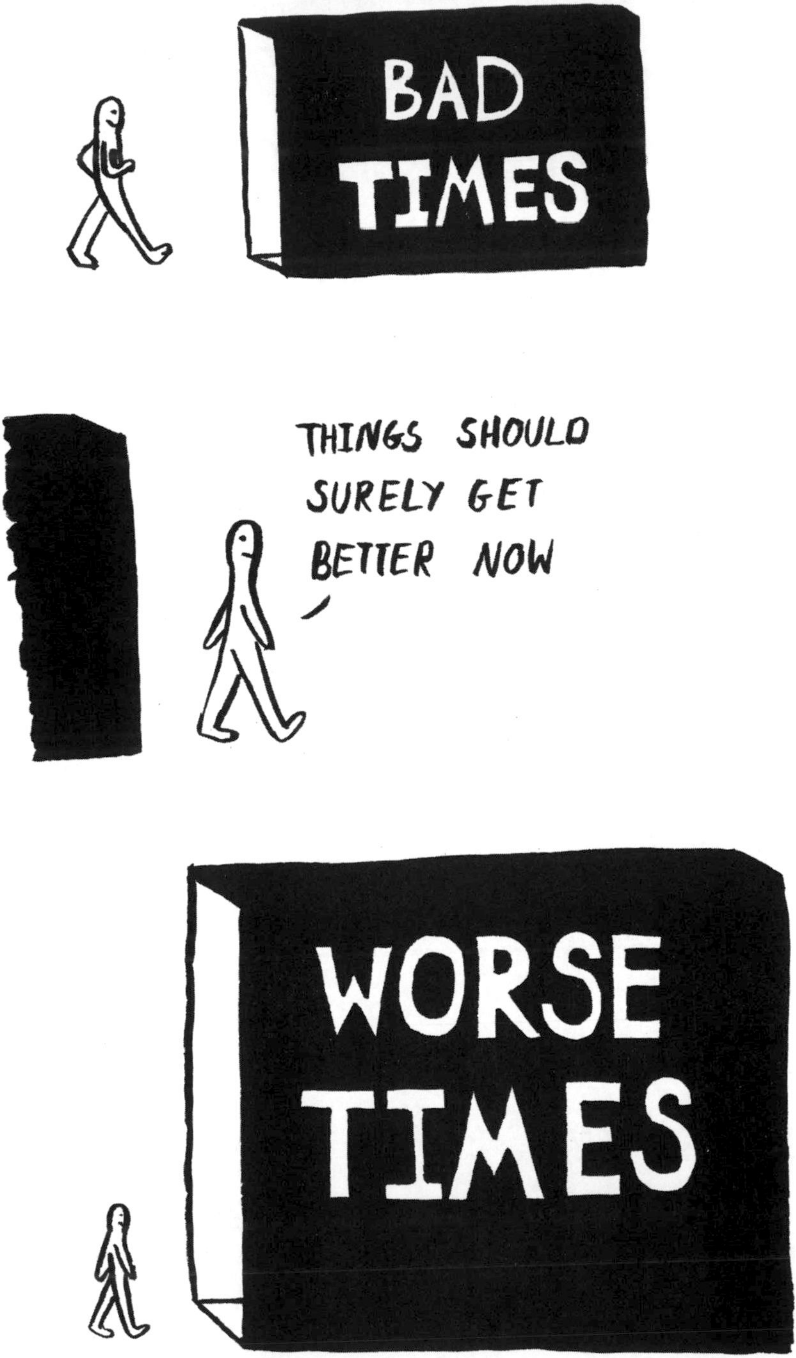
BAD TIMES
THINGS SHOULD SURELY GET BETTER NOW
WORSE TIMES

THERE WILL ALWAYS BE
PEOPLE MORE SUCCESSFUL,
POPULAR, RICH, OR BEAUTIFUL
THAN YOU.

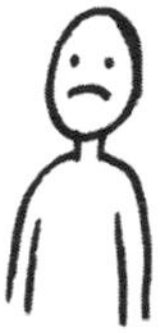

BUT...?

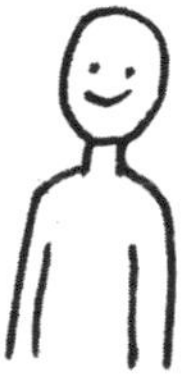

NO, THAT'S IT.
THERE WILL ALWAYS
BE PEOPLE BETTER THAN YOU.

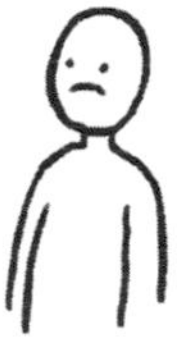

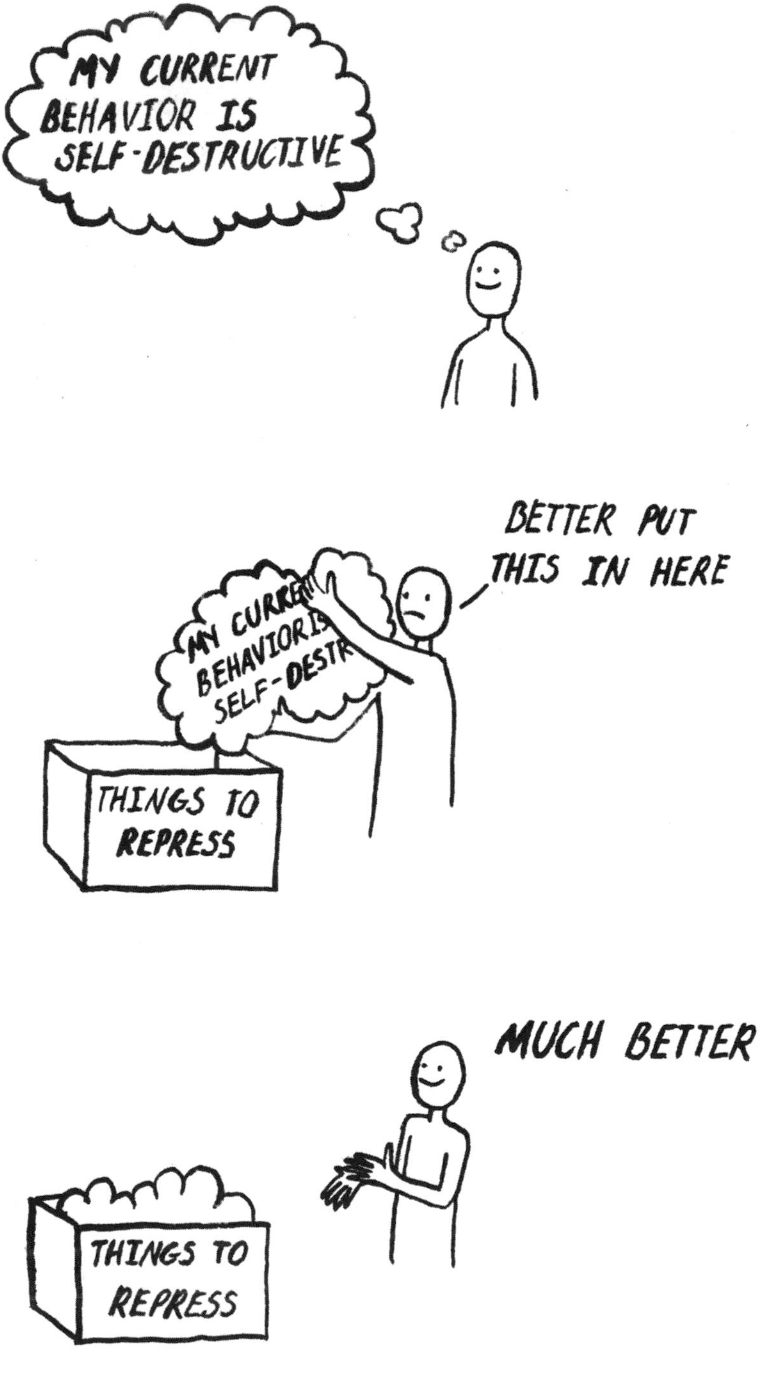
MY CURRENT BEHAVIOR IS SELF-DESTRUCTIVE
BETTER PUT THIS IN HERE
MY CURRE BEHAVIORIS SELF-DESTR
THINGS TO REPRESS
MUCH BETTER
THINGS TO REPRESS

THE FOUR BIGGEST CONS IN LIFE

ONE: IF YOU EXERCISE AND GET FIT, YOU HAVE TO KEEP DOING IT, OR LOSE ALL YOUR PROGRESS.

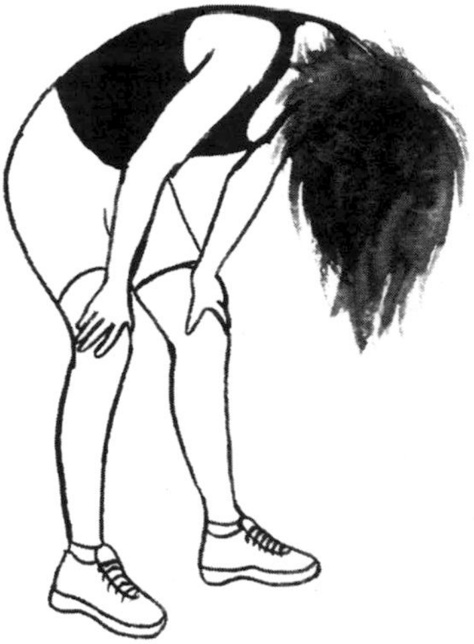

I'VE DONE THE WORK, I SHOULD BE ALLOWED TO RELAX FOR 3-130 MONTHS NOW.

TWO: IF YOU WANT TO FALL IN LOVE, YOU HAVE TO MAKE THE EFFORT TO MEET AND TALK TO NEW PEOPLE.

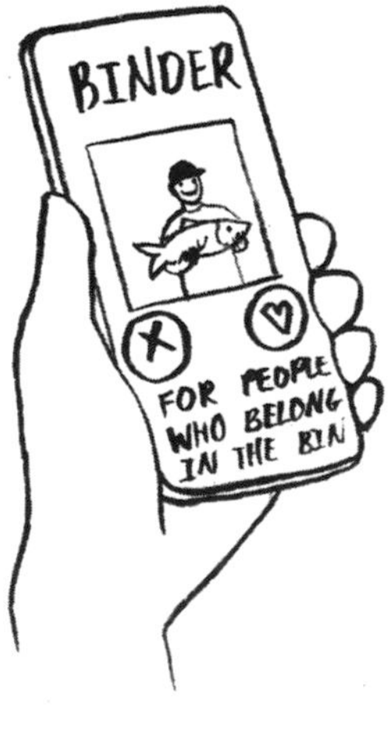
BINDER
FOR PEOPLE WHO BELONG IN THE BIN

SURELY IF IT WAS TRUE LOVE, ABSOLUTELY NO EFFORT OR INVOLVEMENT WOULD BE REQUIRED FROM ME.

THREE: WORKING HARD IS ENOUGH TO BECOME WEALTHY.

WHY DIDN'T I
HAVE THE FORESIGHT
TO BE BORN RICH?

FOUR: YOUR BEST YEARS ARE NOT YOUR
HIGH SCHOOL YEARS.

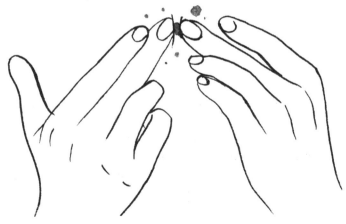

WHOEVER THOUGHT THIS WAS THE BEST LIFE HAS TO
OFFER HAS NEVER KNOWN THE JOYS OF A PROPER
SKIN-CARE ROUTINE.

I'VE DECIDED I'M TAKING
SOME TIME OFF TO FOCUS
ON MYSELF.

NOT FOR SELF-IMPROVEMENT,
JUST SELF-INVOLVEMENT.

DO THIS WHEN YOU'RE SAD

LIST THREE THINGS YOU'RE GRATEFUL FOR:

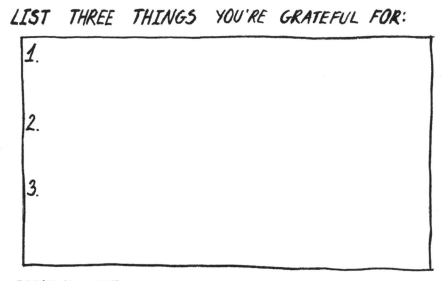

1.

2.

3.

FEELING BETTER? NO? OK, THEN...

LIST THREE THINGS THAT MAKE YOU ANGRY:

1.

2.

3.

YOU DON'T FEEL BETTER AFTER THAT, ONLY ANGRIER?

YEAH, I DON'T KNOW WHERE I WAS GOING WITH THAT EITHER.

OK, LIST YOUR TOP THREE FILMS:

1.

2.

3.

YOU'RE WELCOME!

NO, THAT DIDN'T MAKE YOU FEEL BETTER EITHER, BUT AT LEAST NOW YOU HAVE YOUR TOP THREE FILMS ON HAND!

MY MIND ALWAYS GOES BLANK WHEN I'M ASKED ABOUT MY FAVORITE FILMS.

PICK ONE

COOL GIRL STATUS

THE FREEDOM TO EXPRESS THE FULL SPECTRUM OF HUMAN EMOTION

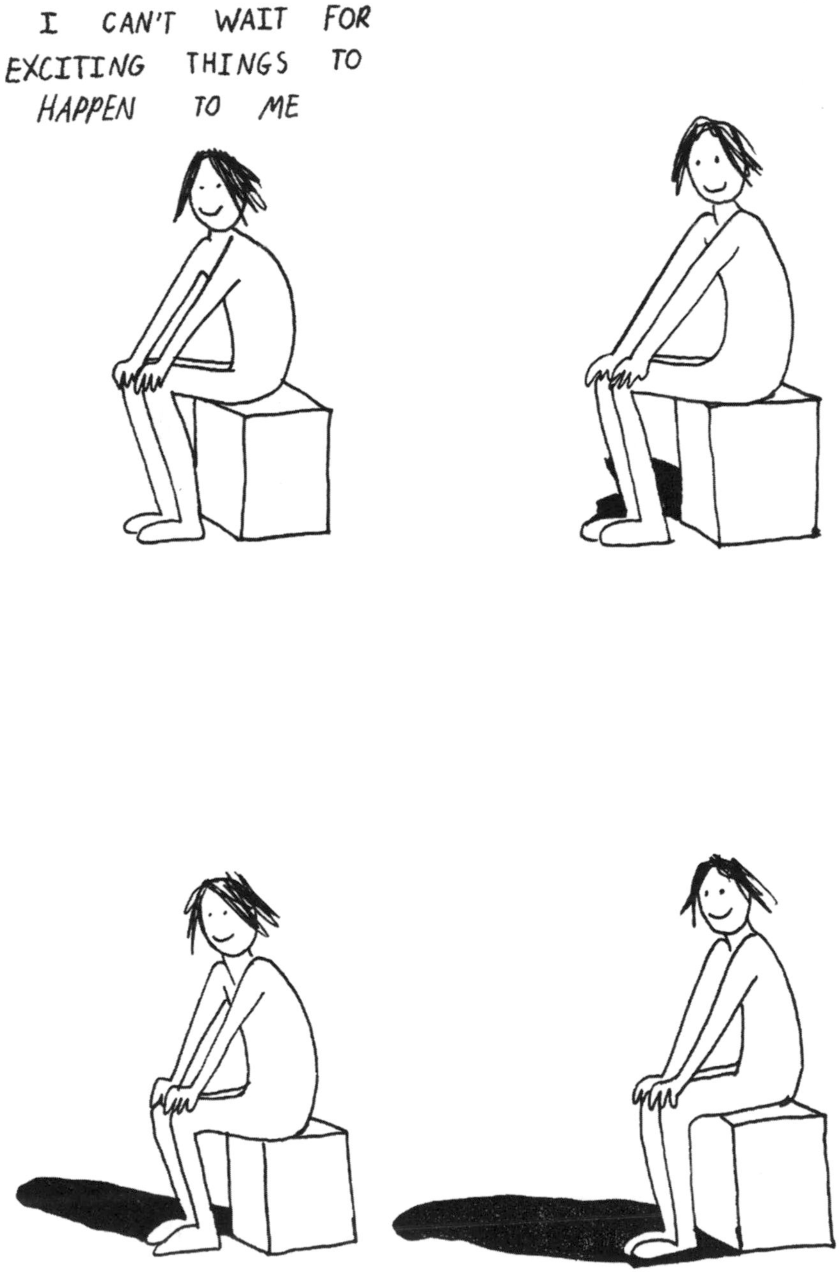
I CAN'T WAIT FOR EXCITING THINGS TO HAPPEN TO ME

THINGS WILL GET BETTER

OR WORSE,

OR THEY'LL STAY THE SAME.

SOME WAYS TO
REFRAME THE
NEGATIVE
AS SOMETHING

POSITIVE

NO, YOU DON'T HAVE A "FLAW"...

YOU HAVE A NEW PROJECT TO WORK ON!

I HAVE A NEW PROJECT
I'M WORKING ON!
IT'S CALLED "SEVERE
EMOTIONAL UNAVAILABILITY"!

COOL! I'M STILL BUSY WITH
"ALCOHOL DEPENDENCE."

BAD THINGS DON'T HAPPEN TO YOU...

ONLY NEW CHALLENGES!

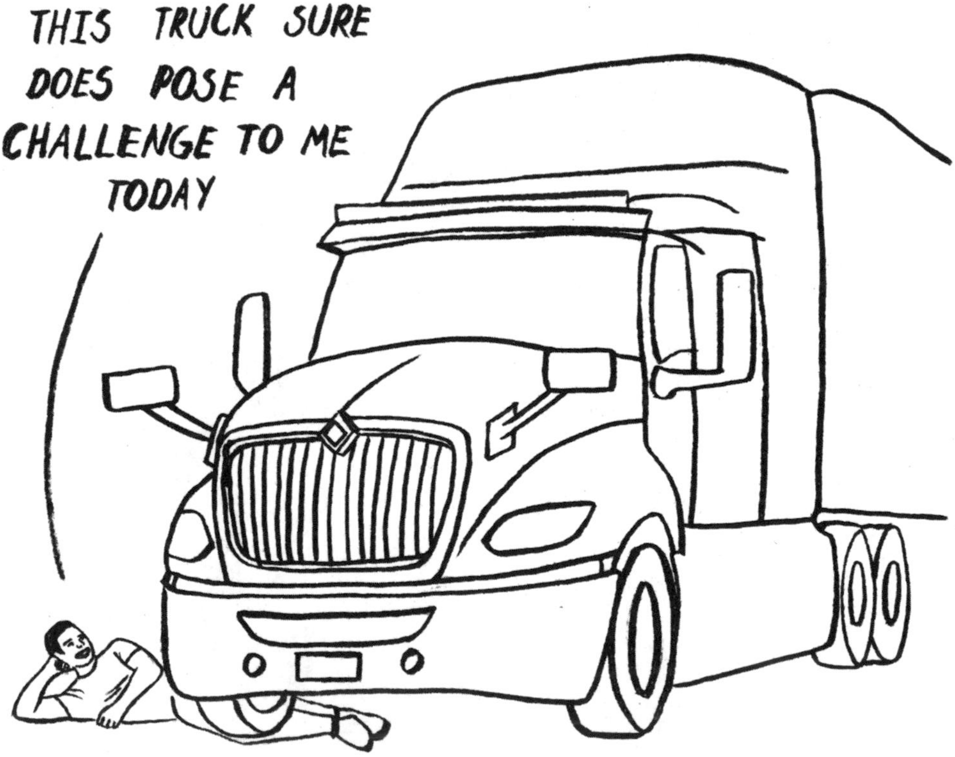
THIS TRUCK SURE DOES POSE A CHALLENGE TO ME TODAY

YOU DON'T HAVE A "PROBLEM," YOU HAVE

AN OPPORTUNITY

YOU'VE BEEN DIAGNOSED
WITH A TERMINAL OPPORTUNITY.
I'M SO SORRY.

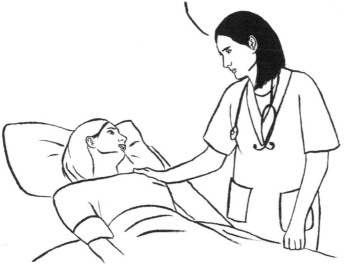

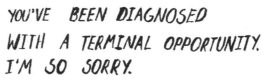

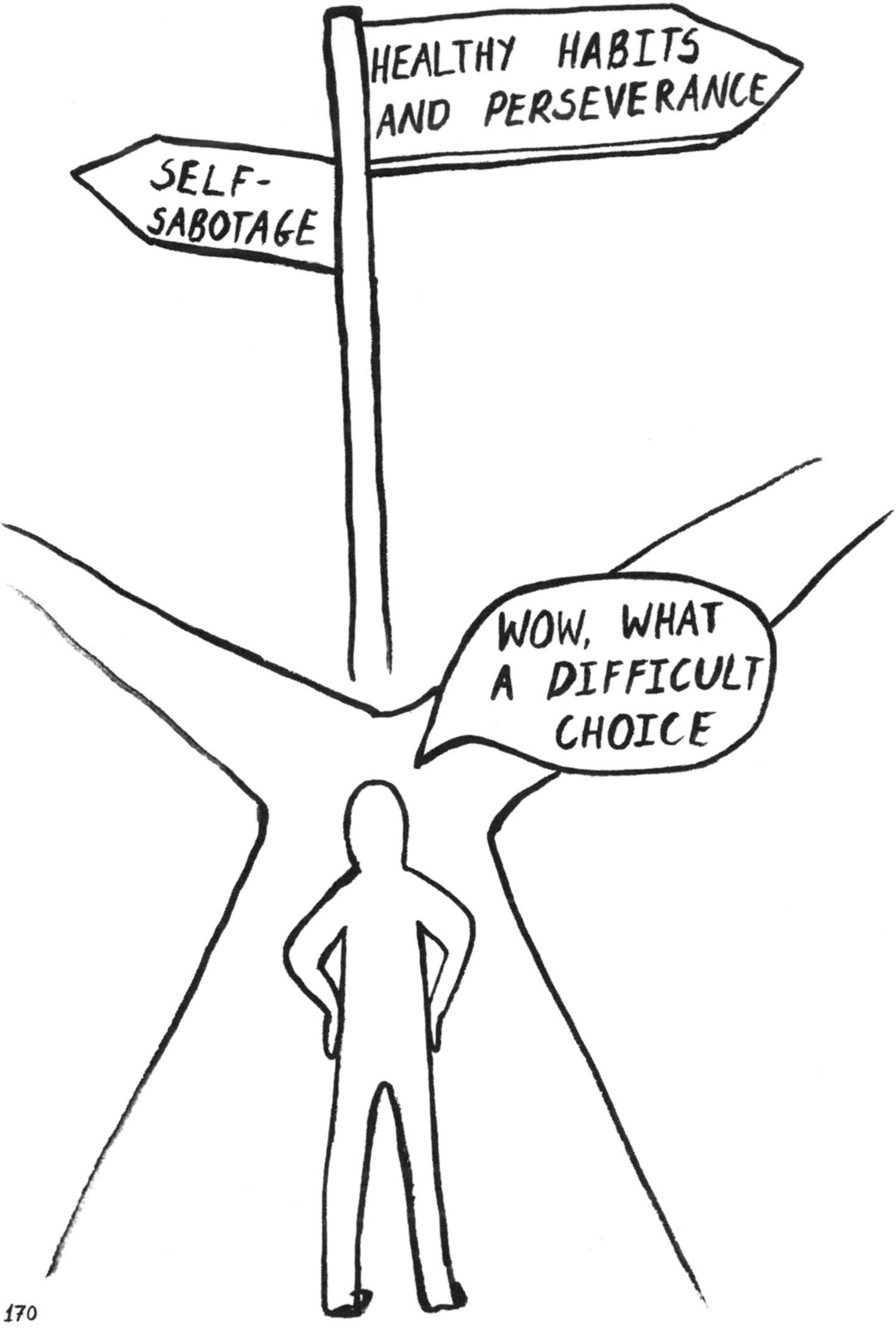
HEALTHY HABITS AND PERSEVERANCE
SELF-SABOTAGE
WOW, WHAT A DIFFICULT CHOICE

WRITE WHAT YOUR DESTINY IS
IN THE CRYSTAL BALL AND IT WILL
COME TRUE *

* 100% GUARANTEED, 0% OF THE TIME

HOW ARE YOU TODAY?

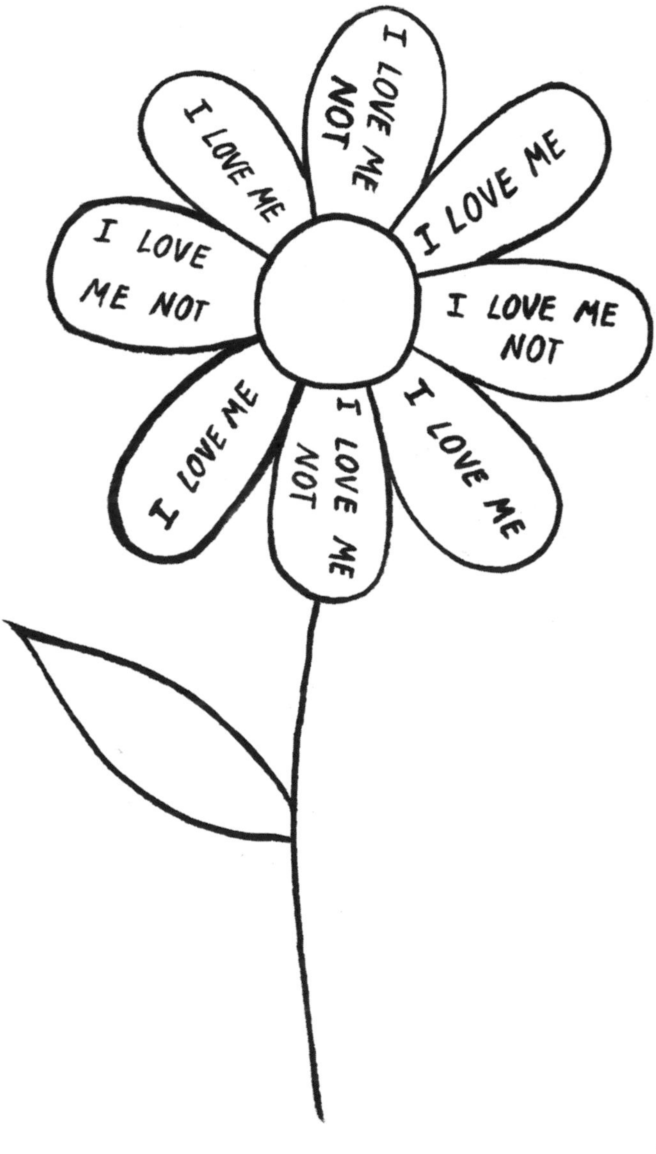
I LOVE ME NOT
I LOVE ME
I LOVE ME NOT
I LOVE ME
I LOVE ME NOT
I LOVE ME
I LOVE ME NOT
I LOVE ME

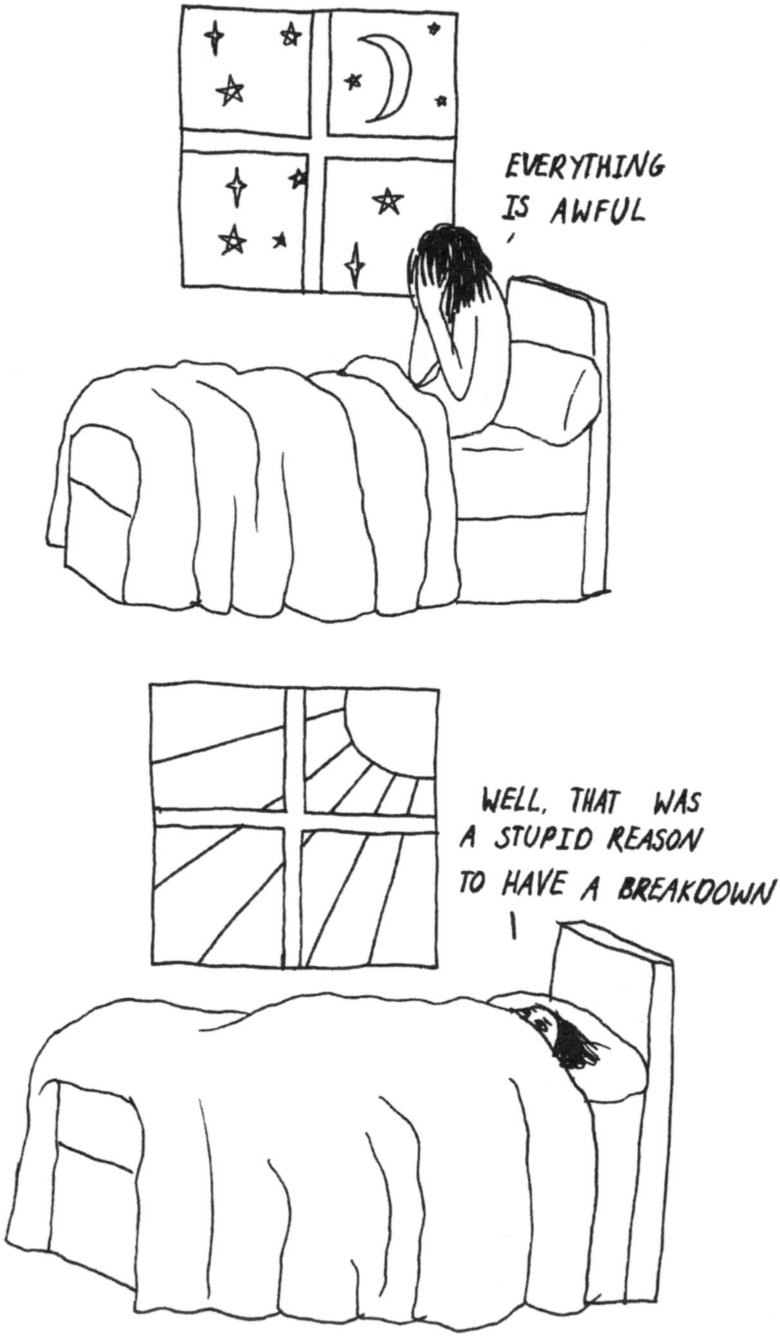
EVERYTHING IS AWFUL
WELL, THAT WAS A STUPID REASON TO HAVE A BREAKDOWN

UNIVERSALLY RELATABLE CONTENT

OPENING AND CLOSING YOUR EYES REPEATEDLY IN ORDER TO KEEP THEM SUFFICIENTLY MOIST

OCCASIONALLY BEING ALL TOO AWARE OF THE LOOMING INEVITABILITY OF DEATH

BEING OVERWHELMED BY THE CRUSHING TOIL OF WORK UNDER CAPITALISM

SOMETIMES THE SHOWER IS TOO HOT

ARE YOU SICK OF SELF-CARE?

WHY NOT TRY...

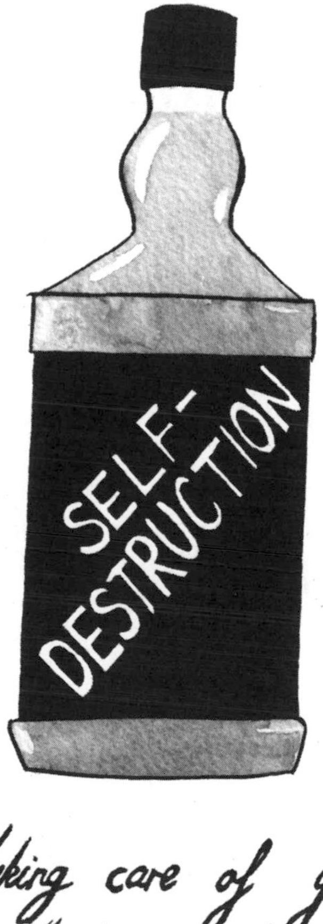
SELF-
DESTRUCTION

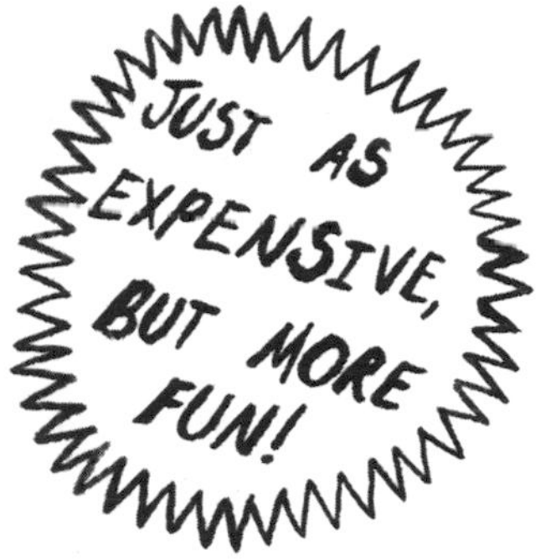
JUST AS
EXPENSIVE,
BUT MORE
FUN!

Because taking care of you should be someone else's problem, for once...

THINGS THAT I, A
FULLY GROWN ADULT,
SHOULD NOT FIND
EMBARRASSING, BUT
NEVERTHELESS DO

1. CROSSING THE ROAD.

2. IT IS EVEN MORE MORTIFYING IF YOU HAVE TO DO THE LITTLE JOG AT THE END BECAUSE YOU'RE RUNNING OUT OF TIME.

3. WHEN YOU'RE IN A RELATIONSHIP AND HAVE TO REFER TO THEM AS "MY PARTNER/BOYFRIEND/GIRLFRIEND/HUSBAND/WIFE/SIGNIFICANT OTHER." I SHOULD JUST BE ABLE TO SAY THEIR NAME AND EVERYONE CAN JUST FIGURE IT OUT FROM CONTEXT.

4. TELLING THE WAITER EVERYTHING IS FINE WHEN THEY CHECK UP ON YOU.

5. WALKING DOWN THE STREET IN A GROUP THAT'S MADE UP OF MORE THAN TWO PEOPLE.

6. ASKING SOMEONE, "IS THIS THE LINE?"

7. THEN QUIETLY STANDING IN THE LINE AND AVOIDING EYE CONTACT.

8. TAKING PICTURES. NOT EVEN SELFIES OR PICTURES OF PEOPLE, JUST PICTURES OF ANY KIND.

9. APPLYING FOR A JOB. WRITING A COVER LETTER IS PARTICULARLY HUMILIATING.

10. ASKING A SALES ASSISTANT FOR HELP, EVEN THOUGH THEY ARE THERE TO HELP.

DOT-TO-DOT FOR ADULTS

START

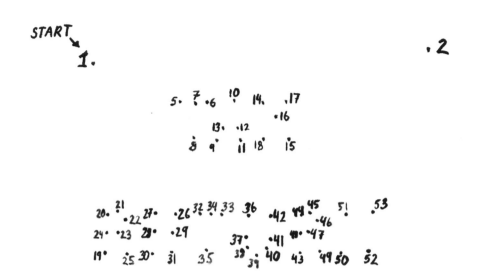

"FRIENDLY" REMINDERS

YOUR CLOTHES ARE
EXTREMELY FLAMMABLE

YOUR ANCESTORS LIVED
THROUGH EVERY POINT
IN HUMAN HISTORY

FOR AS LONG AS YOU
HAVE BEEN ALIVE, YOUR
SKELETON HAS BEEN
WARM AND WET

YOUR TEETH ARE AN
EXPOSED PART OF YOUR
SKELETON

YOU SHOULD DRINK
SOME WATER ♡

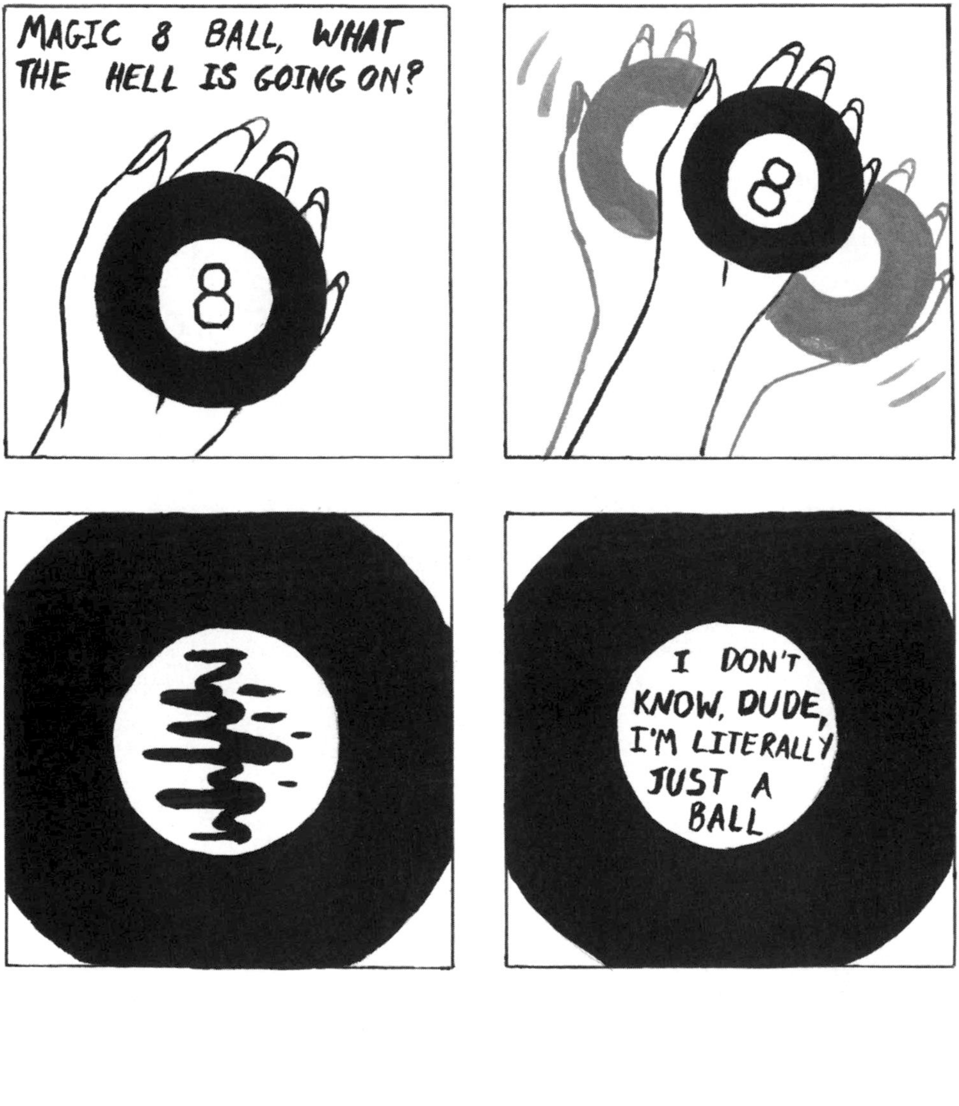
MAGIC 8 BALL, WHAT THE HELL IS GOING ON?
8
8
I DON'T KNOW, DUDE, I'M LITERALLY JUST A BALL

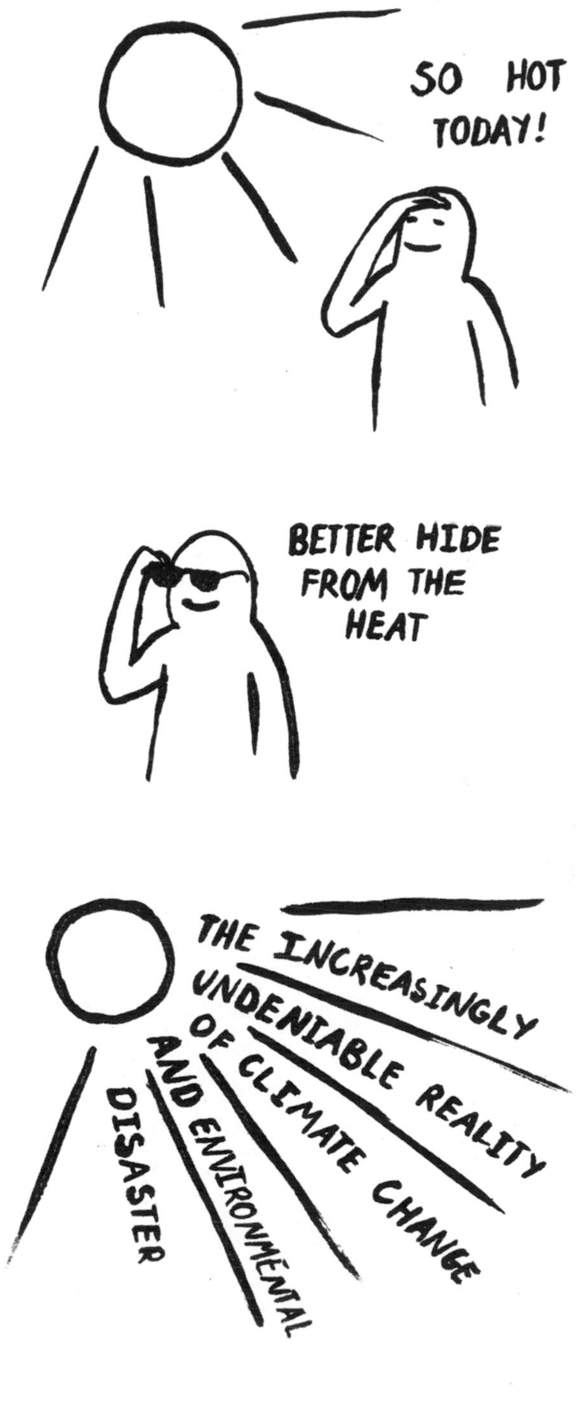
SO HOT TODAY!
BETTER HIDE FROM THE HEAT
THE INCREASINGLY
UNDENIABLE REALITY
OF CLIMATE CHANGE
AND ENVIRONMENTAL
DISASTER

HEALTHIER THINGS TO BASE YOUR ENTIRE SELF-WORTH ON

DO YOU PUT TOO MUCH FOCUS ON THE
AMOUNT OF FOLLOWERS YOU HAVE?

DETOX DIGITALLY AND FOCUS ON THE AMOUNT
OF REAL-LIFE FOLLOWERS YOU HAVE!
START A RELIGIOUS CULT.

DO YOU PLACE YOUR SELF-WORTH ON THE AMOUNT YOU EARN?

REBEL AGAINST THIS CAPITALIST WAY OF THINKING, AND PLACE YOUR WORTH ON MONEY YOU _DIDN'T_ EARN, BY ROBBING A BANK!

DO YOU CARE TOO MUCH ABOUT YOUR APPEARANCE AND HOW OTHERS PERCEIVE YOU?

THIS IS A FRUITLESS AIM, AS BEAUTY STANDARDS ARE EVER SHIFTING AND YOUR FALLIBLE BODY IS ALWAYS DETERIORATING, AND YOU NEED TO FOCUS YOURSELF INTERNALLY.

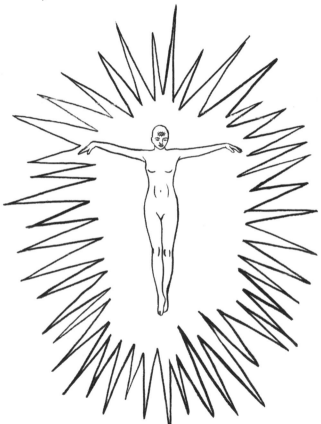

TRY TRANSCENDING THE MORTAL REALM ENTIRELY AND BECOME AN AGELESS, CELESTIAL BEING, ENCAPSULATING ALL THAT IS BEAUTIFUL AND DIVINE.

HOW TO DEAL WITH NEGATIVE EMOTIONS:

YOU WILL NEED:

1

YOUR REPRESSED EMOTIONS
(BOTTLED)*

* IF YOU **CANNOT** MANIFEST
THEM PHYSICALLY, METAPHORICAL
IS FINE

2.

HELLFIRE

<u>METHOD</u>:

STEP ONE: THROW

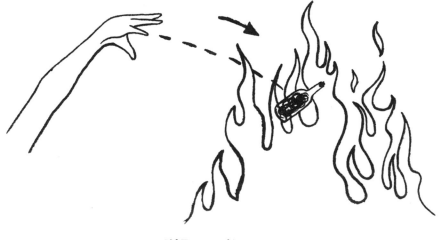

THE END

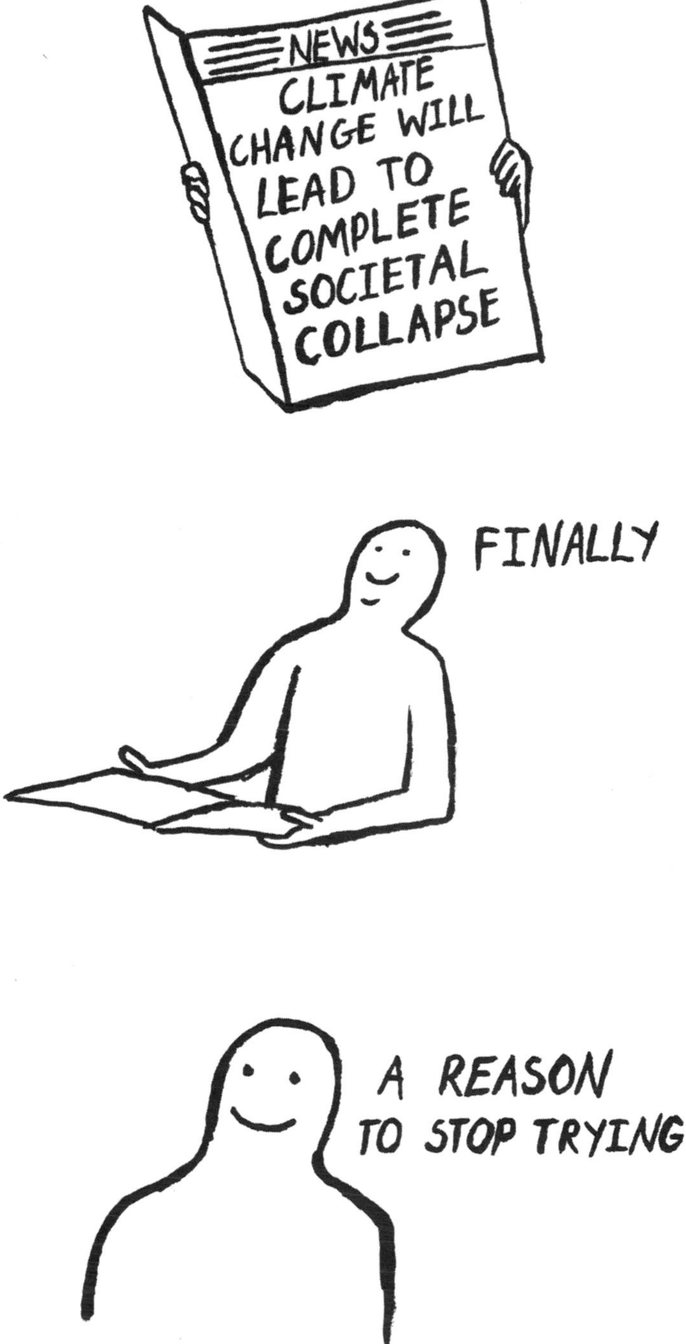
NEWS
CLIMATE CHANGE WILL LEAD TO COMPLETE SOCIETAL COLLAPSE
FINALLY
A REASON TO STOP TRYING

YOU CAN ONLY HAVE TWO

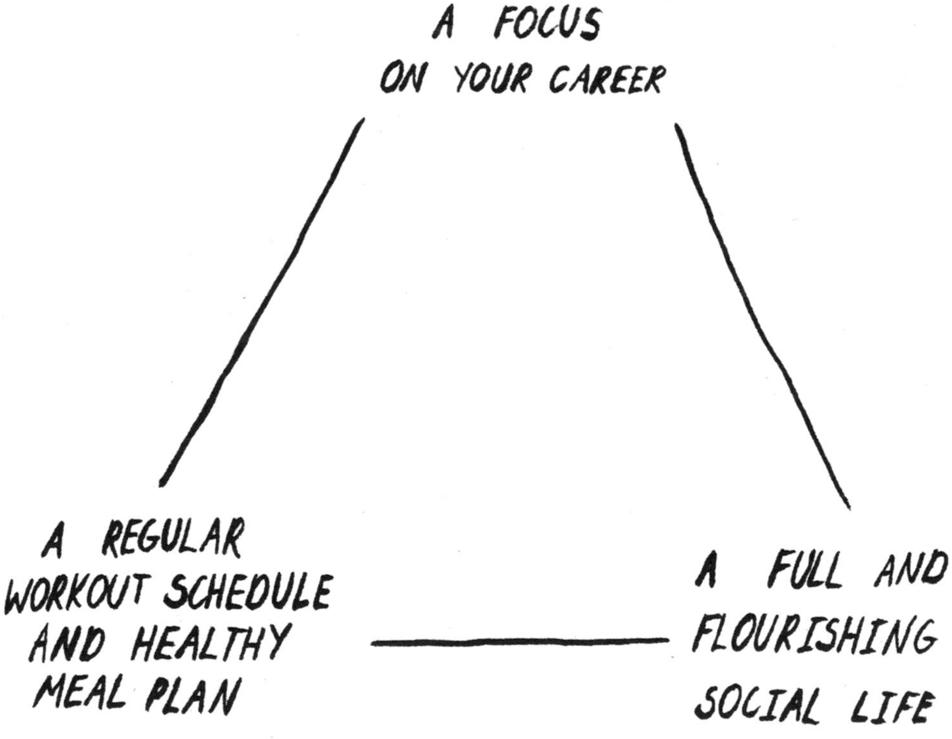
A FOCUS ON YOUR CAREER
A REGULAR WORKOUT SCHEDULE AND HEALTHY MEAL PLAN
A FULL AND FLOURISHING SOCIAL LIFE

CHOOSE YOUR LIFE PATH!

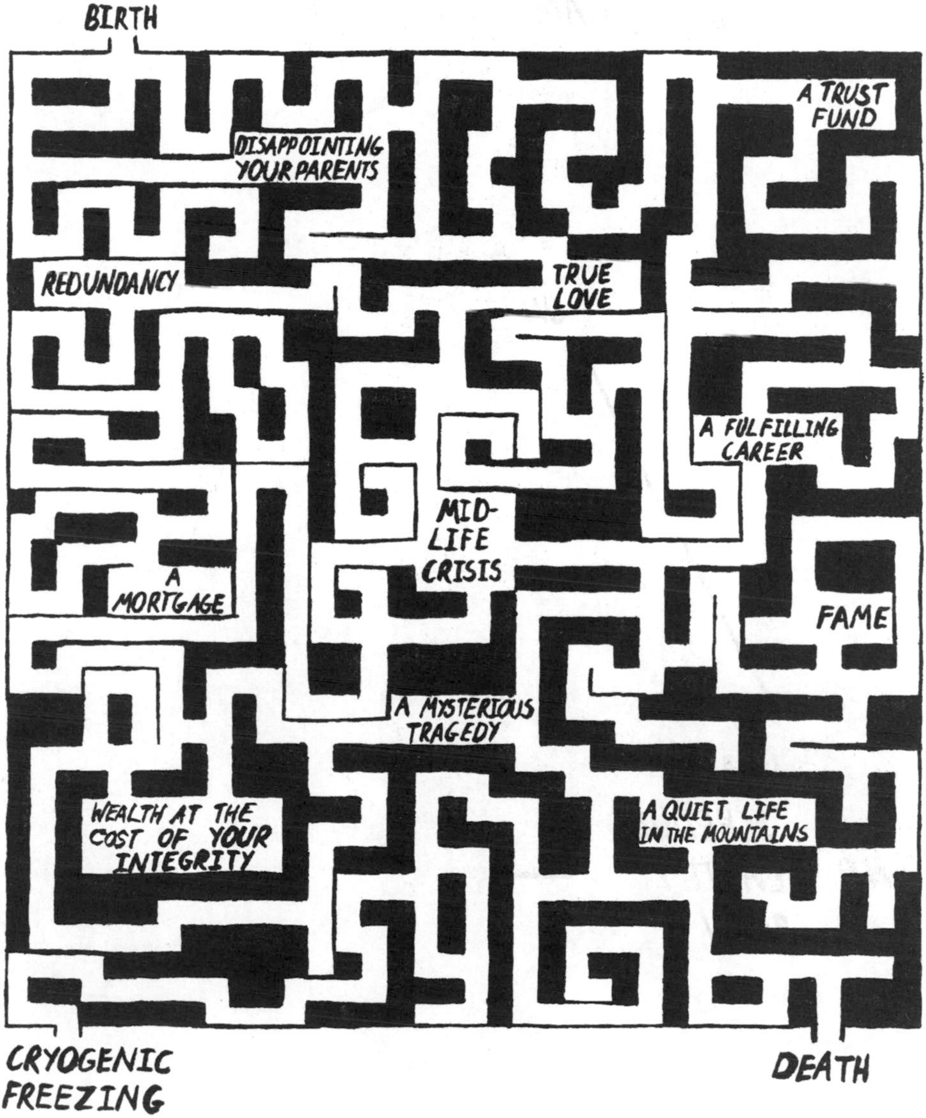
BIRTH
DISAPPOINTING YOUR PARENTS
A TRUST FUND
REDUNDANCY
TRUE LOVE
A FULFILLING CAREER
MID-LIFE CRISIS
A MORTGAGE
FAME
A MYSTERIOUS TRAGEDY
WEALTH AT THE COST OF YOUR INTEGRITY
A QUIET LIFE IN THE MOUNTAINS
CRYOGENIC FREEZING
DEATH

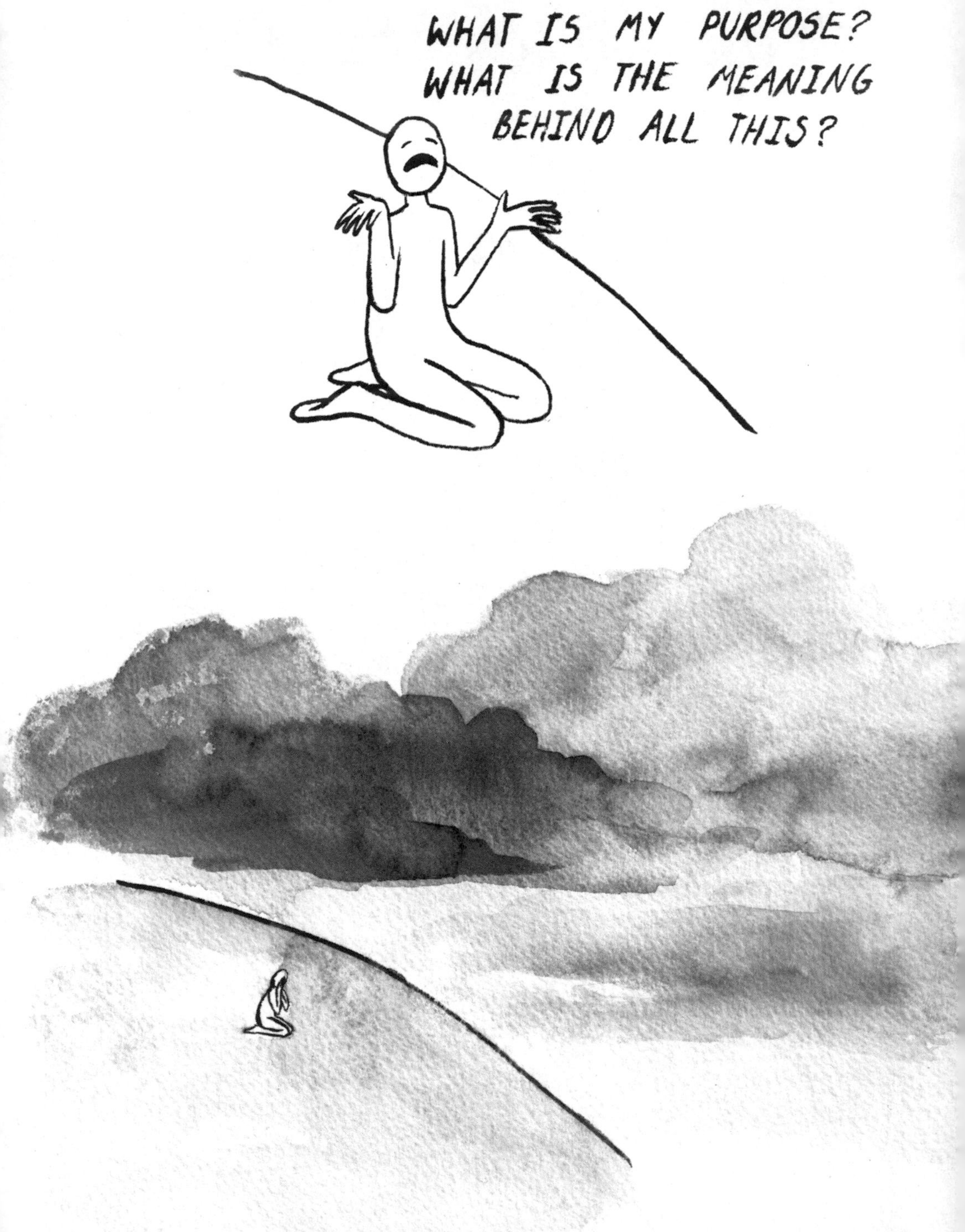
WHAT IS MY PURPOSE?
WHAT IS THE MEANING
BEHIND ALL THIS?

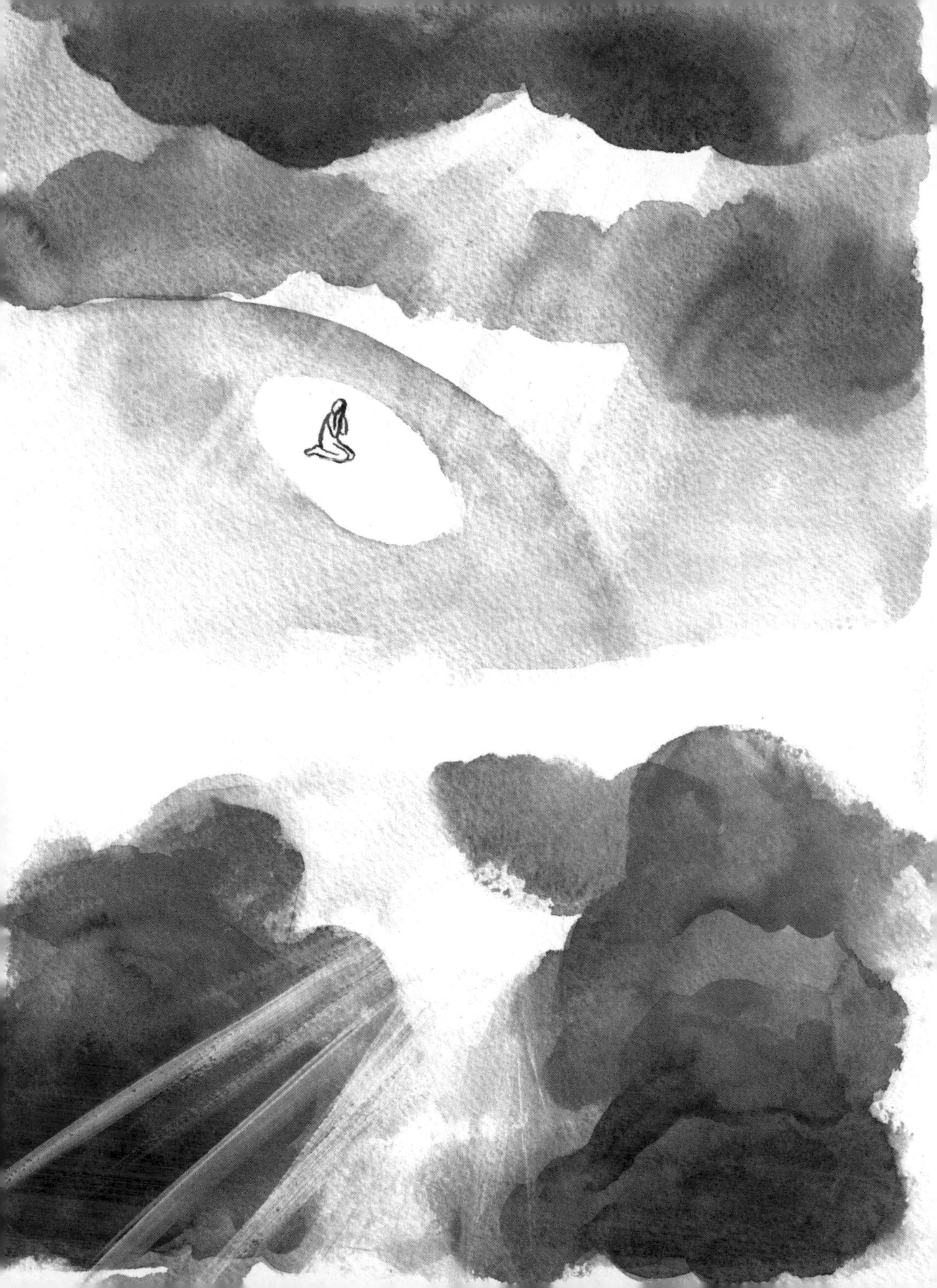

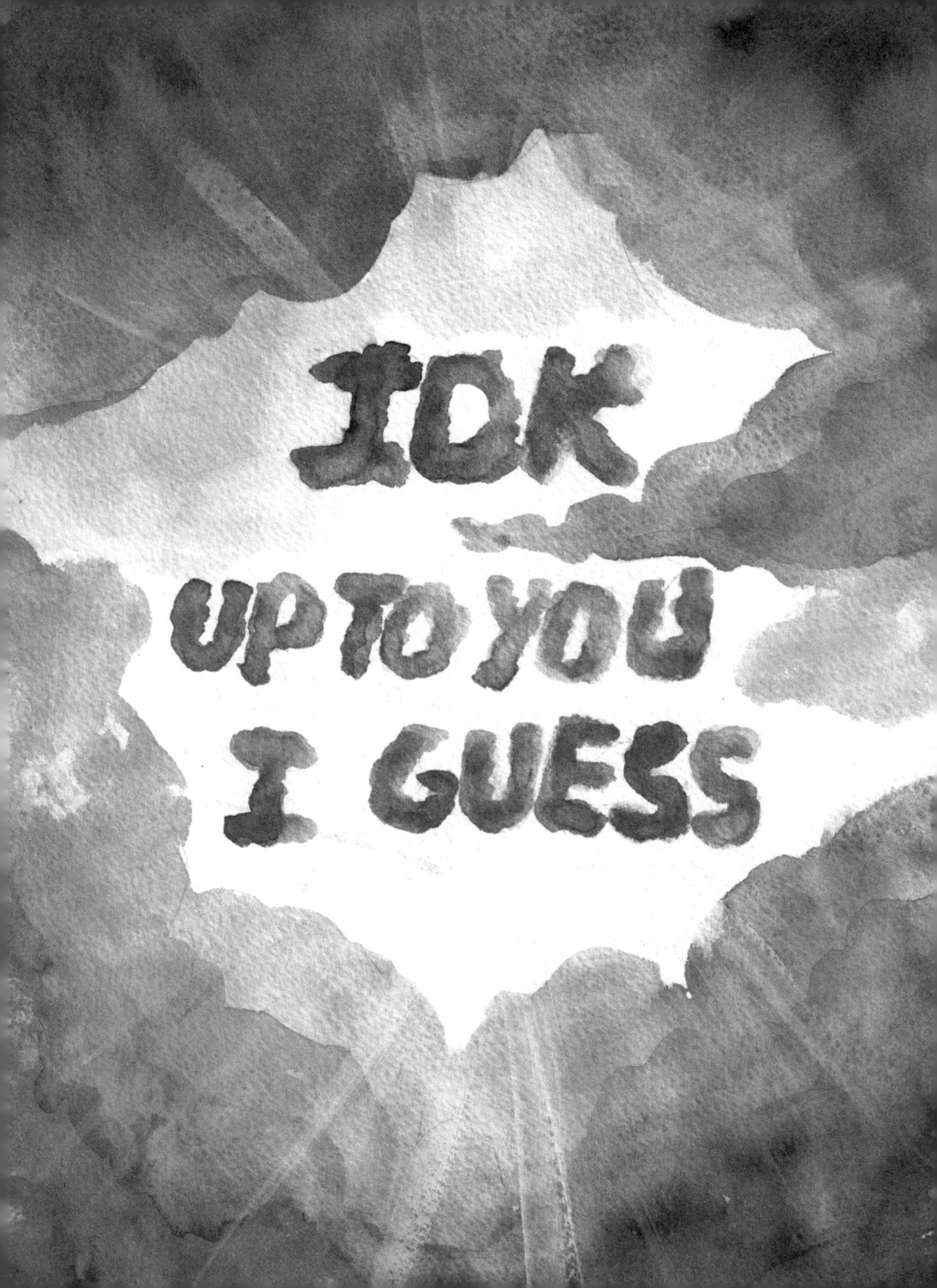
IDK
UP TO YOU
I GUESS

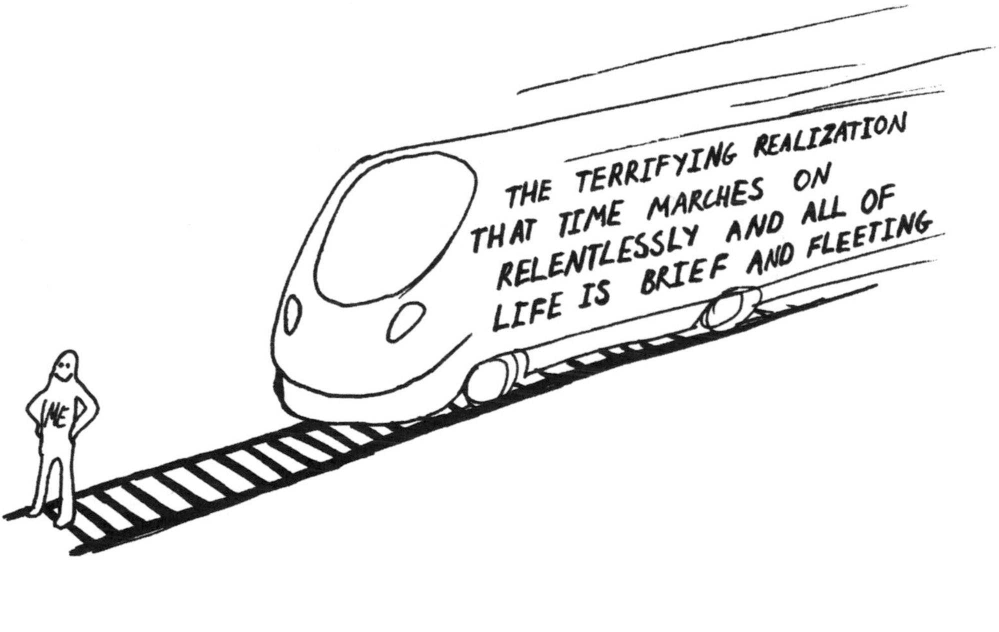
THE TERRIFYING REALIZATION THAT TIME MARCHES ON RELENTLESSLY AND ALL OF LIFE IS BRIEF AND FLEETING
ME

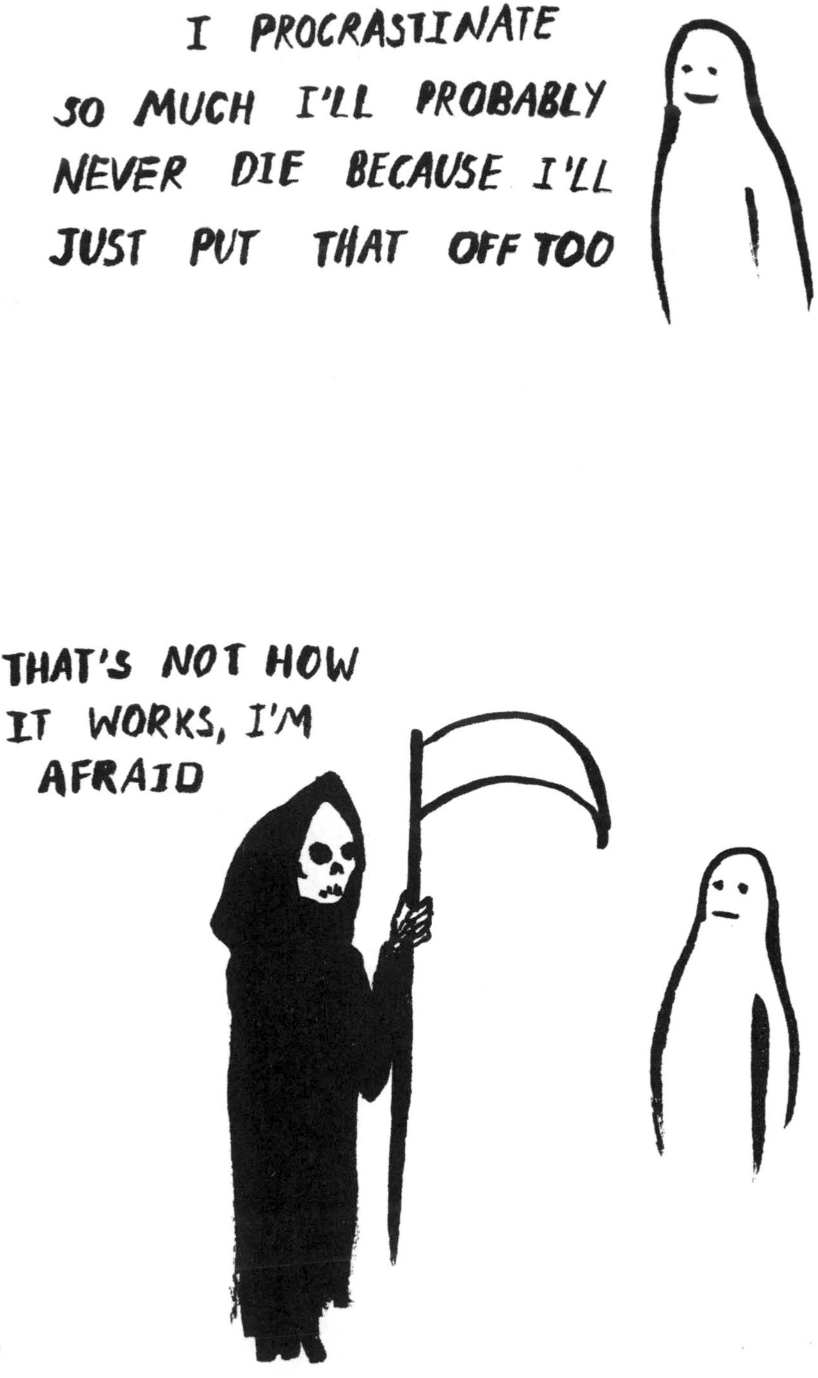
I PROCRASTINATE SO MUCH I'LL PROBABLY NEVER DIE BECAUSE I'LL JUST PUT THAT OFF TOO
THAT'S NOT HOW IT WORKS, I'M AFRAID

ARE YOU DEALING WITH NEGATIVE EMOTIONS?

HERE'S SOME HELLFIRE TO BURN THEM IN, SO YOU NEVER HAVE TO FEEL AGAIN:

WRITE YOUR FEELINGS HERE

ROMANTICIZE THE MUNDANITY OF EVERYDAY LIFE

THE MUNDANITY IN QUESTION:

SITTING **ON** THE TOILET SO LONG THAT YOUR LEGS GO NUMB BECAUSE YOU GOT SUCKED INTO *A SCROLLING VORTEX*

WALKING INTO A ROOM AND IMMEDIATELY FORGETTING WHY YOU ARE THERE

PUTTING YOUR PLASTIC BAGS INTO ANOTHER PLASTIC BAG

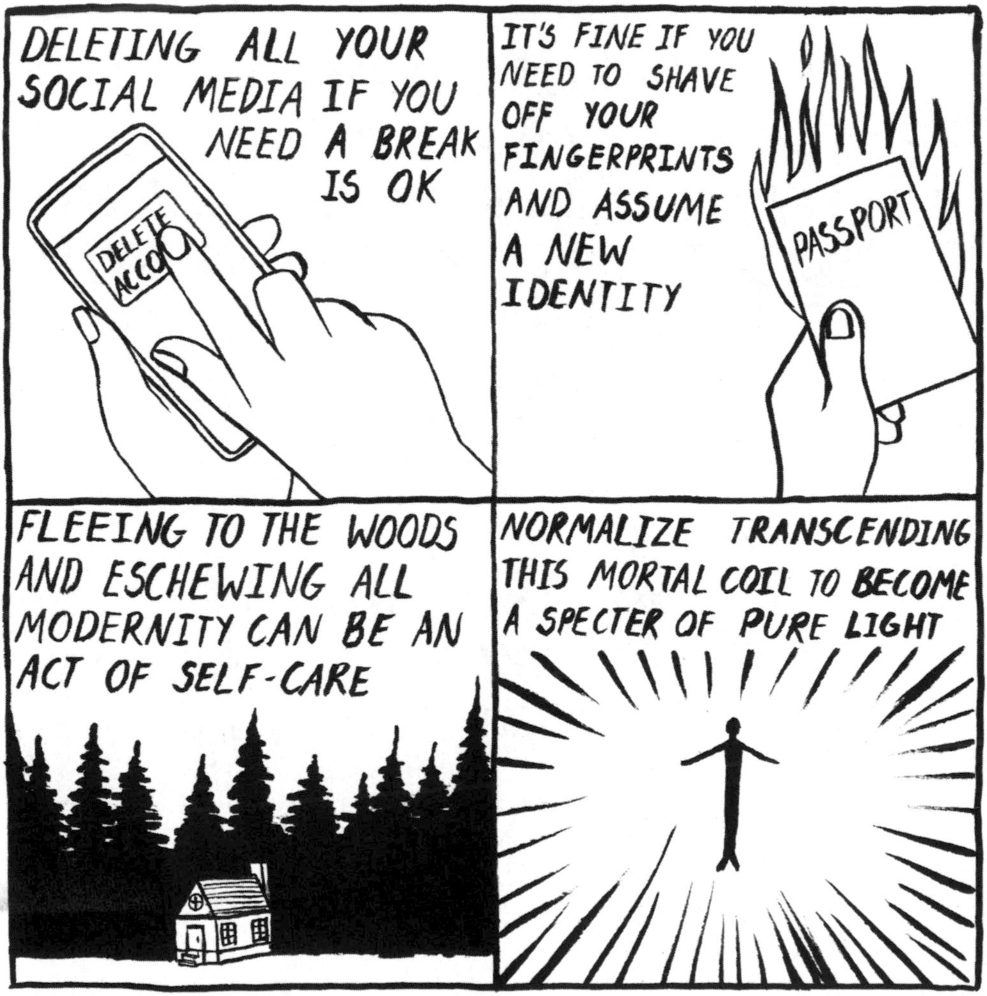
DELETING ALL YOUR SOCIAL MEDIA IF YOU NEED A BREAK IS OK
DELETE ACCO
IT'S FINE IF YOU NEED TO SHAVE OFF YOUR FINGERPRINTS AND ASSUME A NEW IDENTITY
PASSPORT
FLEEING TO THE WOODS AND ESCHEWING ALL MODERNITY CAN BE AN ACT OF SELF-CARE
NORMALIZE TRANSCENDING THIS MORTAL COIL TO BECOME A SPECTER OF PURE LIGHT

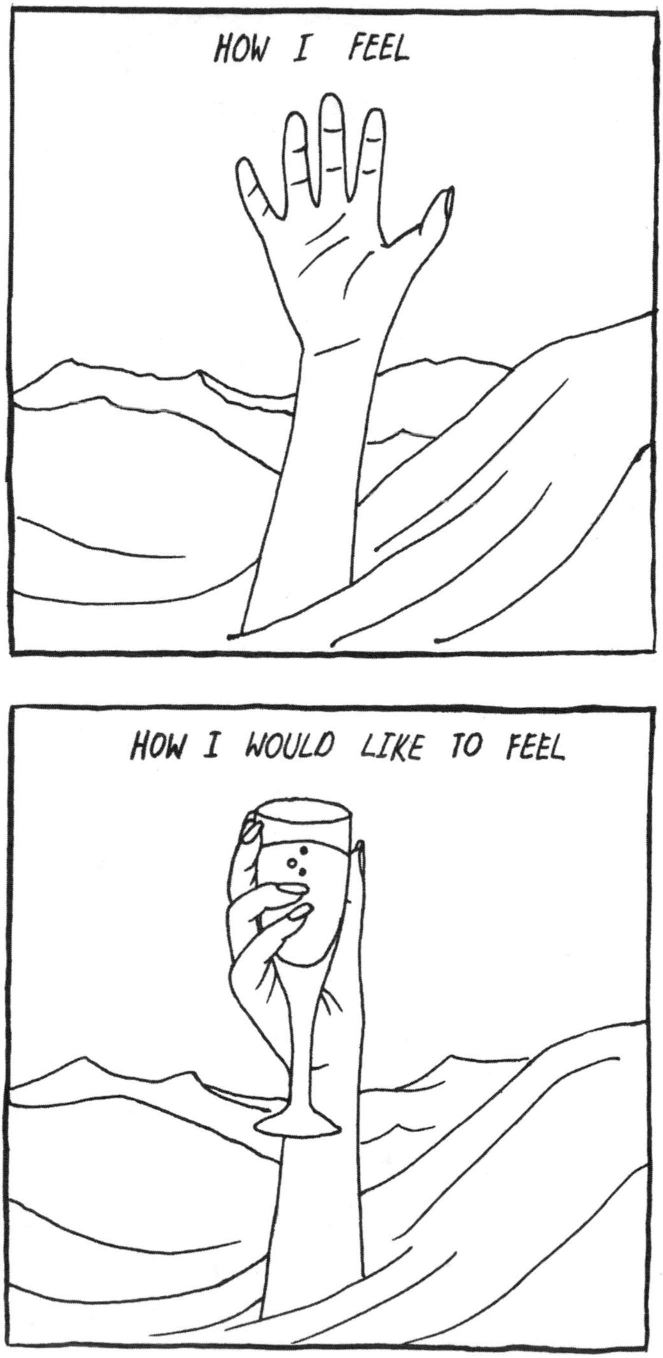
HOW I FEEL
HOW I WOULD LIKE TO FEEL

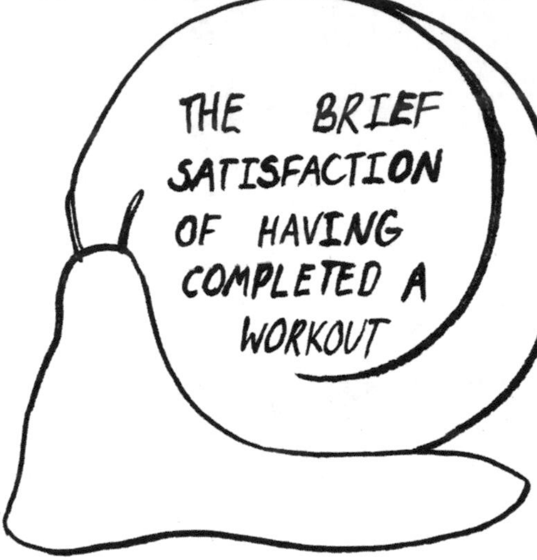
THE BRIEF SATISFACTION OF HAVING COMPLETED A WORKOUT

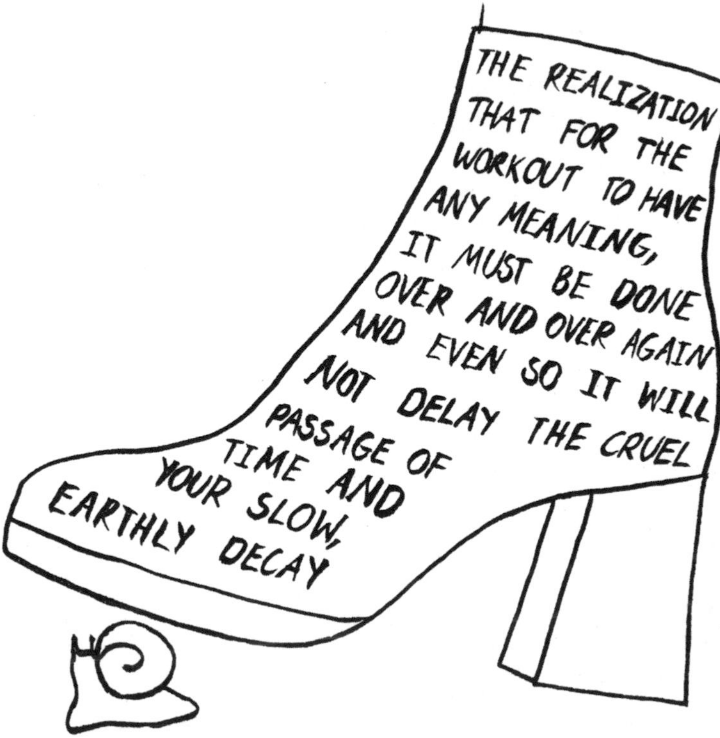
THE REALIZATION THAT FOR THE WORKOUT TO HAVE ANY MEANING, IT MUST BE DONE OVER AND OVER AGAIN AND EVEN SO IT WILL NOT DELAY THE CRUEL PASSAGE OF TIME AND YOUR SLOW, EARTHLY DECAY

A PAINFUL LIST OF LIES THAT HAS TAKEN ME ALMOST THREE DECADES TO REALIZE ARE LIES

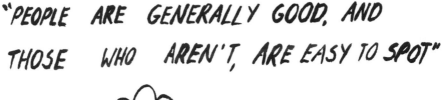

"PEOPLE ARE GENERALLY GOOD, AND THOSE WHO AREN'T, ARE EASY TO SPOT"

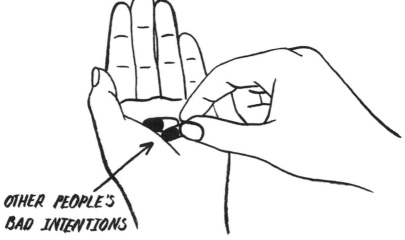

OTHER PEOPLE'S
BAD INTENTIONS

"PEOPLE NEVER INTENTIONALLY
WANT TO HURT YOU AND
IF THEY DID, YOU'D
ALWAYS BE ABLE TO TELL"

"IF YOU BEHAVE LIKE THE WORLD IS ALREADY EQUAL, YOU WILL BE TREATED AS AN EQUAL"

SURE, I DON'T MIND SPLITTING THE BILL FOR THIS DATE YOU INVITED ME ON, EVEN THOUGH I'M PAID MUCH LESS FOR THE SAME JOB AND HAVE ALREADY SPENT MORE MONEY TO REACH A A SOCIALLY ACCEPTABLE LEVEL OF FEMININE BEAUTY, WITHOUT WHICH YOU WOULD NOT BE INTERESTED IN ME DUE TO YOUR OWN SOCIETAL CONDITIONING. ANYWAY, I'M SURE LATER DOWN THE LINE YOU'LL DEFINITELY SPLIT ALL DOMESTIC AND CHILDCARE LABOR EVENLY WITH ME, INSTEAD OF ONLY DOING TASKS WHEN YOU'RE ASKED, BUT LEAVING THE BURDEN OF PLANNING, DELEGATING, AND ORGANIZING ENTIRELY TO ME... RIGHT?

"HARD WORK ALWAYS PAYS OFF"

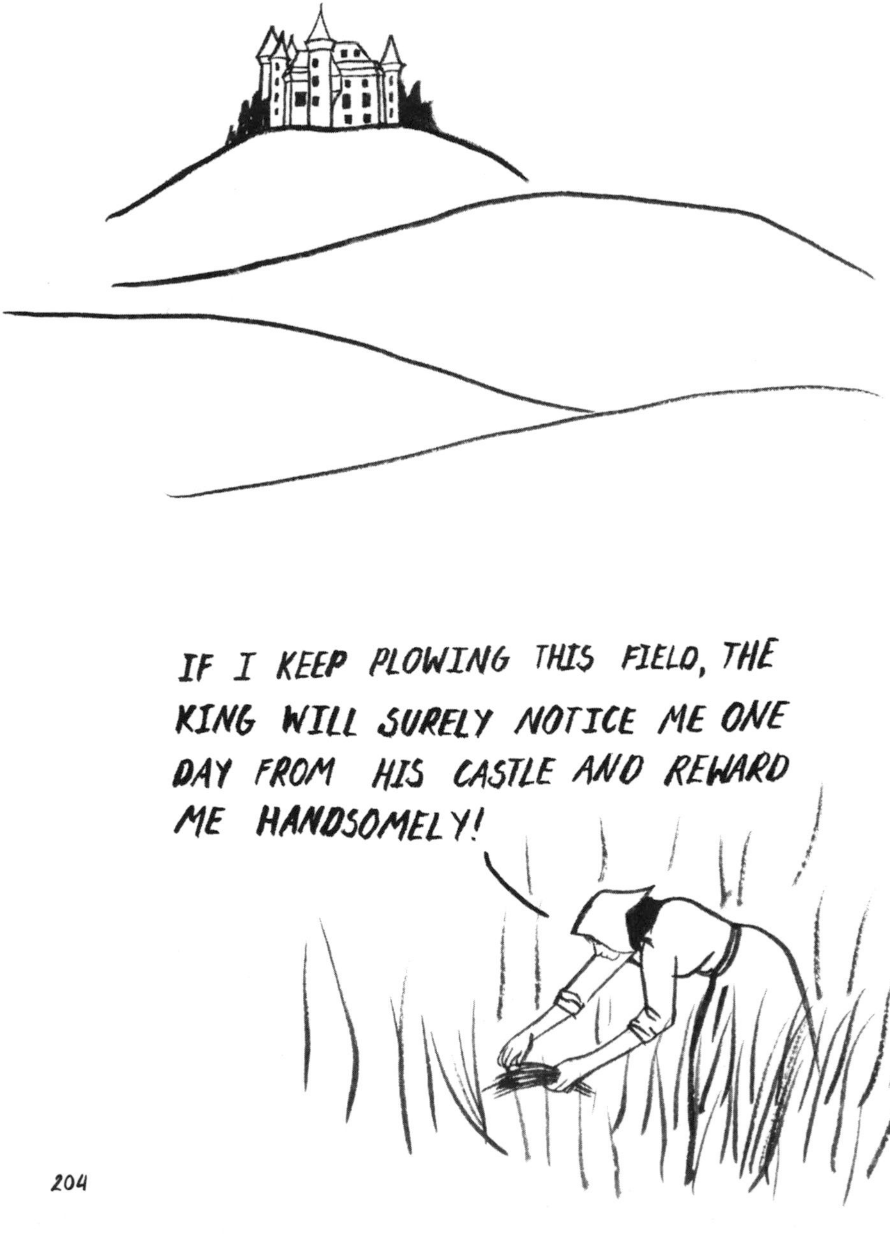
IF I KEEP PLOWING THIS FIELD, THE KING WILL SURELY NOTICE ME ONE DAY FROM HIS CASTLE AND REWARD ME HANDSOMELY!

"THE KEY TO SOLVING ALL ISSUES IS COMMUNICATION"

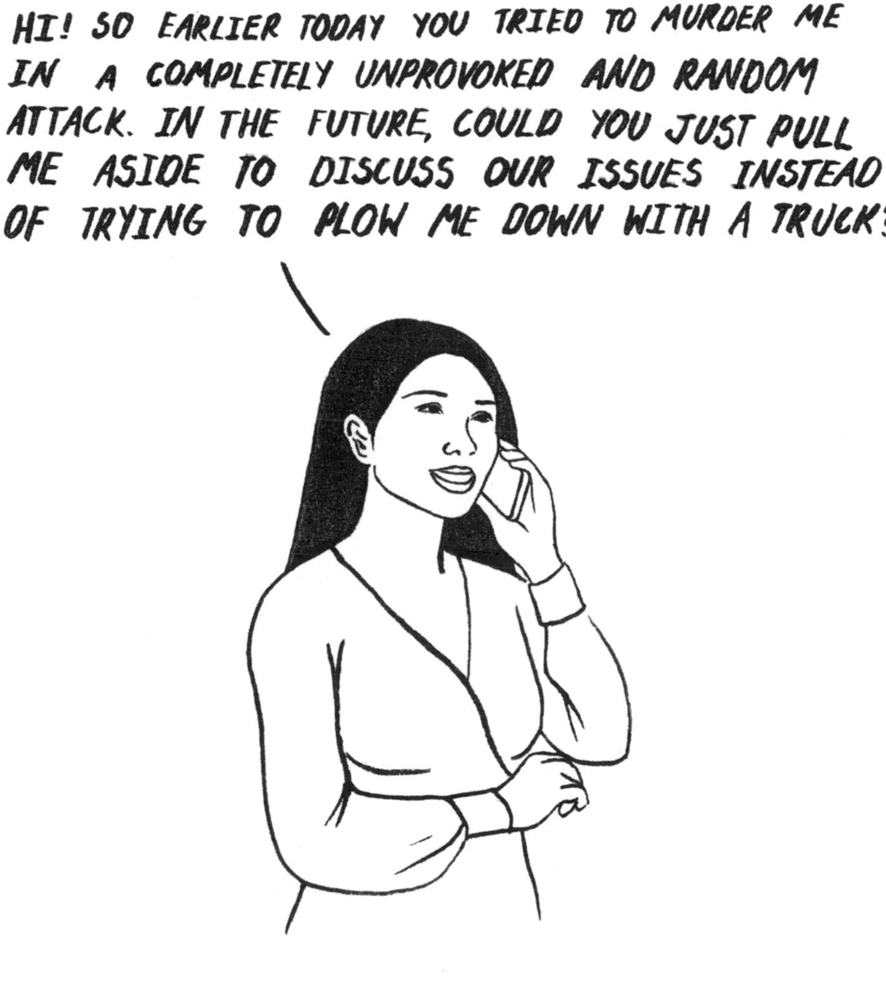
HI! SO EARLIER TODAY YOU TRIED TO MURDER ME IN A COMPLETELY UNPROVOKED AND RANDOM ATTACK. IN THE FUTURE, COULD YOU JUST PULL ME ASIDE TO DISCUSS OUR ISSUES INSTEAD OF TRYING TO PLOW ME DOWN WITH A TRUCK?

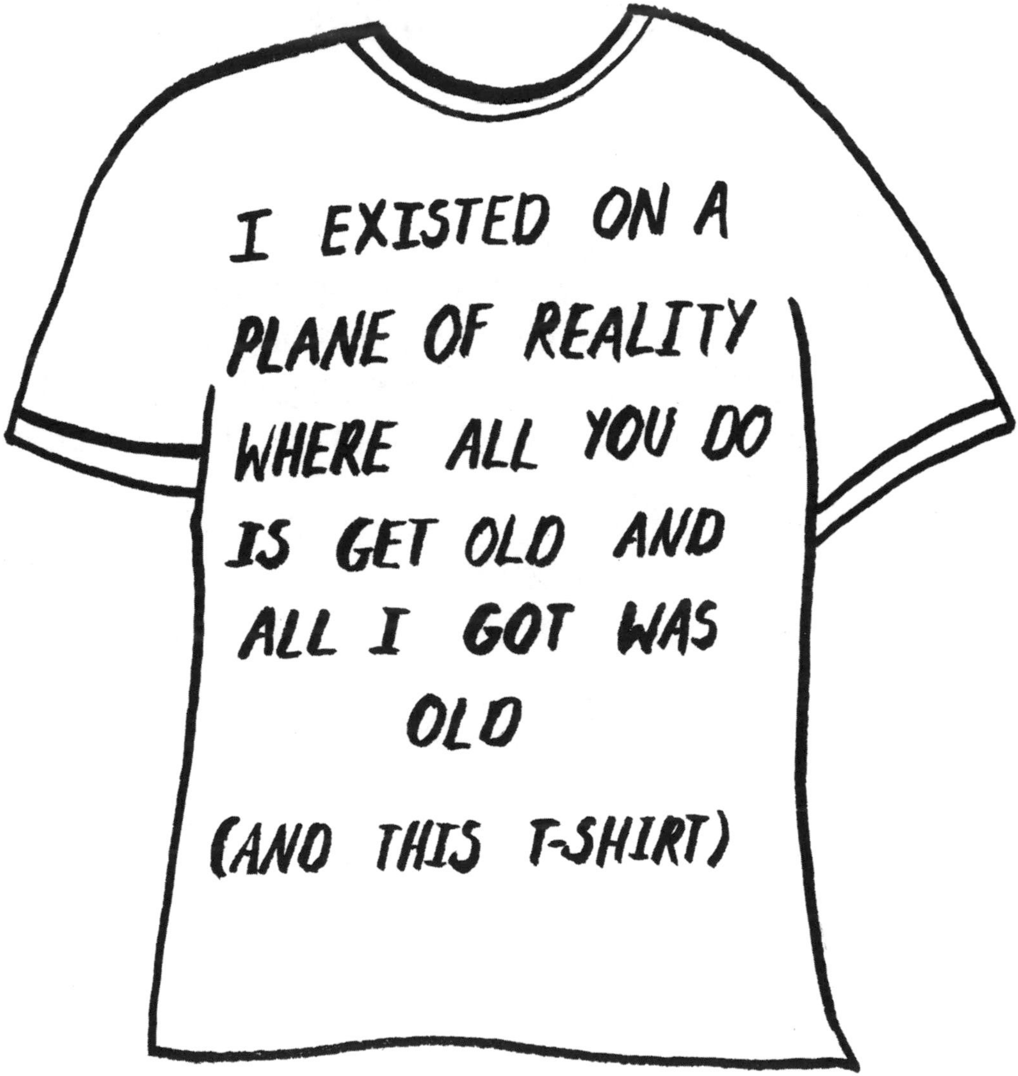
I EXISTED ON A
PLANE OF REALITY
WHERE ALL YOU DO
IS GET OLD AND
ALL I GOT WAS
OLD
(AND THIS T-SHIRT)

LISTS TO MAKE YOU FEEL BETTER, OR WORSE, OR NEUTRAL

LIST THREE THINGS YOU'RE GRATEFUL FOR

1 _____
2 _____
3 _____

NOW LIST THREE THINGS YOU DO NOT NEED IN YOUR LIFE

1 _____
2 _____
3 _____

OK, NOW LIST THREE BUGS YOU THINK ARE COOL

1 _____
2 _____
3 _____

NOW LIST THREE THINGS ABOUT ME THAT YOU THINK ARE PRETTY

1 _____
2 _____
3 _____

LIST YOUR TOP THREE PREFERRED WAYS FOR THE WORLD TO END

1 _____
2 _____
3 _____

FINALLY, LIST YOUR TOP THREE WIKIPEDIA LISTS

1 _____
2 _____
3 _____

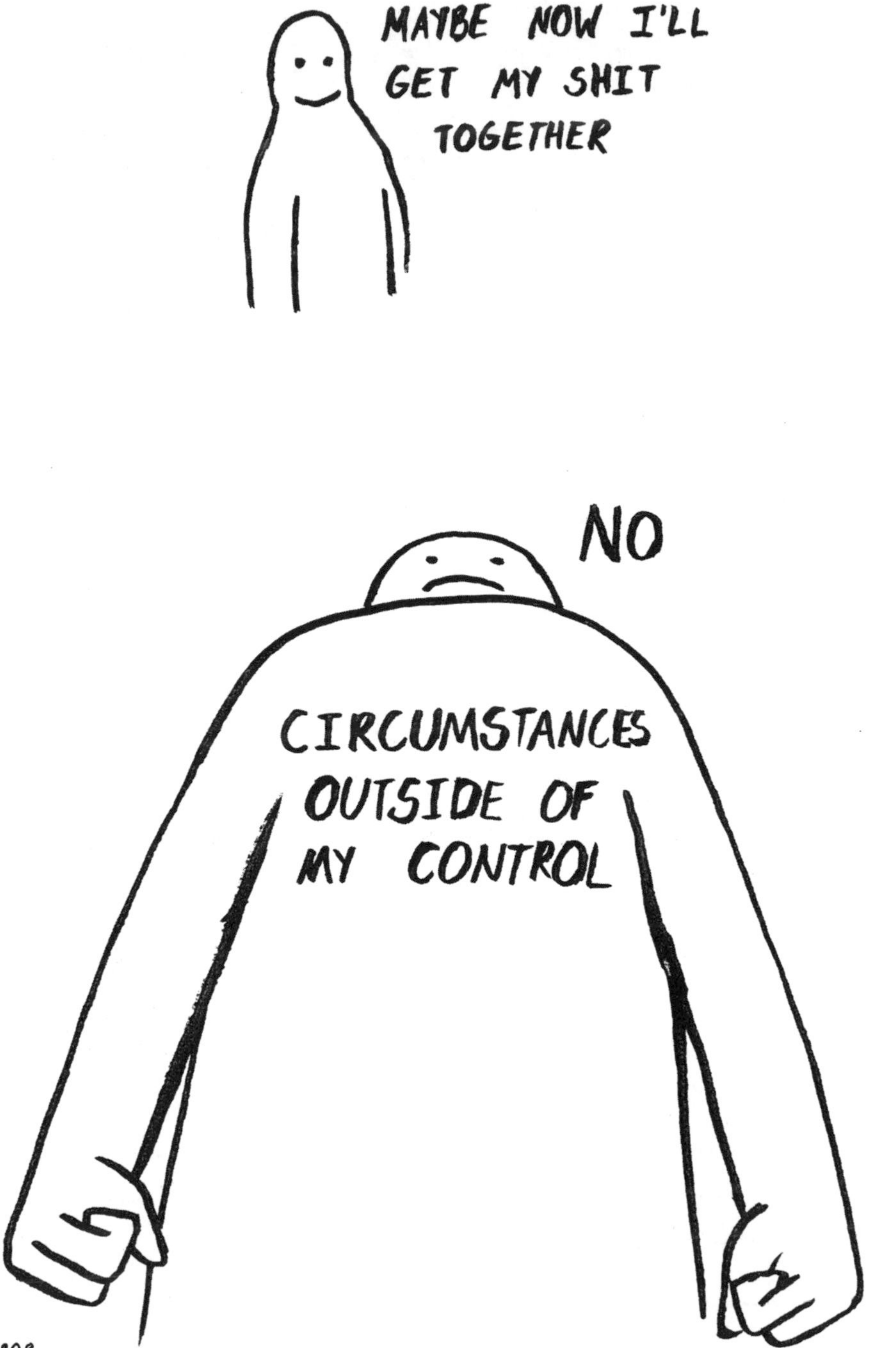
MAYBE NOW I'LL GET MY SHIT TOGETHER
NO
CIRCUMSTANCES OUTSIDE OF MY CONTROL

PEOPLE WHO SPENT THEIR 20s TRAVELING AND LIVING FOR THE MOMENT OFTEN REACH A POINT OF WISHING THEY'D BEEN MORE **CAREFUL** AND FRUGAL, THINKING THEY'D BE HAPPIER **IF** THEY'D BEEN PRUDENT.

HOW DID I CONVINCE MYSELF THAT LIVING IN A VAN WAS A GOOD IDEA?

CONVERSELY, THOSE WHO SPENT THEIR 20s WORKING HARD AND DOING WHAT WAS EXPECTED OF THEM ARE FILLED WITH REGRET THAT THEY DIDN'T TAKE FULL ADVANTAGE OF THEIR YOUTH, DESPITE THEIR MORTGAGE AND WELL-PAYING JOB.

WHY DIDN'T I TRY HARD DRUGS WHEN I HAD THE CHANCE...

THERE IS NO WAY OF **KNOWING** IF YOU WOULD BE HAPPIER NOW IF YOU'D GONE BACKPACKING IN CAMBODIA INSTEAD OF TAKING THAT INTERNSHIP, OR IF YOU DIDN'T GET MARRIED SO YOUNG, OR IF YOU'D LIVED WITH YOUR PARENTS TO SAVE MONEY INSTEAD OF MOVING AWAY.

ALL YOU HAVE IS NOW, AND THE KNOWLEDGE THAT IF YOU SPEND THE PRESENT MOMENT LAMENTING PAST DECISIONS, YOU WILL ONLY BE ADDING TO YOUR LIST OF REGRETS.

WHY AM I INCAPABLE OF COMING UP WITH ANY NEW IDEAS
POP!
COULD IT BE BECAUSE MY BRAIN HAS BEEN CRUSHED INTO A TINY LITTLE BALL FROM THE STRESS OF EXISTENCE?

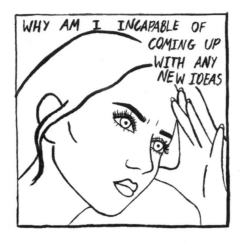

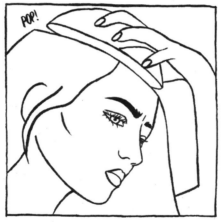

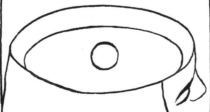

WHAT IS THE PURPOSE OF LIFE?

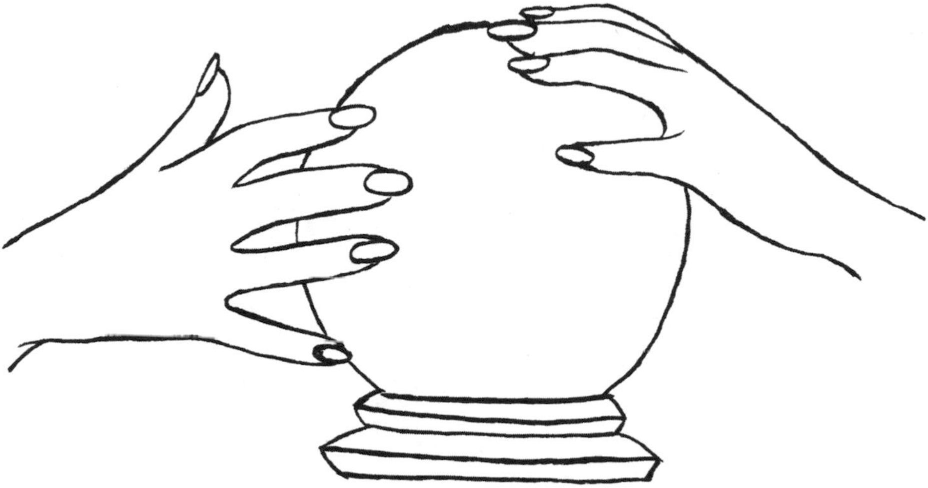

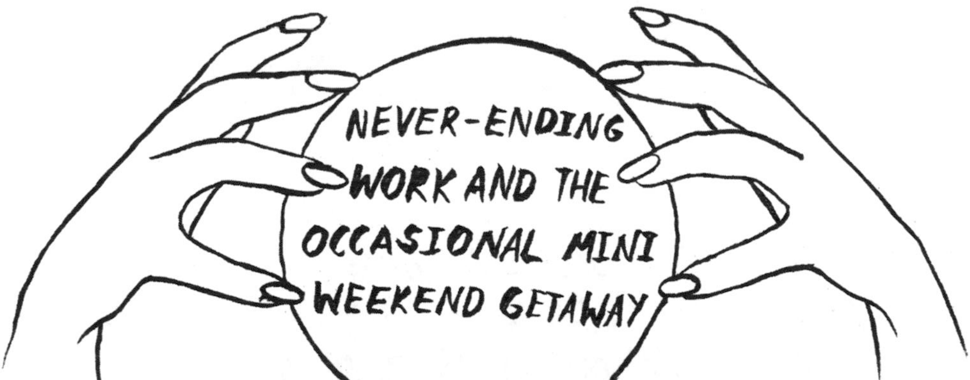
NEVER-ENDING
WORK AND THE
OCCASIONAL MINI
WEEKEND GETAWAY

I REGULARLY FEEL LIKE I AM RUNNING OUT OF TIME AND THAT I AM LIVING LIFE INCORRECTLY.

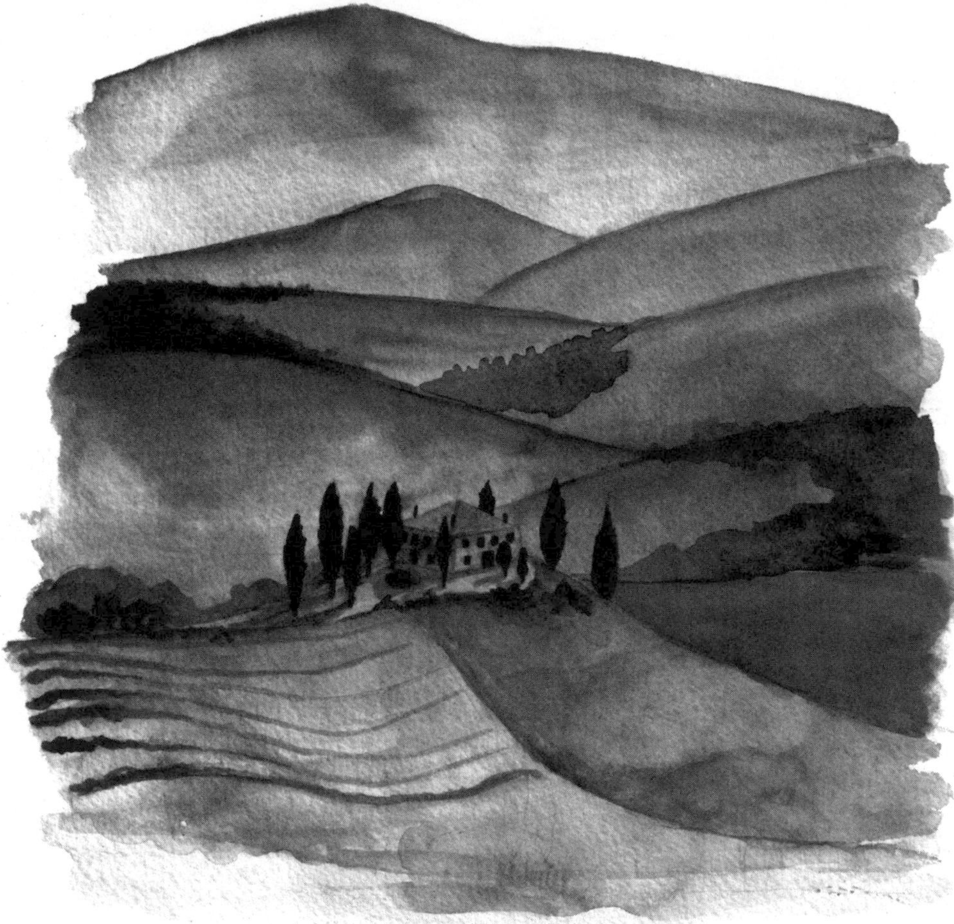

THAT THERE ARE PEOPLE OUT THERE IN FLOWING GOWNS, SIPPING CHAMPAGNE, AND DANCING WITH THEIR ITALIAN LOVERS IN THEIR MANSIONS OVERLOOKING THE TUSCAN HILLS.

THERE ARE PEOPLE LIVING ADVENTURES AND
CARPE DIEM-ING EVERY DAY, AND I'M SITTING
HERE, LIKE A FOOL, ON THE PHONE TO MY
BROADBAND PROVIDER FOR TWO HOURS, PRECIOUS
SECONDS OF MY LIFE SLIPPING AWAY UNNOTICED.

THEN I REALIZE THAT LIFE, GENERALLY, FOR ALL ANIMALS, IS MOSTLY JUST SLEEPING, EATING, SHITTING, AND WAITING.

LIFE WOULD BE BETTER IF I WERE RICH, FOR SURE, NO DOUBT, BUT I WOULD STILL HAVE NO SIGNAL IN THAT TUSCAN VILLA AND THE WAY THAT TANNED ITALIAN LOVER BREATHES WOULD START TO ANNOY ME.

MUNDANITY, EMBARRASSMENT, AND FRUSTRATION
ARE AN INEVITABLE PART OF LIFE.

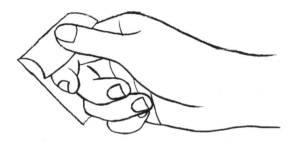

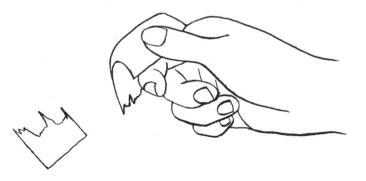

TAKE THE BEAUTIFUL, EPIC MOMENTS
YOU EXPERIENCE AND SAVOR THEM LIKE A
BEAUTIFULLY EDITED TRAILER FOR YOUR LIFE.

THEN, TAKE THE BORING, HUMILIATING, AND MUNDANE PARTS,

AND TURN THEM INTO A BOOK OF

RELATABLE COMICS SOLD TO A MAJOR PUBLISHER.

CONCLUSION

WE ARE ALL LIVING THE SAME LIVES
IF YOU CONSIDER ONLY THE MEDIOCRE PARTS

It's so frustrating that there's no one weird trick to lose weight, sort out my sleep schedule, make everyone like me, and email everyone back promptly. It is even more annoying that life is mostly just waiting around in a line, washing and feeding my silly little human body, and then not even being conscious for about 33 percent of the time.

Yet, knowing that everyone else is experiencing the same relentless mundanity is a small reassurance. Being underwhelmed and feeling like an underachiever is as much a part of the human experience as love and grief are, if not more.

I hope that this little book has made you feel less alone about our individual and collective awfulness. If not, then I don't know what to tell you.

Maybe you're just perfect, unlike the rest of us, and simply couldn't relate.

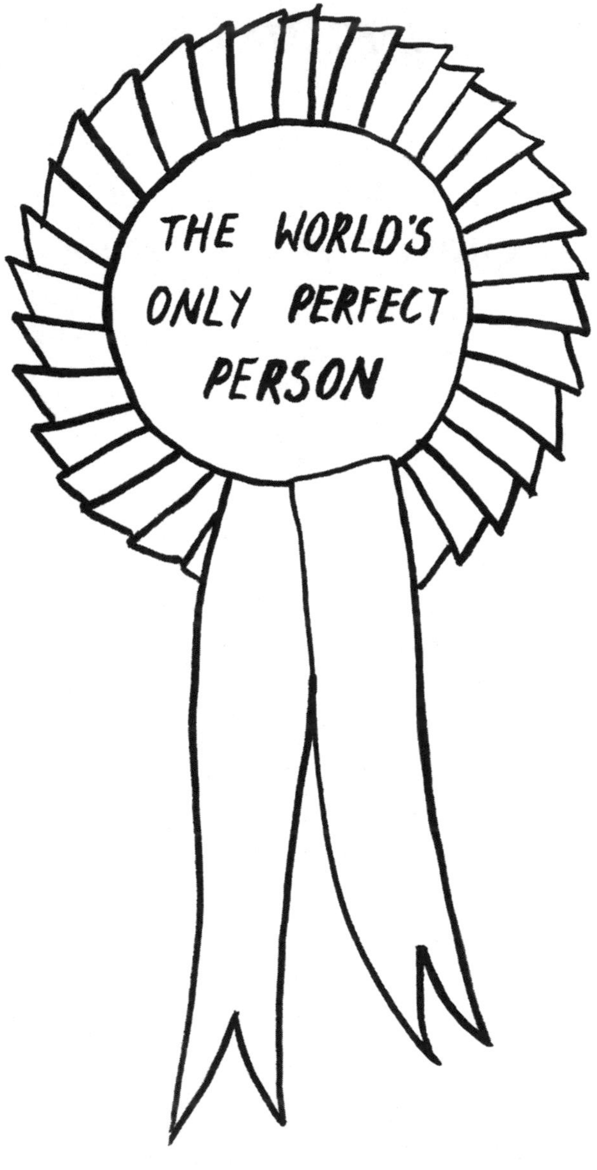
THE WORLD'S
ONLY PERFECT
PERSON

ACKNOWLEDGMENTS

A big thank-you to my parents for going through all the trouble of immigrating and nevertheless being tirelessly supportive of me when I chose to become an artist instead of a lawyer or doctor.

Also thank you to Hannah Street, Hannah Jewell, and Emma Cooke for their thoughtful notes. Thank you to my editor, Lauren Appleton, for always being patient with me, and thank you to my agent, Jennifer Chen Tran, for her relentless optimism and enthusiasm.

ABOUT THE AUTHOR

NATALYA LOBANOVA is an artist, writer, and animator based in London. She completed an art foundation course at Central Saint Martins, then went on to study philosophy and politics at the University of Edinburgh. She formerly worked at *BuzzFeed* as a writer and illustrator, and is now a regular contributor to *The New Yorker*. She is struggling to think of a joke to end this bio on.